WORDS
AND MORE WORDS

Babs Bell Hajdusiewicz

Good Year Books
Parsippany, New Jersey

Dedication

To Nick and Alison

Good Year Books

are available for most basic curriculum subjects plus many
enrichment areas. For more Good Year Books, contact your local
bookstore or educational dealer. For a complete catalog with
information about other Good Year Books, please write:

Good Year Books
An imprint of Pearson Learning
299 Jefferson Road
Parsippany, New Jersey 07054-0480
1-800-321-3106
www.pearsonlearning.com

Book design and illustration by Amy O'Brien Krupp.

ISBN 0-673-36320-1

5 6 7 8 9 - CR - 03 02 01

Preface

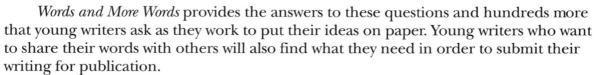

How do you find a word in the dictionary if you can't spell the word?

What are some words that mean the same as very?

Is affect *or* effect *the right word to use in your sentence?*

What words rhyme with the word fast?

When do you drop the final e *before adding a suffix to a word?*

Words and More Words provides the answers to these questions and hundreds more that young writers ask as they work to put their ideas on paper. Young writers who want to share their words with others will also find what they need in order to submit their writing for publication.

Words and More Words provides a single source where young writers can quickly and easily find key information about words and how to use them effectively.

- Thousands of words have been carefully selected and organized in the section "Words . . . and More Words." Here, young writers have at their fingertips comprehensive lists of synonyms and antonyms, metaphors and similes, homophones and homographs, compound words and contractions, words and their origins, fun words, and more than 500 families of rhyming words.

- The "Making Words Count" section provides young writers with invaluable help in organizing, spelling, and punctuating words. Here, writers can locate correct spellings of the most commonly misspelled words, even if they don't know how a word is spelled. Other helpful information includes: frequently misused words and their meanings; characteristics and uses of parts of speech; common verb forms; collective nouns; agreement of subjects and verbs; plural forms of words; prefixes and suffixes; and tips for using capital letters and marks of punctuation.

- The "Sharing Your Words" section gives writers helpful suggestions for submitting their writing for publication. It also provides names and addresses of publications that welcome manuscripts from young writers.

- In the "Putting Knowledge to Work" section, young writers will find a host of practical and enjoyable activities that encourage experimentation with words.

In addition to a glossary and index, *Words and More Words* includes proofreader's marks, library classifications, and specialized indexes that help young writers find particular synonyms and rhyming-word families.

Whether writing for school assignments or for pleasure, young writers will find *Words and More Words* an invaluable single-volume resource to assist them in becoming the best writers they can be.

Contents

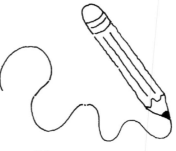

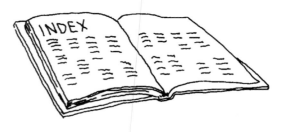

Kinds of Writing

Did you know that everyone is a writer? It's true. Chances are, before today is over, you will use a pen or pencil or a computer keyboard to write something. Look at some of the reasons you may write.

You want to explain something:

      a sign

      directions

      a caption

      rules or instructions

      a label

      an excuse

      a note

      a recipe

You want to convince someone:

      an advertisement

      graffiti

      an application form

      a sign

      a complaint

You need to ask a question or get someone's attention:

      a sign

      an announcement

      an advertisement

      a lost or found notice

      an invitation

      a survey

      an interview

      a questionnaire

You want to answer a question:

        a definition

        an essay

        an application

        a questionnaire

You want to keep a record of events:

        a list

        a diary

        a journal

        a biography

        a autobiography

You want to share thoughts and ideas or tell a story:

        a letter

        a diary

        a journal

        a story

        a poem

        a play

        a joke or riddle

        a letter to the editor

        a biography

        a autobiography

Whether you write a note to a classmate, record your thoughts in a diary or journal, make a sign to ask for help in finding a lost pet, or write "This belongs to" and your name on a notebook, you are using words to communicate with yourself or others.

So what words will you choose to use in your writing? And how will you organize these words on paper or the computer screen? The kind of writing you do depends on the words you choose to use and how you choose to use them.

Words . . .
and
More Words

It Came from Where?!

(Word Origins)

If you had lived before 1762, you might have lunched on "two slices of bread with filling in the middle." The word *sandwich* was not used until John Montagu, the fourth Earl of Sandwich, ordered a servant to deliver to him some roast beef between two slices of toast. The Earl did not want to have to stop playing cards to go eat. Hawaii's Sandwich Islands are also named for the Earl of Sandwich.

Every word has its own roots or history. When new ideas or objects need names, people create new words or borrow from other words or languages. Here are some other words and their origins:

à la carte

as listed on a menu: Borrowed from French.

à la mode

a pie or other dessert served with ice cream: Borrowed from French.

Achilles heel

the weak part of anything: Named for Achilles, a Greek hero who was killed in the Trojan War when an arrow pierced his heel, the only part of his body that had not been coated with a magical protective shield.

Adam's apple

a bulge of cartilage on the windpipe: Named for Adam, a biblical character who ate a forbidden piece of fruit.

amazon

a very tall and strong woman: Named for fierce female warriors in Greek mythology.

a

andante

slowly: Borrowed from Italian.

atlas

a book of maps: Named in the 1500s for Atlas, a Greek mythological character who held the heavens apart from the Earth.

au revoir

good-bye for now: Borrowed from French.

beef stroganoff

beef strips cooked with onions, mushrooms, and sour cream: Named for Count Paul Stroganoff, a nineteenth-century Russian diplomat.

bon jour

daytime "hello" greeting: Borrowed from French.

bon voyage

have a good trip: Borrowed from French.

bona fide

real; genuine: Borrowed from Latin.

bowie knife

a knife with a long double-edged blade: Named for Jim Bowie who made the knife famous at Natchez, Mississippi, in 1827.

boycott

refusal to buy, sell, or use a person's or company's products: Named for Charles Cunningham Boycott, an estate manager whose life in 1880 was made difficult by angry Irish farm tenants.

Braille

a system of raised dots used by people with visual impairments to read and write: Named for Louis Braille who improved on an earlier system.

cardigan

a long-sleeved sweater with buttons down the front: Named for the Earl of Cardigan whose soldiers wore knitted vests during the wintry Crimean War.

cashmere

a very soft wool from goats of Kashmir: Named for Kashmir, India.

Celsius

a scale where water freezes at 0 degrees and boils at 100 degrees: Named for Swedish astronomer Anders Celsius, who in 1742 introduced his system to measure temperature as an improvement over the Fahrenheit scale.

cereal

food made from oat, rice, and wheat grains: Named for Cerus, the Romans' Mother Earth goddess.

chauvinist

a person who favors his own kind and speaks ill of others: Named for Frenchman Nicolas Chauvin who worshipped Napoleon.

chicken tetrazzini

baked casserole of diced chicken, cream sauce, and cheese over thin spaghetti: Named for 1920s Italian opera star Luisa Tetrazzini.

circa

around the time of, usually followed by a specific year: Borrowed from Latin.

cologne

a mildly perfumed liquid: Named for Cologne, Germany, where it has been produced since 1709.

cul-de-sac

a dead-end street: Borrowed from French.

decibel

a measurement of a sound's loudness: Named for Scottish American Alexander Graham Bell, who invented the first useful telephone.

denim

a strong cotton cloth: Named for the city of Nimes, France.

diesel motor

a motor that burns fuel oil: Named for Dr. Rudolph Diesel, the German engineer who developed the engine in the 1890s.

d

doily

a small decorative mat: Named for a London cloth dealer in the early 1700s.

double entendre

a word or phrase with a double meaning: Borrowed from French.

dunce

a person who has difficulty learning: Named for John Duns Scotus, a respected thirteenth-century Scottish scholar whose teachings were ridiculed some two hundred years later.

echo

a sound that bounces back: Named for Echo, a Greek mythological character whose punishment for talking too much was being unable to speak except to repeat what others said.

Epsom salts

a white powder that is a salt of magnesium: Named for the magnesium sulphate springs in Epsom, England.

etcetera

etc.; and a number of others: Borrowed from Latin.

Fahrenheit

a scale in which water freezes at 32 degrees and boils at 212 degrees: Named for Gabriel Daniel Fahrenheit, a German physicist who invented a system for measuring temperature in 1714.

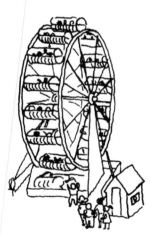

Ferris wheel

an amusement park ride: Named for George Washington Gale Ferris, who introduced a new amusement ride at the World's Columbian Exposition in Chicago in 1893.

forsythia

a yellow-flowered shrub: Named for William Forsyth, a Scottish gardener who introduced the shrub to England in the eighteenth century.

frankfurter

a smoked beef or pork sausage: Named for Frankfurt, Germany, where it was created.

frisbee

a plastic saucer tossed between players: Named for William Frisbie, whose pie company's pans were tossed back and forth by Yale students in 1871.

gardenia

a flower with white or yellow petals: Named for Dr. Alexander Garden, a Scottish American medical doctor who collected plants.

Geiger counter

a clicking device used to measure radioactivity: Named for Hans Geiger, a German physicist and one of three inventors of the device.

Gideon Bible

a Bible found in every hotel room in America: Named for Gideon, a biblical character.

graham cracker

a whole-wheat cracker: Named for Sylvester Graham, a nineteenth-century minister who encouraged Americans to eat low-fat vegetarian diets including whole-wheat products.

guillotine

a device for chopping off someone's head: Named for Dr. Joseph Ignace Guillotin, a French medical doctor who favored replacing the sword and rope as beheading devices.

hamburger

a patty of ground beef: Named for the city of its origin, though opinions differ whether that city is Hamburg, New York, or Hamburg, Germany.

hors d'oeuvre

bite-sized food served before a main meal: Borrowed from French.

hygiene

keeping clean to prevent disease: Named for a character in Greek mythology, Hygeia, goddess of health.

jumbo

very large: Borrowed from Swahili.

jungle

land overgrown with trees and plants: Borrowed from Hindi.

k

khaki

a yellowish-brown color: Borrowed from Hindi.

kiwi

a sweet green fruit grown in New Zealand: Borrowed from Maori.

leotard

one-piece snug-fitting garment worn by dancers and acrobats: Named for its inventor, Jules Leotard, a nineteenth-century French circus performer.

loganberry

a reddish-purple berry: Named for James Harvey Logan, a California judge who grew the plant from a seed in 1880.

lynch

to hang an accused person without a legal trial: Named for one of several men, possibly Captain William Lynch, a Virginian whose followers sought to get rid of a neighborhood's troublemakers in the late 1700s.

mackintosh

a waterproof coat: Named for Scottish chemist Charles Macintosh (the word's incorrect spelling remains), who invented waterproof cloth in 1823.

magnolia

a tree or shrub with large fragrant flowers: Named for French medical doctor and botany professor Pierre Magnol, after his death in 1715.

Manila paper

strong paper used for envelopes and wrapping: Named for Manila hemp, a product from the leaves of the abaca plant of Manila, the Philippines.

mason jar

a canning jar with screw-on lid: Named for John Mason, who introduced the jar in New York in 1857.

maverick

an unbranded animal: Named for Samuel Augustus Maverick, a Texas lawyer and rancher whose cattle were never marked with his brand.

mentor

one who acts as a teacher or role model: Named for Greek mythology's Mentor who offered advice to Odysseus's son.

mesmerize

to grab someone's full attention: Named for Franz Anton Mesmer, an Austrian medical doctor who practiced hypnosis early in the nineteenth century.

never-never land

an imaginary place: Borrowed from Australian slang.

Nobel Prize

annual award in chemistry, literature, medicine and physiology, peace, and physics for outstanding work that benefits all people: Named for Swedish inventor Alfred Nobel whose estate has funded the awards since 1901.

ohm

a measure of electrical resistance: Named for Georg Simon Ohm, a German physicist who introduced the measure early in the nineteenth century.

panacea

something that can make everything okay: Named for Panacea, daughter of the Greek god of medicine, who could cure the ill.

paparazzi

eager photographers: Borrowed from Italian.

pasteurize

special heating process to kill harmful bacteria: Named for Louis Pasteur, a French chemist who discovered how to sterilize, or remove germs from, milk by heating the milk and then quickly cooling it.

poinsettia

a red leafed tropical plant: Named for U.S. ambassador Joel R. Poinsett who discovered the plant in Mexico in the 1800s.

Pollyanna

one who expects the best regardless of the situation: Named for a character created by American author Eleanor Porter.

p

prima donna

> *a temperamental person:* Borrowed from Italian.

Pulitzer Prize

> *annual monetary award to newspaper writers, photographers, and cartoonists:* Named for Hungarian-American journalist and newspaper owner Joseph Pulitzer whose estate has funded the awards since 1917.

Pullman

> *a sleeping car on a train:* Named for its inventor, George Mortimer Pullman.

raglan

> *a sleeve whose seam goes from the underarm to the neck:* Named for Lord Raglan, who wore a coat with raglan-type sleeves during the Crimean War.

résumé

> *a brief summary of qualifications:* Borrowed from French.

Richter scale

> *a scale used to measure earthquakes:* Named for C. F. Richter, an American who studied earthquakes.

safari

> *a long or adventurous journey:* Borrowed from Arabic.

salmonella

> *a bacteria that causes food poisoning:* Named for Daniel Elmer Salmon, an American veterinarian.

saxophone

> *a woodwind instrument:* Named for Antoine Joseph Sax who, in 1840–1844, perfected his father's earlier creation.

sayonara

> *good-bye:* Borrowed from Japanese.

sequoia

> *a very large evergreen tree of California and Oregon:* Named for Cherokee leader Sequoyah after he died in 1847.

shampoo

> *to wash the hair:* Borrowed from Hindi.

sideburns

unshaven hair in front of the ears: Named for General Ambrose Everett Burnside, a governor of Rhode Island and U.S. senator, who first wore the side whiskers.

silhouette

a shadow outline of a figure: Named for Étienne de Silhouette, a Frenchman who failed in his effort to help his financially troubled country following the Seven Years War.

sousaphone

a bass tuba: Named for its inventor, John Philip Sousa, an American composer and bandmaster of the U.S. Marine Corps band.

spoonerism

accidental transposition of words, letters, or syllables: Named for Reverend William Archibald Spoon, an English college dean whose many accidental mix-ups included speaking of Queen Victoria as a "queer old dean" when he meant to say "dear old queen."

status quo

the current state of things: Borrowed from Latin.

stetson

a large hat often worn by cowboys: Named for John Batterson Stetson who manufactured the hats in Philadelphia around 1865.

taco

a tortilla rolled or folded in half: Borrowed from Spanish.

teddy bear

a stuffed toy: Named for bear-hunter President Theodore Roosevelt in 1902.

tortilla

a round, flat unleavened bread: Borrowed from Spanish.

tundra

a treeless plain: Borrowed from Lappish.

V

vandalism

destroying another's property: Named for the Vandals, a German tribe who destroyed many treasures when they invaded Rome in the fifth century.

vermicelli

very thin long pasta: Named for an Italian word meaning "little worms."

Victorian

having to do with Queen Victoria's reign in England from 1837 to 1901: Named for Queen Victoria.

voilà

an interjection meaning "There it is!" or "Look!": Borrowed from French.

volcano

an eruption of ash and molten rock from a hole in the Earth: Named for Vulcan, the Roman god of fire.

volt

a measure of electrical current: Named for Count Alessandro Guiseppe Antonio Anastasion Volta, an Italian who in 1800 invented the first device that produced an electric current.

watt

a measure of electrical power: Named for Scotland's James Watt, who invented the first practical steam engine around 1765.

zinnia

a plant with brightly colored flowers: Named for Johann Gottfried Zinn, a German botanist and physician.

Another Way to Say It

(Synonyms, Metaphors, Similes)

As a writer, you want your reader to be able to "picture" what you are saying. *Synonyms, metaphors,* and *similes* are words and phrases that help you "paint" your pictures.

Synonyms, such as *annoying* and *bothersome,* are words that mean the same or nearly the same. Using synonyms helps you vary the language you use; it also helps you "paint" a clearer and more interesting picture for your reader.

When writing, you use *idioms,* also called *figures of speech* or *figurative language,* for the same reasons you use synonyms. Figures of speech include *metaphors* and *similes.* Metaphors and similes compare two ideas. For example, suppose a character in your story has a habit of bothering others. If you say the character is a "pain in the neck," you'd be using a metaphor to compare the character's annoying behavior to pain. You could also express this comparison in a simile, using the words *like* or *as.* You might say the character in your story is "like a pain in the neck" or "as bothersome as a pain in the neck."

Another kind of figurative language is a *cliché.* A cliché is a figure of speech that is used so often that it is said to be "overworked." You could use the cliché "runs like a racehorse" to describe a fast runner. But your language would be more original if you said the runner was "like a champion sprinter" or "as swift as a fleeting deer."

You can use the following alphabetical lists when you're looking for "another way to say it." Look for your word among the words in bold type. Then choose from the ideas listed below it to find a synonym, metaphor, or simile that says exactly what you want to say. You might want to add some of your own ideas to the lists.

a

A

able adjective

able-bodied
apt
capable
competent
experienced
knowledgeable
qualified
ready and willing
trained
up for anything
versed

act noun

a stroke of genius
accomplishment
achievement
action
deed
duty
feat
job
performance
project
task
transaction
work

alike adjective

allied
complementary
equal
equivalent
like two peas in a pod
parallel
resembling
same
similar
symmetrical

synonymous
twin

almost adverb

about
approximately
around
as good as
bordering on
close to
for the most part
in the neighborhood of
more or less
nearly
not quite
on the verge of
roughly
within a stone's throw

angry adjective

about to explode
as mad as a hornet
at the end of your rope
at your wit's end
blowing a fuse
boiling
burned up
coming unglued
cross
enraged
fed up
fit to be tied
flying off the handle
furious
going ballistic
going berserk
going haywire
going off the deep end
had it up to here
having a bee in your
    bonnet
having your feathers
    ruffled
hitting the ceiling

hot under the collar
hysterical
incensed
inflamed
infuriated
irate
losing your temper
like a wild animal
mad
on fire
out of control
peeved
raging
seeing red
seething
sore
stark-raving mad
steamed
surly

answer verb

acknowledge
confirm
explain
interpret
R.S.V.P.
reply
respond
retaliate
satisfy
solve
tell

argue verb

attack
battle
bicker
contest
debate
differ
disagree
discuss
dispute
explain

go at it
haggle
hash over
lock horns
pick a fight
quarrel
quibble
riot
spat
struggle
war
wrangle

ashamed adjective

abashed
chagrined
embarrassed
feel like two cents
guilty
humiliated
like the cat that swallowed
    the canary
mortified
red-faced
remorseful
shamefaced
sheepish
taking the rap
without a leg to stand on

ask verb

appeal
beckon
beg
demand
examine
fish for
grill
inquire
interrogate
invite
plead
probe
query

question
quiz
request
require
summon

avoid verb

abstain
avert
beat around the bush
circumvent
dodge
elude
escape
evade
give a cold shoulder to
hem and haw
make yourself scarce
not touch with a ten-foot
    pole
refrain
retreat
shirk
shun
shy away from
steer clear of
turn a deaf ear

awkward adjective

accident-prone
all thumbs
bumbling
can't walk and chew gum
    at the same time
clumsy
gawky
graceless
inept
klutzy
like a bull in a china shop
like an accident that's
    about to happen
uncoordinated
ungraceful

B

bad adjective

a lemon
atrocious
awful
corrupt
criminal
crooked
defective
dishonest
evil
for the birds
foul
harmful
horrible
immoral
inferior
like a dead rat
like yesterday's garbage
mean
nasty
notorious
poor
rotten
rude
scum of the earth
spoiled
terrible
unacceptable
unfit

begin verb

break ground
break into
break the ice
call to order
catch fire
come out of nowhere
commence
cut the ribbon
dedicate

b

b

dive in
embark
fire away
get cracking
get going
get off the ground
get the show on the road
get your feet wet

go ahead
inaugurate
initiate
instigate
kick off
launch
lay the foundation
make a move
open
originate
plunge forward
roll up your sleeves
start
start the ball rolling
take effect
take off
take the first step

believe verb

acknowledge
be convinced
depend on
get it through your head
have faith in
recognize
rely on
swallow
take to heart
trust
value

best adjective

choice
chosen
excellent
fine
highest
matchless
outstanding
perfect
prime
select
starred
super
superb
superlative
supreme
tops
utmost

big adjective

as big as all outdoors
colossal
cumbersome
elephantine
enormous
expansive
famous
gargantuan
gigantic
glorious
grand
great
heavy
hefty
huge

humongous
immense
inflated
large
larger than life
majestic
massive
monstrous
monumental
outstanding
ponderous
prominent
spacious
Texas-sized
titanic
tremendous
vast

blame verb

accuse
bawl out
call on the carpet
censor
charge
chew out
come down on
criticize
denounce
disapprove
find fault
give a piece of your mind
give a tongue lashing
hold accountable
indict
lecture
point the finger at
put in the hot seat
read the riot act
reprimand
scold
tell off
throw the book at

bother verb

annoy
bug
disturb
drive up the wall
drive you crazy
get under your skin
give fits
harass
hassle
heckle
hound
irritate
mock
needle
perturb
pester
pick on
taunt
tease
torment

brag verb

blow your own horn
boast
break your arm patting
    yourself on the back
crow
flaunt
gloat
make yourself larger than
    life
show off
sing your own praises

brave adjective

bold
courageous
daring
dashing
fearless
gallant
gutsy
heroic
nervy
spunky
unafraid

break verb

crack
crumble
damage
demolish
destroy
fracture
make mincemeat of
mutilate
pull to shreds
pulverize
ruin
shatter
smash
snap
splinter
split
tear
total
wreck

bright adjective

beaming
brilliant
dazzling
glaring
gleaming
glowing
illuminated
light
like a million stars
like a newly polished
    dance floor
like diamonds
like the noonday sun
lucid
radiant
shining
shiny
sparkling
sunny
vivid
well-lit

build verb

assemble
construct
create
develop
devise
erect
establish
fabricate
fashion
found
make
manufacture
mold
originate
produce
raise
rear
shape

burn verb

char
go up in smoke
incinerate
inflame
scorch
sear
set on fire
singe
smolder

busy adjective

absorbed
active
burning the candle at
    both ends

b

bustling
engaged
engrossed
in perpetual motion
industrious
intent
involved
laboring
no time to blink
occupied
on the go
racing against time
studious
working

buy verb

acquire
bargain for
barter
get your hands on
obtain
pay for
pick up
procure
purchase
secure
swap

calm adjective

collected
composed
cool
motionless
placid
restful
serene
smooth
still
tranquil
undisturbed

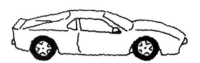

car noun

auto
automobile
caboose
coach
convertible
coupe
diner
dragster
limousine
motorcar
Pullman
rattletrap
sedan
sleeper
streetcar
taxicab
tram
trolley
van
vehicle
wheels

careful adjective

accurate
alert
apprehensive
attentive
canny
cautious
concerned
conscientious
considerate
deliberate
detailed
discrete
exacting
fastidious
fearful
finicky
fussy

guarded
heedful
hesitant
meticulous
mindful
observant
painstaking
particular
picky
precise
prudent
taking your time
thorough
thoughtful
using kid gloves
walking on eggshells
wary

careless adjective

forgetful
heedless
hit-or-miss
inattentive
inconsiderate
inexact
lackadaisical
messy
neglectful
negligent
nonchalant
rash
reckless
remiss
sloppy
thoughtless
unconcerned
unthinking

carry verb

bear
bring
cart
conduct
convey

deliver
dispatch
ferry
fetch
haul
lug
move
pack
pass along
send
ship
take
tote
transport

catch verb

ambush
apprehend
arrest
capture
clutch
discover
ensnare
entrap
grab
grasp
grip
hold
hook
net
pluck
receive
seize

snare
snatch
take
trap

celebrate verb

commemorate
dedicate
eulogize
go out on the town
honor
keep
kick up your heels
memorialize
observe
party
praise
raise the roof
remember
whoop it up

change verb

alter
diversify
do an about-face
exchange
improve
make over
modify
mutate
reorganize
replace
shuffle
substitute
swap
switch
trade
transform
turn color
turn over a new leaf
turn the tide
vary
whistle a different tune

chase verb

dog
follow
hound
hunt
pursue
run after
seek
shadow
stalk
tag along
tail
track
trail

cheap adjective

discounted
economical
inexpensive
low-priced
reasonable
shabby
worthless

cheat verb

bamboozle
beguile
con
deceive
defraud
do out of
hoodwink
hornswoggle
mislead
outwit
plagiarize
pull a fast one
pull the wool over your
  eyes
short-change
stack the deck
swindle
take advantage of
trick

C

choose verb

adopt
cull
elect
embrace
pick
prefer
select
single out
vote for

clean adjective

bathed
dusted
fresh
healthy
laundered
polished
pure
scoured
scrubbed
shiny
sparkling
spick-and-span
spotless
stainless
swept
tidy
vacuumed
washed

clear adjective

apparent
as clear as a bell
as clear as day
as plain as the nose on
    your face
certain
cloudless
conspicuous
definite
distinct
evident
exposed

like handwriting
    on a wall
obvious
plain
prominent
transparent
unobstructed

cold adjective

airy
an ice cube
bitter
breezy
chilly
cooled
crisp
depressing
distant
freezing
frigid
frosted
frosty
iced
icy
lifeless
like a witch's heart
listless
polar
refrigerated
remote
shivering
standoffish
unfriendly
windy
wintry

color noun

hue
intensity
pigment
shade
tinge
tint
tone

come verb

appear
approach
arrive
bear down upon
gain
reach
show up
turn up

complain verb

bellyache
bewail
crab
fume
gripe
grouch
growl
grumble
lament
nag
squawk
yammer

confused adjective

at a loss for words
baffled
bewildered
buffaloed
can't make heads nor tails
    of it
confounded
discombobulated
disconcerted
disturbed
don't know if you're
    coming or going
don't know which end is
    up
draw a blank
flipped out
flustered
foggy

going in circles
hazy
in a maze
like a train with no engine
lost at sea
mystified
out of it
perplexed
spaced out
taken aback
thrown off balance
torn
troubled
uncertain
upset

cost noun

a king's ransom
a pretty penny
an arm and a leg
charge
dues
expenditure
expense
fare
payment
price
toll
value
worth

country noun

area
district
land
nation

people
province
region
territory

crazy adjective

absurd
asinine
batty
bonkers
crazed
daffy
daft
demented
dippy
foolish
goofy
has a screw loose
   somewhere
idiotic
insane
irrational
loony
lunatic
mad
mad as a March hare
nonsensical
not playing with a full deck
off the wall
out in left field
preposterous
schizo
silly
stark-raving mad
stupid
unbalanced
wacko

crowd noun

bevy
drove
flock
horde
jam

masses
mob
multitude
swarm
throng

cruel adjective

barbaric
bloodthirsty
brutal
cold-blooded
evil
harsh
heartless
inhuman
like an old buzzard
mean
ruthless
savage
severe
unfeeling
vicious
wicked
witchy

cry verb

bawl
blubber
break down
lament
moan
snivel
sob
wail
weep
whimper
whine

curious adjective

inquiring
inquisitive
investigative
itching to know

c

like a cat
nosy
questioning
quizzical
searching
snoopy
wide-eyed

cut verb

amputate
carve
dissect
divide
gash
prune
rip
saw
score
sever
shave
shear
slash
slice
slip
slit
split
tear
trim

dangerous adjective

a red light
alarming
chancy
hazardous
like an open pit
like jumping into a fire
ominous
perilous
risky
sounds an alarm
treacherous
unsafe

dark adjective

black
dim
dismal
dreary
dull
evil
faint
gloomy
lightless
murky
opaque
shadowy
wicked

dead noun

like a corpse
deceased
departed
dormant
extinct
gone
history
inorganic
lifeless
numb
passed away
perished
smothered
suffocated
terminated
tired

deep adjective

bottomless
cavernous
fathomless
in the bowels of the earth
like the ocean
way down

different adjective

assorted
contrasting
dissimilar
distinctive
extraordinary

like night and day
odd
unique
unlike
unusual
varying

difficult adjective

a losing battle
as clear as mud
can't scratch the surface
complex
exhausting
hard
having your work cut out
    for you
laborious
like beating your head
    against a brick wall
like being in a maze
like duck soup

like finding your way in
the dark
like having your hands tied
behind your back
like rowing upstream
like trying to find a needle
in a haystack
like trying to move
mountains
mind-boggling
no bed of roses
no picnic
perplexing
puzzling
rigorous
strenuous
taxing
tedious
troubling
trying

dirty adjective

dusty
filthy
foul
grimy
a pigsty
a pit
messy
muddy
soiled
spotted
stained
unclean
unkempt

disappointed adjective

betrayed
dejected
discouraged
disenchanted
disillusioned
feeling like you lost your
song

feeling like your bubble
burst
feeling like your dog just
died
having lost heart
let down

dry adjective

arid
as dry as a bone
bare
boring
dehydrated
like a desert
parched
thirsty
tiresome

dull adjective

boring
clouded
dense
disinteresting
dismal
dreary
lifeless
pointless
tarnished

easy adjective

a cinch
a piece of cake
an ace in the hole
all in a day's work
elementary
full speed ahead
like taking candy from a
baby
like turning on a faucet

natural
obvious
like being on automatic
pilot
plain
simple
uncomplicated

eat verb

bolt
consume
devour
dine
feast
gobble up
gorge
gulp down
pack it in
pig out
put away
ravage
scarf down
snack
stuff your face
wolf it down

empty adjective

a bottomless pit
abandoned
blank
deserted
hollow
unfulfilled
unfurnished
unoccupied
vacant
a void

enjoyable adjective

amusing
delightful
entertaining
exciting
fun

like a day with your best
    friend
like a hot fudge sundae
like ice on a hot day
playful
pleasurable

especially adverb

by and large
chiefly
first of all
in particular
mainly
mostly
notably
particularly
primarily
uncommonly
uniquely
unusually

excited adjective

a live wire
agitated
alive
all pumped up
animated
anxious about
bustling
eager
energetic
enthusiastic
eyes popping out
full of steam
gung-ho
hyped

hyper
keen on
keyed up
like running on new
    batteries
spirited
worked up

fall verb

cascade
collapse
crumple
descend
drop
go head over heels
keel over
plummet
sink
slide
slip
slump
stumble
take a nose dive
take a spill
topple
trip
tumble

family noun

ancestors
ancestry
background
bloodline
children
dynasty
folks
heritage
household
kin
offspring

origin
pedigree
people
relatives
roots
tribe

famous adjective

a shining star
big cheese
celebrated
distinguished
esteemed
great
king of the mountain
popular
prominent
renowned
respected
top banana
well-known

fast adjective

a race horse
accelerated
ahead of time
brisk
expeditious
express
lightning-swift
like Jackie Joyner-Kersee
like a speeding bullet
like a streak of lightning
quick
rapid
speedy
swift

f

fat adjective

ample
as fat as a pig
big
broad
bulky
chubby
heavy
husky
large
massive
obese
overweight
plump
portly
solid
stout
wide

few adjective

atypical
bare
deficient
exceptional
few and far between
inadequate
insufficient
lacking
meager
measly
nominal
paltry
rare
scanty
scarcer than hen's teeth
skimpy
uncommon
unheard-of

find verb

come across
come upon
detect
discern
discover
espy
get to the bottom of
locate
note
notice
pinpoint
place
procure
solve
spot
turn up
uncover

first adjective

beginning
chief
earliest
foremost
initial
leading
main
major
opening
original
premiere
primary
principal

fix verb

cobble
correct
do up
doctor up
mend
mend fences
patch
prepare
put right
rectify
remedy
repair
restore
solve

straighten
touch up

friend noun

acquaintance
ally
buddy
chum
classmate
companion
comrade
helper
pal
peer
playmate
sidekick
teammate

full adjective

ample
brimming
chock full
crammed full
crowded
developed
filled
jam-packed
overflowing
packed
stuffed
thorough

fun noun

amusement
enjoyment
entertainment
gaiety
hobby
joy
pastime
play
pleasure
recreation

funny adjective

amusing
bringing down the house
comical
entertaining
hilarious
humorous
hysterical
jovial
laughable
like a clown
like an elephant on stilts
like Laurel and Hardy
like something from
    "Saturday Night Live"
ridiculous
riotous
side-splitting
silly
witty

game noun

competition
contest
joke
match
meet
prank
recreation
sport
tournament

good adjective

a perfect ten
a role model
acceptable
accurate
all right
angelic

appropriate
authentic
believable
best
correct
courteous
delicious
excellent
fine
first-class
fitting
flawless
genuine
godly
great
healthful
helpful
hits the spot
honorable
innocent
magnificent
mannerly
moral
not bad
obedient
okay
perfection-plus
permissible
praiseworthy
real
reliable
respectable
right
righteous
safe
satisfactory
sound
suitable
super
superb
superior
takes the cake
time-honored
trustworthy
valid
valuable

virtuous
well-behaved
well-mannered
wholesome

grow verb

add to
amplify
augment
become greater
bloom
bulge
deepen
develop
double
enlarge
expand
fill out
flourish
germinate
heighten
increase
lengthen
magnify
mature
multiply
prosper
shoot up
snowball
spread
spring up
sprout
stretch
supplement
swell
thicken
thrive
triple
wax
widen

happy adjective

as happy as a lark
at peace with the world
blissful
blithe
cheerful
contented
delighted
ecstatic
elated
exultant
glad
gleeful
in seventh heaven
jolly
jovial
joyful
joyous
jubilant
lighthearted
like a clam at high tide
like a million bucks
merry
mirthful
on cloud nine
on top of the world
optimistic
overjoyed
pleased
positive
satisfied
sunny
ten feet tall
thrilled
tickled
tickled pink
untroubled
upbeat
walking on air
without a care in the world

hard adjective

demanding
grim
inelastic
inflexible
poker-faced
relentless
rigid
set in your ways
stiff
stiff as a board
taut
tense
unbending
unyielding

hate verb

abhor
abominate
bear a grudge against
can't bear
can't stand
despise
detest
dislike
have no use for
loathe

have verb

acquire
hold
include
keep
obtain
own
possess
procure
receive
retain
secure

help verb

aid
assist
boost
come through
do the honors
give a hand
nurse
prevent
rescue
serve
stick together
support
work

hide verb

camouflage
conceal
disappear from sight
disguise
stash
take cover
veil

high adjective

elevated
heavenly
like a kite
lofty
out of sight
steep
tall
towering

hire verb

appoint
assign
employ
engage
enlist
retain

h

hit verb

bash
beat up
conk
cream
hammer
knock
pound
slap
smack
strike
thump
whack

home noun

abode
address
apartment
bungalow
cabin
castle
condominium
cottage
hotel
house
pad
residence
shelter
tent
townhouse
trailer

hopeful adjective

confident
expectant
keeping your fingers
    crossed
looking forward to
optimistic
wishful

hot adjective

boiling
burning
feverish
fiery
flaming
heated
roasting
sultry
sweating
sweltering
torrid

hungry adjective

famished
hungering
like a bottomless pit
like a marooned sailor
malnourished
ravenous
starving
voracious

hurry verb

accelerate
burn rubber
bustle
fly on the wings of the
    wind
get a move on
get cracking
get in gear
go all out
go at full blast
go like greased lightning

hasten
hightail it
hotfoot it
hustle
lose no time
make haste
make hay while the sun
    shines
make it snappy
move quickly
press on
push on
race
ride hard
run like mad
rush
scurry
shake a leg
skedaddle
speed
step on it
step on the gas
step tall

hurt adjective

abused
broken
bruised
damaged
harmed
impaired
injured
like a piece of bruised fruit
like a pincushion
feeling like you've lost your
    best friend
mistreated
pained
ruined
sprained
tormented
wasted
wounded

I

ill adjective

ailing
diseased
indisposed
sick
sickly
sore
unhealthy
unwell

innocent adjective

a babe in the woods
blameless
faultless
guiltless
impeccable
in the clear
irreproachable
pure
righteous
sinless
upright
virtuous

interesting adjective

absorbing
amusing
attractive
charming
enchanting
engaging
engrossing
entertaining
exciting
fascinating
gripping
intriguing
inviting
riveting
spellbinding
stimulating
tempting
thought-provoking

invite verb

attract
beckon
call for
entice
flirt with
invoke
look for
lure
petition
plead
request
seek
solicit
summon
tempt

J

jealous adjective

begrudging
covetous
desirous
eating your heart out
envious
green with envy
itching
yearning

join verb

bind
bridge
connect
consolidate
converge
couple
link
marry
meet
merge
seam
span
team up
tie
unite

jump verb

bounce
bound
hop
hurdle
leap
like a kangaroo
like a leapfrog
pounce
spring
vault

K

kill verb

assassinate
butcher
execute
finish off
knock off
liquidate
massacre
murder
polish off
slaughter
slay
snuff out
waste
wipe out
zap

last noun

all she wrote
closing
concluding
end
end of the line
ending
eventual
final
hindmost
latest
posterior
rearmost
ultimate

late verb

behind
behind schedule
belated
delayed
overdue
past due
postponed
tardy

laugh verb

be in stitches
cackle
chortle
chuckle
crow
double up
giggle
guffaw
hoot
howl
make fun of
roar
roll on the floor

snicker
split your sides
tee-hee
titter

lazy adjective

a couch potato
idle
inactive
indolent
inert
lax
lethargic
listless
shiftless
unmotivated

let verb

admit
allow
approve of
authorize
entitle
permit
sanction

light adjective

airy
buoyant
delicate
feathery
like a spider's web
nimble
slight
spry
tiny
weightless

little adjective

ant-sized
brief
dinky

dwarfed
itty-bitty
measly
mini
miniature
minuscule
minor
peewee
piddling
scanty
short
small
teeny
tiny
wee

lonely adjective

alone
companionless
cut off
desolate
forlorn
friendless
haven't a friend in the
    world
isolated
lonesome
separate
withdrawn

lots noun

a flood
a great deal
acres
an army
an excess of
aplenty
as plentiful as water
considerable amount
enormous amount
extra
gobs
heaps
innumerable

loads
many
masses
more than you can handle
mountains of
much
multitudinous
numerous quantities
oodles
quite a few
scads
tons
tremendous amount
umpteen
volumes

loud adjective

blaring
booming
clamorous
deafening
earsplitting
earthshaking
fortissimo
harsh
intense
noisy
roaring
thunderous
vociferous

love verb

admire
adore
be fond of
be infatuated with
care for
cherish
delight in
enjoy
esteem
get a kick out of
have a liking
hold dear

idolize
like
long for
prize
relish
savor
smitten with
think the world of
treasure
worship

middle noun

average
bull's eye
center
core
dead-center
focus
heart
hub
like sandwich spread
mean
median
midpoint
midsection
nucleus
on target
par for the course

money noun

bill
bread
bucks
change
coins
deposit
dollar
dough
income

pay
riches
salary
savings
wealth
worth

never adverb

at no time
not a fat chance
hardly ever
not at all
not ever
not in a million years
rarely
the second Tuesday of next
    week
under no circumstances

new adjective

contemporary
extraordinary
fresh
hot
latest
modern
recent
unexplored
unfamiliar
unused
unusual
up-to-the-minute

nice adjective

a fountain of kindness
a good egg
agreeable
amiable

n

appropriate
benevolent
comfortable
congenial
cordial
correct
delightful
enjoyable
fitting
friendly
genial
good
good-natured
gracious
kind
likable
neighborly
pleasant
pleasing
polite
proper
refined
right
satisfactory
sociable
thoughtful
suitable
welcome

night noun

bedtime
dark
darkness
dusk
evening
nighttime
sunset
twilight

noise noun

bedlam
clamor
clatter
commotion

din
fracas
hubbub
hullabaloo
pandemonium
racket
ruckus
tumult
turmoil
uproar
yelling

O

often adverb

a lot
every time you turn around
frequently
habitually
oft
over and over
periodically
regularly
repeatedly
time after time
time and time again
usually

old adjective

a dinosaur
a fossil
aged
ancient
antique
as old as Methuselah
as old as the hills
dilapidated
elderly
extinct
getting on in years
obsolete

old-fashioned
outdated
over the hill
passé
prehistoric
senile
used
worn

P

painful adjective

aching
achy
annoying
burning
difficult
hurting
irritating
like a stab in the back
raw
sore
throbbing

part noun

bit
chip
chunk
crumb
division
element
fair share
fraction
fragment
morsel
part and parcel
particle
piece
portion
scrap
section
segment

share
shred
slice

people noun

country
everybody
family
humankind
humans
individuals
inhabitants
masses
mortals
nation
persons
population
race
residents
society

picture noun

artwork
drawing
film
likeness
movie
painting
photograph
portrait
snapshot

playful adjective

energetic
feeling your oats
frisky

frolicsome
full of vim and vigor
fun-loving
gamesome
skittish
sportive
teasing

poor adjective

bankrupt
broke
destitute
don't have two pennies
    to rub together
financially challenged
half-baked
hard up
impoverished
indigent
needy
penniless
poverty-stricken
strapped

pretty adjective

appealing
as lovely as a rose
attractive
beautiful
becoming
chic
comely
cool
cute
delicate
delightful
divine
elegant
exquisite
eye-catching
fair
fetching
fine
glamorous

good-looking
gorgeous
handsome
lovely
magnificent
neat
nice
pleasing
seemly
sightly
striking
stunning
stylish

Q

quiet adjective

calm
hushed
like a church mouse
on cat feet
passive
peaceful
serene
silent
still
tranquil

R

ready adjective

about to
agreeable
all set
available
on tap
on top of things

r

on your toes
prepared
primed
prompt
punctual
willing

rich adjective

affluent
loaded
moneyed
opulent
prosperous
rolling in dough
wealthy
well-off

right adjective

aboveboard
accurate
constitutional
correct
exact
fair
fair and square
flawless
honest
impartial
just
lawful
legal
licensed
logical
moral
perfect
precise
rational
reasonable
responsible
rightful
straightforward
true

rough adjective

bumpy
coarse
crinkly
difficult
irregular
jagged
like sandpaper
uneven

rub verb

brush
curry
groom
knead
massage
pat
pet
polish
scour
scrub
smooth
stroke

rule noun

code
command
decree
guideline
law
order
power
principle
regulation
standard

run verb

beat it
bolt
canter
dart
dash
depart

flee
gallop
hurry
jog
leave
lope
race
retreat
rush
scamper
scoot
scramble
scurry
speed
sprint
tear out
trot
zoom

sad adjective

broken-hearted
cheerless
crestfallen
crummy
crushed
dejected
depressed

despondent
discouraged
disheartened
dismal
down in the dumps
downcast
downhearted
feeling blue
forlorn
gloomy
heartbroken
joyless
lifeless
like a piano without its keys
like hitting rock bottom
melancholy
miserable
pitiable
sorrowful
sorry
tearful
unhappy
wearing a long face
woebegone
woeful
wretched

safe adjective

all right
guarded
harmless
home free
in good shape
invulnerable
like money in the bank
okay
on solid ground
out of harm's way
out of reach
out of the woods
protected
secure
sheltered
undamaged
under lock and key

said verb

added
admitted
admonished
announced
answered
argued
bawled
bragged
breathed
called
cautioned
challenged
claimed
commanded
commented
cried
croaked
declared
demanded
described
exclaimed
explained
gasped
hinted
informed
lamented
laughed
lied
mentioned
mouthed
murmured
offered
ordered
outlined
panted
pleaded
praised
prayed
preached
promised
proposed
quipped
quoted
ranted

recited
remarked
reminded
replied
reported
responded
roared
sassed
screamed
shouted
shrieked
sighed
smirked
snapped
spoke
sputtered
stammered
stated
stuttered
suggested
testified
told
uttered
volunteered
wailed
warned
wept
whispered
wondered
yelled

save verb

conserve
preserve
protect
recycle
rescue
reserve
safeguard
salvage
secure
squirrel away

S

saw verb

beheld
discerned
examined
eyed
gaped at
gazed at
glanced at
glimpsed
got an eyeful
inspected
kept your eyes peeled
laid eyes on
noted
noticed
observed
paid attention to
perceived
pictured
probed
realized
scrutinized
sighted
spied
spotted
stared at
surveyed
took a gander at
took note of
understood
viewed
watched
witnessed

scared adjective

a real chicken
afraid
afraid of your own shadow
alarmed
as white as a sheet
fearful
frightened
getting cold feet
hair-raising

horrified
intimidated
like a toddler in a haunted
   house
like you've seen a ghost
paralyzed
petrified
quivering like a bowl of
   jelly
terrified
turning turtle
your hair's standing on
   end

seat noun

bench
bleacher
chair
couch
cushion
highchair
loge
lounge
pew
rocker
sofa
stool
throne

shiny adjective

bright
clean
gleaming
glistening
glossy
glowing
like a newly polished
   dance floor
luminous
polished
radiant

shout verb

bellow
cheer
cry
exclaim
holler
howl
let off steam
make yourself heard
roar
scream
whoop it up
yap
yell
yelp
yip

shy adjective

a clinging vine
apprehensive
bashful
coy
demure
hesitant
meek as a lamb
modest
reclusive
reluctant
reticent
timid
unasserting

sleep verb

catch forty winks
catnap
conk out
count sheep
crash
doze
drowse
get some shuteye
grab some Z's
hit the hay

hit the sack
nap
retire
sack out
saw logs
slumber
snooze
zonk out

slow adjective

as slow as a seven-year itch
dawdling
deliberate
hesitant
leisurely
lethargic
like a sloth
like molasses in January
pausing
plodding
sluggish
snail-like

smart adjective

a brain
alert
as smart as a whip
brainy
bright
brilliant
capable
clever
ingenious
intelligent
keen
knows the ropes
like a regular computer
like a walking encyclopedia
sensible
sharp
trivia whiz

smooth adjective

flat
flush
glossy
like glass
polished
sanded
satiny
seamless

soft adjective

comfortable
cushiony
flexible
like a baby's bottom
like cotton
like old leather
pliable
plush

stay verb

anchor
continue
dwell
halt
inhabit
linger
plant your feet
remain
reside
set your feet in concrete
settle
sit tight
stop

steal verb

cabbage onto
con
hustle
pilfer
plunder
rip off
rob

shoplift
snitch
swindle
thieve

stop verb

abandon
back off
break up
call a halt
call it a day
call it quits
cease
come off it
complete
cut off
discontinue
end
finish
give up the ship
halt
hit the road
hold your fire
hold your horses
lay off
nip in the bud
pull up stakes
put an end to
put to bed
quit
throw in the sponge
wrap up
yield

storm noun

blizzard
cloudburst
cyclone
downpour
gale
hurricane
monsoon
sandstorm
snowfall

tornado
typhoon

story noun

adventure
anecdote
biography
epic
fable
fantasy
folktale
legend
memory
myth
narrative
novel
opera
play
report
saga
serial
tale
yarn

street noun

alley
avenue
boulevard
driveway
freeway
highway
lane
pavement
road
route
strip
superhighway
thoroughfare
toll road
turnpike

strong adjective

durable
hardy
Herculean
mighty
powerful
rugged
sturdy
tough
as strong as an ox

suddenly adverb

abruptly
all at once
all of a sudden
before you can say, "Jack
    Robinson"
hastily
hurriedly
immediately
in a flash
instantly
on short notice
on the spur of the moment
out of the blue
posthaste
promptly
quickly
rapidly
speedily
swiftly
unexpectedly
without warning

take verb

accept
achieve
acquire
embrace
engage
gain
gather
grasp
grip
hold
obtain
pick
possess
procure
receive
secure

talk verb

address
blow the lid off
break the news
call the shots
chatter
chatter like a monkey
come clean
communicate
converse
convey
declare
exchange ideas
express
give a song and dance
    about
lay down the law
let the cat out of the bag
make a point
pipe up
point out
proclaim
put in two cents' worth
rap
relate
say
speak
speak like an orator
state
utter
vent

tall adjective

aerial
as tall as the Empire State
    Building
elevated
full-grown
high
like Kareem Abdul-Jabbar
lofty
towering

teacher noun

advisor
boss
coach
counselor
educator
employer
fellow
guide
instructor
leader
master
model
pedagogue
professor
schoolmaster
trainer
tutor

thin adjective

all skin and bones
as skinny as a rail
gaunt
lanky
lean
narrow
pencil-thin
scrawny
skeletal
skinny
slender
slight
slim
threadlike
willowy
wispy

think verb

conceive
contemplate
meditate
ponder
reason
reflect
speculate
visualize

tight adjective

compact
compressed
fastened
fixed
immovable
restricted
rigid
secure
snug
stationary
taut

time noun

break
century
day
hour
instant
minute
moment
month
once
period
second
shift
term
week
year

tired adjective

beat
bored
bushed
dead to the world
dead-tired
dog-tired
drowsy
exhausted
fatigued
ready to drop
restless
sleepy
spent
tuckered out
weary
wiped out
worn out

top noun

acme
apex
ceiling
cover
crest
crown

t

lid
peak
pinnacle
roof
summit
utmost

touch verb

caress
feel
finger
handle
knead
manipulate
pet
press
put your mark on
rub
stroke

true adjective

a charm
accurate
actual
authentic
confirmed
correct
dependable
exacting
factual
flawless
genuine
legitimate
literal
natural
nonfictional
official
perfect
precise
proper
pure
real
reliable
sincere
tried and true

trusted
truthful
valid
verified

try verb

attempt
consider
endeavor
examine
experiment with
give it a whirl
have a go at it
inspect
look over
make a stab at it
sample
seek
strive
struggle
take a risk
taste
test
think about
try your hand at it
undertake

ugly adjective

an ugly duckling
bad-looking
disagreeable
disfigured
displeasing

hideous
homely
like Frankenstein
messy
nasty
objectionable
plain
repugnant
repulsive
unappealing
unattractive
unpleasant
unsightly

under preposition

at the bottom of
below
beneath
immersed in
submerged in
underneath

understand verb

be in the know
catch on
comprehend
deduce
discern
fathom
figure out
get it
get it through your head
get the drift of
get the hang of
get the message
get the picture
grasp
psych out
read it like a book
read your mind
realize
reckon
savvy
see the light
the lightbulb goes on

W

use verb

apply
consume
employ
exercise
handle
make use of
occupy
operate
practice
spend
utilize

terribly
thoroughly
to the nth degree
totally
uncommonly
uncontrollably
unquestionably
unusually
vastly

want verb

aspire toward
be attracted to
be in need of
covet
crave
desire
fancy
feel inclined toward
feel like
hanker after
have occasion for
hope for
hunger for
long
long for
need
prefer
set your heart on
thirst for
wish for
yearn

very adverb

abnormally
absolutely
altogether
awfully
completely
considerably
decidedly
deeply
downright
drastically
enormously
entirely
exceedingly
excessively
extraordinarily
extravagantly
extremely
highly
mighty
notably
outrageously
profoundly
quite
radically
remarkably
supremely

walk verb

advance
amble
go
hoof it
lumber
meander
pace
pad
plod
prance
ramble
roam
saunter
shuffle
stagger
step
stride
stroll
strut
swagger
tiptoe
totter
trek
trudge
waddle
wander

warm adjective

friendly
hearty
heated
hot
lukewarm
sincere
tepid
toasty

weak adjective

a pushover
a wet noodle
delicate
diluted
faint
feeble
flimsy
fragile
frail

puny
shaky
unstable

well adverb

ably
adequately
efficiently
like a charm
properly
right
satisfactorily
skillfully
successfully
sufficiently

went verb

abandoned
absconded
advanced
ambled
budged
defected
departed
descended
deserted
disappeared
embarked
emigrated
escaped
fled
flew
gallivanted
journeyed
left town
made headway
made off
migrated
paced
passed
proceeded
rambled
ran off
retreated

roved
scrammed
stole away
strayed
strode
traveled
trekked
vamoosed
wandered
withdrew

wet adjective

damp
drenched
humid
like a drowned rat
moist
saturated
soaked
soggy
sopping

whisper verb

hint
mumble
murmur
mutter
say under your breath
sigh
speak in hushed tones

wide adjective

ample
boundless
broad

capacious
expansive
extensive
far-flung
full
immense
massive
roomy
spacious
spread out
sweeping
thick
vast

won verb

accomplished
achieved
attained
bagged
brought home the bacon
came in first
came into
came out ahead
carried the day
conquered
excelled
gained a victory
harvested
nailed down
netted
pulled down
realized
reaped
sacked
scored
succeeded
swept
took by storm
triumphed
walked away with
waltzed off with
won the jackpot

ill-at-ease
itching
nervous
on edge
on pins and needles
perturbed
tormented
troubled
under the gun
uneasy
upset

improper
inaccurate
incorrect
infernal
irrational
mistaken
mixed-up
out in left field
screwy
sinister
unlawful
untrue

work noun

assignment
business
career
chore
drudgery
duty
effort
elbow grease
employment
errand
homework
industry
job
labor
project
schoolwork
task
toil
vocation

write verb

communicate
compose
drop a line
inscribe
jot
note
pen
record
scribble
scribe
transcribe

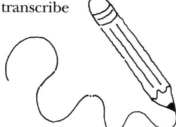

Y

young adjective

childlike
fresh
immature
infantile
minor
naive
new
recent
undeveloped
youthful

worried adjective

anxious
apprehensive
at loose ends
behind the eight ball
concerned
distressed
disturbed
down to the wire
fearful
fretful

wrong adjective

awful
corrupt
criminal
erroneous
flawed
groundless
illegal
illegitimate
illicit
immoral

Opposites Attract
(Antonyms)

ancient – modern

Antonyms are words that have opposite meanings.

B

back – front
backward – forward
bare – covered
beautiful – ugly
before – after
beginning – end
below – above
big – little
birth – death
black – white
blunt – sharp
bold – fearful
boring – exciting
bottom – top
boy – girl
break – repair
bright – dim
bright – dull
busy – idle
buy – sell

C

calm – panic
careful – rambunctious
cause – effect
child – adult
clean – dirty
cold – hot
come – go
comedy – tragedy
common – unique
complicated – simple
compliment – insult
conceal – expose
contract – expand
cooked – raw
cool – warm
covered – bare
coward – hero
cruel – kind
cry – laugh
curved – straight

A

above – below
absent – present
add – subtract
adult – child
after – before
against – for
aged – youthful
agree – refuse
alive – dead
all – none
allow – forbid
alone – together
always – never
amateur – professional
ancient – modern
answer – question
arrival – departure
ascend – descend
ask – tell
asleep – awake
attack – defend
awake – asleep

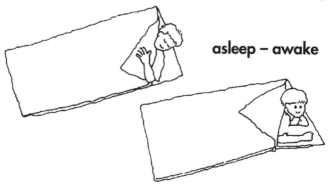

asleep – awake

D

dangerous – safe
dark – light
dawdle – hurry
day – night
dead – alive
death – birth
deep – shallow
defend – attack

departure

arrival

departure – arrival
descend – ascend
different – same
difficult – easy
dim – bright
dirty – clean
divide – unite
divorced – married
down – up
dry – wet
dull – bright
dull – shiny
dumb – smart
dwarf – giant

E

early – late
earn – spend
east – west
easy – difficult
easy – hard
effect – cause
empty – full
end – beginning
enemy – friend
entrance – exit
even – odd
evening – morning
evil – good
exciting – boring
exit – entrance
expand – contract
expand – shrink
expose – conceal

F

fact – fiction
fail – pass
fail – succeed
failure – success
false – true
fancy – plain
far – near
fast – slow
fat – thin
father – mother
fearful - bold
female – male
few – many
fiction – fact
figuratively – literally
find – lose
finish – start

fire – hire
first – last
float – sink
follower – leader
foolish – wise
for – against
forbid – allow
forget – remember
forward – backward
fresh – spoiled
friend – enemy
from – to
front – back
frozen – melted
full – empty

G

generous – selfish
gentle – rough
giant – dwarf
girl – boy
give – receive
go – come
go – stop
good – evil
guilty – innocent

fearful – bold

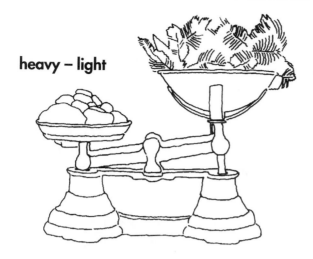

heavy – light

late – early
laugh – cry
leader – follower
learn – teach
least – most
left – right
less – more
lie – truth
light – dark
light – heavy
literally – figuratively
little – big
long – short
loose – tight
lose – find
loss – profit
lost – won
loud – soft
love – hate
low – high

happy – sad
hard – easy
hard – soft
hate – love
healthy – ill
heavy – light
hero – coward
hide – show
high – low
hire – fire
horizontal – vertical
hot – cold
hurry – dawdle

inferior – superior
innocent – guilty
inside – outside
insult – compliment

joy – pain

kind – cruel
knowledgeable – ignorant

major – minor
male – female
many – few
married – divorced
melted – frozen
messy – tidy
minor – major
modern – ancient
more – less
morning – evening
most – least
mother – father
multiple – single

idle – busy
ignorant – knowledgeable
ill – healthy
imagined – real
increase – reduce

large – small
last – first

narrow – wide
near – far
negative – positive
never – always
new – old
night – day
no one – everyone
no – yes
noise – silence
noisy – quiet
none – all
north – south
nothing – something

odd – even
off – on
often – seldom
old – new
old – young
on – off
opaque – transparent
open – shut
optimist – pessimist
outside – inside
over – under

pain – joy
panic – calm
pass – fail
permanent – temporary

pessimist – optimist
plain – fancy
play – work
polite – rude
poor – rich
positive – negative
present – absent
private – public
professional – amateur
profit – loss
public – private
pull – push
purchase – return
push – pull

question – answer
quick – slow
quiet – noisy

rambunctious – careful
raw – cooked
real – imagined
receive – give
reduce – increase

refuse – agree
remember – forget
repair – break
return – purchase
rich – poor
right – left
rough – gentle
rough – smooth
rude – polite

sad – happy
safe – dangerous
same – different
seldom – often
selfish – generous
sell – buy
serious – silly
shallow – deep
sharp – blunt
shiny – dull
short – long
short – tall
shout – whisper
show – hide
shrink – expand

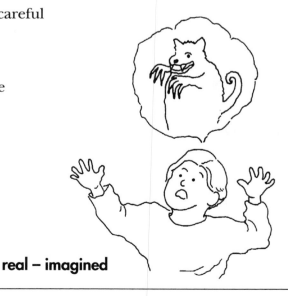

real – imagined

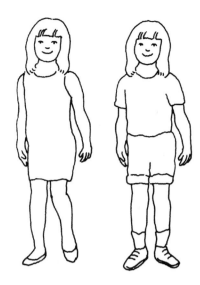

same – different

shut – open
shy – talkative
sick – well
silence – noise
silly – serious
simple – complicated
single – multiple
sink – float
sit – stand
slow – fast
slow – quick
small – large
smart – dumb
smooth – rough
soft – hard
soft – loud
something – nothing
sour – sweet
south – north
spend – earn
spoiled – fresh
stand – sit
start – finish
start – stop
stop – go
stop – start
straight – curved
subtract – add

succeed – fail
success – failure
sunrise – sunset
superior – inferior
sweet – sour

talkative – shy
tall – short
tame – wild
teach – learn
tell – ask
temporary – permanent
thick – thin
thin – fat
thin – thick
tidy – messy
tight – loose
to – from
together – alone
top – bottom
tragedy – comedy
transparent – opaque
true – false
truth – lie

ugly – beautiful
under – over
unique – common
unite – divide
up – down
use – waste

valuable – worthless
vertical – horizontal

warm – cool
waste – use
well – sick
west – east
wet – dry
whisper – shout
white – black
wide – narrow
wild – tame
wise – foolish
won – lost
work – play
worthless – valuable

yes – no
young – old
youthful – aged

They Look the Same, But . . .

(Homographs)

bank

Homographs are words that have the same spelling but have very different meanings. The words also have different origins or histories. To remember that homographs are words that *look* the same, you may want to think of a graph—you *look* at a graph.

Here are some common homographs. You may want to add more homographs to this list.

arms I held my new puppy in my *arms.* (body parts)
It is illegal to bear *arms* in some states. (weapons)

bail The judge set a high *bail* for the prisoner. (money for release)
Hold the bucket by its *bail.* (wire handle)

ball A dog ran off with the golf *ball.* (round object)
My parents went to the holiday *ball.* (formal dance)

band The marching *band* will play at the game. (group of musicians)
The striped *band* is missing from my hat. (thin strip around)

bank I have a savings account at the *bank.* (a business place)
The water rose over the *bank.* (edge along a river)

bark She'll *bark* at any new sound. (dog's noise)
The *bark* has been peeled away. (tree covering)

baste Grandma likes to *baste* a roast. (cover with liquid while cooking)
The tailor must first *baste* the hem. (to sew with long stitches)

b

bat
We saw a *bat* in our attic. (animal)
Who will *bat* first? (strike a ball)
Baseball players use a leaded *bat* for practice. (club)

batter
Andy is the first *batter*. (baseball player)
The cake *batter* tastes good.
   (uncooked mixture)

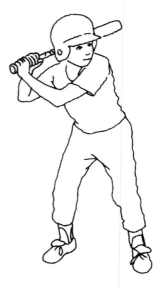

bay
Dad put a *bay* leaf in the stew. (leaf used in cooking)
We live near the *bay*. (part of a sea)

bear
The *bear* broke into our camp. (large furry animal)
This wagon won't *bear* all that weight. (support or carry)

bill
You can send me a *bill*. (statement of what is owed)
The bird's *bill* is stuck. (beak)

bit
May I have a *bit* of that? (small piece)
Mom bought a new *bit* for the drill. (pointed tool)
Sadie *bit* into a rotten apple. (did bite)

blaze
They put out the *blaze* in record time. (fire)
We will *blaze* a trail for you. (make a path)
Tomorrow's headlines will *blaze* the story. (publish)

blow
That news was a *blow*. (sudden attack)
This storm will *blow* over. (move swiftly)

bluff
We hiked around the *bluff*. (steep cliff)
Don't *bluff* me! (fool)

boil   The water will *boil* soon! (liquid heated till bubbling)
             My dad had a *boil* on his leg. (infected sore)

boom   That *boom* was an explosion! (loud and deep noise)
             Ships couldn't go past the *boom*. (chain barrier)

bounds   My dog *bounds* over fences. (leaps)
             You're out of *bounds*. (borders)

bow   I would *bow* before a king. (bend in respect)
             The *bow* is damaged. (front of a ship)

bow   My little sis wears a *bow* in her hair. (looped ribbon)
             I have a *bow* and no arrows. (wood weapon)

bowl   Put some cereal in a *bowl*. (deep dish)
             I like to *bowl*. (a game)

box   Please put it in a *box*. (container)
             Phil will *box* tonight. (sport played while wearing gloves)
             We planted a *box* border. (small evergreen plant)

bridge   The *bridge* connects two cities. (crossover)
             My parents play *bridge*. (card game)

brush   I use a *brush* on my dog every day.
                (grooming tool)
             He had a *brush* with the police.
                (problem)

can   No one *can* reach the cave. (is able to)
             I'd like a *can* of blue paint. (container)

capital I don't have the *capital* to do that. (money)
             Murder is sometimes a *capital* crime. (punishable by death)
             Tallahassee is Florida's *capital*. (place of government)

chops   He *chops* vegetables. (cuts)
             I turned and hit my *chops*. (jaws)

C

chord   She played the wrong *chord*.
              (three or more musical notes sounded together)
              I used a ruler to draw a *chord*. (line between two points on a circle)
              The news struck a *chord* with us. (a feeling)

chow   That dog is a *chow*. (a breed)
              I'd love some *chow*. (slang for food)

clip   Please *clip* these tags. (cut off)
              I'll *clip* a note to it. (fasten)

cobbler   My dad is a *cobbler*. (shoemaker)
              We had *cobbler* for lunch. (fruit pie)
              This looks as if a *cobbler* did it. (one who does a poor job)

colon   The *colon* is in your digestive tract. (part of large intestine)
              That sentence needs a *colon*. (mark of punctuation)

count   My sister is learning to *count*. (number items in order)
              Your opinion doesn't *count*. (have worth)
              Randolph is a *count*. (nobleman)

crow   A *crow* is in that tree. (large bird)
              The rooster's *crow* woke me.
              (loud cry)
              This is nothing to *crow* about.
              (slang for brag)
              My uncle is descended from the *Crow*.
              (American Indian group)

cue   Watch for a *cue*. (signal)
              We lost the *cue*. (long rod for playing pool)

date   The *date* is wrong on the form. (specific day)
              We have a *date* tomorrow. (planned meeting)
              I would rather not eat the *date*. (fruit of a date palm)

dock   We went out on the *dock*. (long platform)
              My boss will *dock* my pay. (cut out a part of)

down   We went *down* the stairs. (toward a lower place)
I'd like a *down* pillow. (soft feathers)
It's only the third *down*. (football term)

dresser   Put it in your *dresser*. (piece of furniture)
He's a stylish *dresser*. (one who dresses)

drove   Mom *drove* me home. (did drive)
I saw a *drove* of cattle. (herd)

duck   There's a *duck* on the pond. (wild bird)
You'd better *duck* fast! (get down)
The doctor's coat was made of *duck*. (cotton cloth)

ear   My *ear* hurts. (hearing organ)
I'd like an *ear* of corn. (part of a plant)

fair   We're going to the county *fair*. (event)
That's not *fair!* (equal; just)
The weather is *fair*. (clear and sunny)
She's *fair*-haired. (light)

fan   The *fan* helps keep us cool. (blowing machine)
My mom is a Celtics *fan*. (admirer)

fast   You did that awfully *fast*. (quickly)
Some people *fast* for a reason. (go without food)

felt   I *felt* sad. (did feel)
The *felt* pads protect the table. (type of cloth)

file   Help me *file* these papers. (put away in an orderly manner)
I need a new *file*. (drawer; folder)
She'll *file* her nails. (smooth with a tool)

fine   That's *fine* with me. (okay)
My brother paid his library *fine*. (money as penalty)

f

firm
I like a *firm* mattress. (not soft)
My aunt's *firm* is downtown. (company)

fit
Nothing will *fit* me! (be the right size)
The toddler had a *fit*. (tantrum)

flat
The land is all *flat*. (not hilly)
Our *flat* is on the second floor. (apartment)

flounder
We had *flounder* for dinner. (kind of fish)
I'm afraid I will *flounder* without help.
    (struggle awkwardly)

fly
The bird is hurt and can't *fly*.
    (soar through air)
A *fly* is on the table. (insect)

found
I finally *found* my radio. (did find)
We'll *found* a new group. (establish)

frank
I'd like a *frank*. (hot dog)
Let's be *frank* with each other. (open and honest)

fret
Grandma will *fret* if I don't call home. (worry)
Stroke the third *fret* for that note. (ridge on a guitar)

fry
My grandma doesn't *fry* much anymore. (cook in oil)
I caught a *fry*. (young fish)

grave
We dug a *grave* for my hamster. (burial hole)
I have *grave* doubts about this. (serious)
He let us *grave* our initials in the wood. (carve)

ground
We sat on the *ground*. (soil; earth)
Hamburger is *ground* beef. (minced by grinding)

gum
There's *gum* stuck to my shoe. (chewing substance from trees)
My *gum* was bleeding a bit. (tissue around teeth)

hail   The *hail* was terrible. (icy rain)

Please *hail* a cab. (call out for)

hamper   Dirty clothes go in the *hamper*. (special container)

That won't *hamper* our plans. (interfere with)

hatch   Please close the *hatch*.
(a cover)

The chicks should *hatch* today.
(be born)

hawk   I saw the *hawk* fly over. (bird)

We can *hawk* what's left. (peddle for sale)

heel   I broke the *heel*. (rear bottom of shoe or foot)

My dog can *heel* now. (stay close behind)

The boat might *heel*. (tip to one side)

hide   I can't *hide* my joy. (keep from showing)

They made things from *hide*. (animal skin)

hold   I'll *hold* the bags. (keep or stop)

The bags are in the *hold*. (cargo place on ship or plane)

The bank put a *hold* on the check. (wait for approval)

jam   I like *jam* on peanut butter. (sweet preserve)

We'll have to *jam* the things in. (pack tightly)

There's a traffic *jam* over there. (crowding)

jar   Put the juice in this *jar*. (container with large opening)

That noise will *jar* the windows. (rattle; shake)

jerky   The ride was *jerky*. (sudden starts and stops)

He acted *jerky*. (slang for foolish)

I snacked on *jerky*. (dried meat strips)

jet   We watched the soaring *jet*. (kind of airplane)

The beads were made from *jet*. (hard black coal)

The *jet* gushed from the tank. (stream of gas or liquid)

j

jumper   She wore a *jumper* to school. (type of garment)

My cat is a real *jumper.* (one who jumps)

keys   We live in the *keys.* (low islands)

I forgot my *keys.* (devices that unlock)

kind   I like it when people are *kind.* (good-natured)

What *kind* of animal is that? (type)

lap   The puppy will *lap* that in a flash. (drink)

I'll go one *lap* with you. (course traveled)

The kitty loves my *lap.* (upper legs when sitting)

last   You won't be *last.* (at the end)

This will never *last.* (go on and on)

lead   We *lead* the others. (are ahead of; guide)

There's no *lead* in my pencil. (soft graphite)

leave   I have to *leave* now. (go away)

My brother is on *leave* soon. (permitted absence)

left   There's no food *left.* (remaining)

Put it on the *left* side. (opposite of right)

We *left* the concert. (did leave)

lie   I would never *lie* about this. (tell untruth)

I need to *lie* down. (stretch out flat)

light   This *light* is too bright. (ray of energy)

The feathers are *light.* (not heavy)

We'll *light* there around ten. (arrive)

m

like
This is *like* a dream. (similar to)
I *like* you. (am pleased with)

line
There's a *line* all the way to the street. (single row)
I helped Mom *line* the drawers. (cover the insides of)
We have a fax *line.* (wire circuit)

loaf
I can't afford to *loaf.* (be idle)
I'll buy a *loaf.* (bread shape)

lock
Please *lock* up when you leave. (fasten the entrance)
Mom kept a *lock* of my baby hair. (piece)

long
I *long* to go to Australia. (wish for)
It's a *long* way away. (great length)

mail
The *mail* hasn't come yet. (letters)
I'll *mail* it tomorrow. (send)
My brother tried to make a suit of *mail.* (armor)

maroon
I wouldn't *maroon* you out here. (leave helpless)
You might like these *maroon* boots. (brownish-red)

mat
Leave it under the *mat.* (small rug)
I like the picture's *mat.* (border)
The dog's hair will *mat* if it gets wet. (tangle)

match
These clothes don't *match.* (go together)
The *match* is tonight. (planned contest)
Don't strike that *match!* (stick that makes fire)

meal
I gave *meal* to the animals. (ground grain)
We had a delicious *meal.* (food served)

m

mean
He is not a *mean* person. (unkind)
I didn't *mean* that! (intend)
The *mean* temperature was 60 degrees. (average)

mine
That's *mine*. (belonging to me)
The workers went into the *mine*. (mineral-filled hole in earth)

miss
I *miss* my best friend. (long for)
Miss Thomas is my teacher. (unmarried woman's title)
Watch out, in case I *miss*. (fail to hit target)

mold
There's *mold* on this bread. (fungus growth)
The coach wants to *mold* the team. (shape)

mole
My grandpa has a *mole* on his arm. (brown skin spot)
We have a *mole* living in our yard. (small animal)

mum
I gave Mom a *mum* corsage. (kind of flower)
Dad said he'd be *mum* about it. (silent)

nag
Our *nag* is in the pasture. (old horse)
I wish you wouldn't *nag* me! (keep telling me)

page
Look at this *page!* (one side of paper)
I get to be a *page* for our congressman. (youth who runs errands)
Page me if you need something. (call on a beeper)

palm
My *palm* itches! (inside of hand)
The *palm* is growing nicely. (kind of tree)

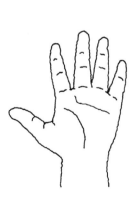

patent   Someone has a *patent* on this gadget. (special right of inventor)
She wore *patent* shoes. (shiny leather)

peck   Birds sometimes *peck* at our windows. (strike at with bill)
Who picked a *peck* of pickles? (a measured amount)

pen   The *pen* won't hold that horse. (enclosed area)
I need some paper and a *pen*. (writing instrument)

pine   A *pine* is one kind of evergreen. (kind of tree)
I *pine* to go visit my old house. (wish strongly)

pitch   *Pitch* the ball to me. (throw)
There's *pitch* on the road. (tar)

pitcher   The lemonade is in the *pitcher*. (jar with spout)
Who's the *pitcher* for your team? (player who pitches)

pool   The *pool* feels great on a hot day. (tank of water)
We played *pool* at my house. (table game)
Let's *pool* our money. (put together)

pop   I heard it *pop*. (quick, short sound)
My *pop* says I can go. (dad)
I like some kinds of *pop*. (soft drink)
I like *pop* art. (popular)

post   The *post* broke off. (support pole)
Your *post* is in the hallway. (appointed duty)
The *post* is rarely late. (mail)

pound   Please get a *pound* of beans. (unit of weight)
We got our dog at the *pound*. (pen)
I'll *pound* on your door to wake you. (hit hard)

present   At the *present*, I'm in fifth grade. (current time)
I want to shop for a *present*. (gift)
All of us are *present*. (not absent)

p

prune   I ate a *prune* for the first time. (fruit)
             We need to *prune* this tree. (trim)

punch   The *punch* is delicious. (beverage)
             No one is going to *punch* me! (hit)

pupils   Our class has two new *pupils*. (students)
             Your *pupils* are so tiny. (black part of eye)

racket   My *racket* is too old. (sports paddle)
             What's all that *racket*? (noise)

rare   This meat is too *rare*. (uncooked)
             It's *rare* to see an ostrich out here. (unusual)

rash   I'd never had a *rash* like this. (itchy spots on skin)
             I did a *rash* thing. (act without thinking)

refrain   I'll try to *refrain*. (hold back)
             Remember to sing the *refrain*. (repeated part)

rest   Here's the *rest* of the news. (what is left)
             I need to *rest* after running. (relax)

ring   My sister has a class *ring*. (finger jewelry)
             Listen and you'll hear it *ring*. (bell sound)
             Elephants have their own *ring*. (circle)

root   We'll *root* for you! (cheer)
             The *root* is showing. (plant's support)

row   You need to help me *row*. (move using paddles)
             I'm in the second *row*. (line)

sage   I like the taste of *sage*. (kind of herb)
             He acts like a *sage*. (wise person)

sash   The *sash* needs new paint. (window frame)
             He wore a *sash* with the tuxedo. (waist band)

saw I *saw* the accident. (did see)

This *saw* is dull. (cutting tool)

Maybe her *saw* will be helpful. (wise saying)

school I'll go to a new *school* next year. (place to learn)

A *school* of fish raced by. (group)

seal This needs an official *seal*. (mark of approval)

The sea lion is one kind of *seal*. (sea mammal)

second Please wait a *second*. (part of a minute)

I was *second* in line. (number two)

This shirt is a *second*, but it looks perfect. (item of lesser quality)

shed I thought I was going to *shed* tears. (pour forth)

I keep my bike in the *shed*. (storage place)

shingles The *shingles* blew off in the storm. (roof covering)

My uncle has *shingles*. (viral blisters)

slip I'll *slip* into my seat. (move easily)

You'll need this *slip* to get back in class. (piece of paper)

Mom's *slip* was showing. (underskirt)

slug She might *slug* her brother. (hit hard)

There's a *slug* on the porch. (kind of snail)

sock One *sock* is always missing. (footwear)

Don't *sock* me with the bill! (hit)

S

soil

This *soil* is moist. (dirt)

Babies *soil* their diapers. (make dirty)

sole

My shoe needs a new *sole*. (bottom of shoe)

We had *sole* for supper. (kind of fish)

This is my *sole* request. (only)

spell

I can *spell* well. (say or write a word's letters)

We're going through a dry *spell*. (period of time)

I felt like I was in a *spell*. (mystical state)

squash

Baked *squash* tastes good. (kind of vegetable)

I'm learning to play *squash*. (kind of sport)

I'm afraid I'll *squash* you. (press flat)

stable

Let's go out to the *stable*. (horse barn)

The stock market is *stable*. (unchanging)

stall

Let's go clean out the *stall*. (pen in a stable)

I hope we can *stall* for a few days. (delay)

steer

Please *steer* me to the software department. (guide)

That's a champion *steer*. (male in ox family)

stoop

We had to *stoop* over. (bend)

The *stoop* needs to be painted. (porch)

story

His office is on the fifth *story*. (building's floor)

Tell me a bedtime *story*. (tale)

strip

My mom will *strip* the paint. (remove)

I need a *strip* of tape. (narrow piece)

stroke

My cat loves for me to *stroke* her fur. (pet)

His *stroke* is powerful. (hit)

sty

Mom says my room is like a *sty*. (pigpen)

I have a *sty* on my eye. (sore swelling)

V

swallow   There's a *swallow* on our bush. (kind of bird)

Some medicines are hard to *swallow*. (move down the throat)

tap   I'll *tap* on your door. (knock lightly)

The water in the *tap* is quite cold. (faucet)

tart   We made two pies and one *tart*. (small pie)

My favorite is the *tart* one. (pleasantly sour)

temple   The wedding is in the *temple*. (place of worship)

My head hurts on my *temple*. (part of the head at the side of the eye)

tick   The clock won't *tick*. (sound)

My dog had a *tick* on his ear. (kind of insect)

The leak didn't go through the *tick*. (pillow cover)

till   We'll be here *till* noon. (until)

I put my allowance in the *till*. (spot for money)

A farmer will *till* our land. (plow)

tip   Be careful not to *tip* it over. (spill slightly)

Let's leave a good *tip*. (money for service)

I'll sharpen the *tip* of the stick. (end)

tire   We had a flat *tire*. (rubber on wheel)

Grandpa might *tire* by then. (get weary)

toast   We'll *toast* the bride and groom. (honor for good luck)

I want to *toast* this bagel. (heat to crispness)

toll   You'll hear the *toll* every hour. (bell sound)

We'll have to pay a *toll* every ten miles. (fee for using)

top   The baby giggled when she saw the *top*. (spinning toy)

The cat is on *top* of the high cupboard. (highest place)

vault   We went into the *vault* at the bank. (place for safekeeping)

I decided to *vault* the fence. (jump over)

w

well   I don't feel *well*. (healthy)
            My uncle's farm has a *well*. (hole as source of water)

will   She *will* be here tomorrow. (is to)
            My dad made his *will*. (instructions for heirs)

yard   I need a *yard* of ribbon. (a measure of three feet)
            My dog will not stay in the *yard*. (grassy area)

They Sound the Same, But . . .

(Homophones)

aisle
isle

Homophones are words that sound alike but have different spellings and meanings. To remember that homophones are words that *sound* the same, you may want to think of a phone—you hear *sounds* when you use a phone.

Here are some common homophones. You may want to add more homophones to this list.

ad means an advertisement. *I read an ad in the newspaper.*
add means to put numbers together. *He'll add the cost of my purchases.*

aid means to help. *Two police officers will aid us.*
aide means an assistant. *Our aide is not here today.*

air means gases that surround the Earth. *The air seems awfully moist.*
heir means one who inherits. *My grandpa says I am his heir.*

aisle means a pathway. *The bride is coming down the aisle.*
I'll means I will. *I'll be there in a minute.*
isle means an island. *We'll take a ferry to the isle.*

all means everything. *Can all of that be true?*
awl means a tool for punching holes. *I used an awl to make a hole in my belt.*

all ready means to be prepared. *I was all ready to go an hour ago!*
already means earlier. *I already brushed the dog.*

allowed means to receive permission. *I'm not allowed to hang out at malls.*
aloud means out loud. *Please read that aloud.*

a

altar means a religious place. *The couple exchanged vows at the altar.*
alter means to change. *I cannot alter how you feel about that.*

ant means an insect. *Mom found a carpenter ant in the drawer.*
aunt means a female relative. *My aunt is coming to visit.*

arc means part of a circle. *I started a rainbow by drawing an arc.*
ark means a type of ship. *Collin built a model of an ark.*

ascent means upward. *The worst part of the hike was the ascent.*
assent means agreement. *Mr. Atterbury hasn't given his assent.*

assistance means help. *Rolf needed assistance with his science project.*
assistants mean helpers. *He now has two assistants.*

ate means to have eaten in the past. *Raoul ate his lunch and much of mine.*
eight means a number. *There are eight parts of speech.*

attendance means being present. *Abra has perfect attendance.*
attendants means those who take care of. *Flight attendants help travelers.*

aye means yes. *Everyone voted by saying, "Aye."*
eye means used for seeing. *Brittany has a sty in her eye.*
I is a pronoun. *I like to write stories.*

ball means a round object. *Milton caught every ball.*
bawl means to cry. *The baby looks like she's going to bawl.*

band means a group. *Our school's band will give a concert today.*
banned means not allowed. *Shorts are banned at my brother's school.*

bare means not covered. *My dad's head is bare.*
bear means an animal. *A bear invaded our campsite.*
bear also means to carry. *The donkey will bear the food up the mountain.*

base means bottom. *Mushrooms are growing at the base of the tree.*
bass means a low sound. *My grandpa is a bass singer in a choir.*

bases means more than one base. *I ran the bases for my injured friend.*
basis means a foundation. *We formed teams on the basis of friendship.*

bazaar means a marketplace. *Grandma sells crafts at the bazaar.*
bizarre means strange. *Today's news is bizarre.*

be means to be alive. *Jacquie will be here any minute.*
bee means an insect. *We stood still when we saw the bee.*

beach means the edge of a lake or sea. *My family's going to the beach.*
beech means a kind of tree. *I think that's a beech tree.*

beat means to whip. *My team beat all the others.*
beet means a red vegetable. *Mom sliced a beet for the salad.*

beau means a male sweetheart. *My grandma has a new beau.*
bow means a knot with loops. *My little sister likes to wear a bow in her hair.*
bow also means a curved object. *This stick might make a good bow.*

been is a form of the verb *be*. *I have not been to Disney World yet.*
bin means a container. *There's a bin for every kind of screw and nail.*

bell means an object you ring. *The bell hasn't rung yet.*
belle means a pretty female. *My sister was the belle of her party.*

berry means a kind of fruit. *There's only one kind of berry in the salad.*
bury means to cover up. *My dog likes to bury things.*

b

bite means to use teeth. *Ruth can't bite into that thick sandwich.*
byte means a computer unit. *A byte contains eight bits.*

billed means charged. *We were billed for someone else's phone calls.*
build means put together. *We plan to build some bookshelves in my room.*

blew is a past tense of the verb *blow*. *The wind blew sand in our faces.*
blue means a color. *Corinne wore a blue shirt.*

boar means a male pig. *My uncle has a boar at his farm.*
bore means to be dull. *Sometimes things bore me.*
bore also means to make a hole. *Dad will use a drill to bore into the wood.*

board means sawed wood. *This board will work as a shelf for books.*
bored means not interested. *Phyllis says she's never bored.*

burrow means to dig into. *A mole will burrow holes in the yard.*
burro means an animal. *The little burro looked so sad.*
borough means a town or village. *Our borough's population is small.*

bough means part of a tree. *The ice has bent more than one bough.*
bow means part of a ship. *We sat up front in the bow.*

brake means a part used for stopping. *Mom slammed her foot on the brake.*
break means to come apart. *I hope we didn't break the window!*
break also means time out. *Our class gets a break from homework.*

bridle means a horse's headpiece. *Jamey's horse has a new bridle.*
bridal means of a bride. *The bridal party has rehearsal tonight.*

but means except. *Stan thinks it's true, but he's not sure.*
butt means the end. *I had to use the butt of my fishing rod to clear a path.*

buy means to purchase. *Natalie needs to buy some pens.*
by means near. *We drove by the radio station.*
bye means good-bye. *No one said "Bye" when we left.*

capital means a city where a state's or country's government is located. *Albany is the capital of New York.*

capital also means chief. *The capital reason we're going is to tour the ruins.*

capitol means a building. *The lawmakers have offices in the capitol.*

carat means a unit used to measure gems. *The diamond is less than a carat.*

caret means an editor's mark. *I put a caret to show where this word goes.*

carrot means a vegetable. *There'll be carrot sticks for everyone.*

around ^the^ corner

ceiling means the top of a room. *Some old houses have wood ceilings.*

sealing means closing tightly. *We're sealing the boxes now.*

cell means a small space. *The coat closet felt like a cell.*

sell means exchange for money. *The new store will sell CDs.*

cent means a penny. *I don't have a cent to my name!*

sent means being asked to go. *Mom sent me to my room.*

scent means an odor. *My dog is tracking some animal's scent.*

cereal means food from grain. *This cereal is fat-free.*

serial means one in a series. *The new TV serial is on Monday nights.*

cheap means of little cost. *I bought a cheap pair of boots.*

cheep means a bird sound. *It sounded like a baby bird's cheep.*

chews means to use teeth. *Meg's sister chews her nails.*

choose means to select. *You may choose whichever one you'd like.*

chute means an inclined trough. *We slid down the grain chute at the farm.*

shoot means to fire at. *I'd never want to shoot an animal.*

cite means to quote someone else's words. *I cited the President's speech in my report.*

sight means can see. *My sight is better now that I have glasses.*

site means a place. *The old Steller house is now a historical site.*

C

claws means an animal's nails. *My friend's kitten has sharp claws.*
clause means a part of a sentence. *I forgot a comma after the opening clause.*

close means to shut. *I have to remember to close the hamster's cage.*
clothes means clothing. *We went shopping for school clothes.*

coarse means not fine. *Some dogs have coarse hair.*
course means a subject. *My brother likes his history course.*
course also means a path. *Did you take the long course through the woods?*

complement means to make whole. *Money would complement my wallet!*
compliment means a nice comment. *My dad gave me a compliment.*

core means the center. *Give your apple core to the hamster.*
corps means a group. *A corps of engineers will study the damaged bridge.*

creak means a noise. *I heard a scary creak in the night.*
creek means a small stream. *Let's wade across the creek.*

crews means workers in groups. *Clean-up crews will take care of this mess.*
cruise means to sail or drive about. *I'd love to go on a cruise to Alaska.*

cruel means hurtful. *Larry would never be cruel to an animal.*
crewel means a kind of stitching. *My aunt does crewel work.*

deer means an animal. *A deer leaped across the road.*
dear means much loved. *My grandma calls me "Dear."*

desert means to go away from. *I promise I won't desert you.*
dessert means part of a meal. *We had bread pudding for dessert.*

die means to stop living. *I don't ever want my pets to die.*
dye means to add color. *The red dye turned everything pink!*

doe means a female deer. *The fawn followed the doe into the stream.*
dough means an unbaked mixture. *Cookie dough tastes good.*
do means a musical note. *We played do, re, mi over and over on the piano.*

do means to work at. *I will do that for you.*
dew means water droplets. *Dew covered the ground this morning.*
due means owed. *My library book is due tomorrow.*

ewe means a female sheep. *That sheep is probably a ewe.*
yew means a shrub. *The bow is made from the wood of a yew.*
you is a pronoun. *You should have seen the sunrise this morning!*

fair means honest or just. *I suppose taking turns is the fair way.*
fair also means an event. *We went to the State Fair last night.*
fare means cost. *Do you need the exact fare to ride the subway?*

feat means a remarkable deed. *Monty's feat was applauded.*
feet means plural of *foot. The donkey stomped his feet.*

find means uncover. *Could you help me find my jacket?*
fined means charged. *I'll get fined if I've lost that book.*

fir means a kind of tree. *The snow-covered fir trees looked like ghosts.*
fur means an animal's coat. *Some animals shed fur in the spring.*

flea means an insect. *I found a flea in the carpet.*
flee means to run away. *Barkley tries to flee when I brush him.*

flew means went away. *The birds flew off when I went outside.*
flu means an illness. *Fever and aching all over are flu symptoms.*
flue means a tube or pipe. *The chimney flue was stuffed with twigs.*

flour means ground grain. *My mom makes gravy with flour.*
flower means a part of a plant. *A wild flower grew in the sidewalk crack.*

for means the purpose of. *I have news for you.*
four means a number. *All four puppies curled up to sleep.*

forth means forward. *We'll go forth when you're ready.*
fourth means after third. *Eddie is fourth in line.*

f

foul means out of bounds. *The umpire called it a foul ball.*
foul also means bad. *A skunk's scent is foul.*
fowl means a bird. *The chicken is one kind of fowl.*

friar means a religious person. *The friar asked directions to the church.*
fryer means a deep pan. *Mom cooked the potatoes in a fryer.*

gnu means an antelope. *The gnu looks much like an ox.*
new means not old. *Our new sofa arrived last night.*
knew is past tense of the verb *know*. *I knew you would understand.*

grate means a pattern of metal bars. *My dog sniffed the sewer grate.*
great means large or very good. *Our school has a great choir.*

grown means to get bigger. *I have grown three inches this year.*
groan means a sound. *Your groan suggests you'd rather not do this.*

guessed means decided without facts. *Tad says he guessed the answer.*
guest means a visitor. *We're having a guest in our class tomorrow.*

hair means a head covering. *My hair won't cooperate today!*
hare means a rabbit. *We had a pet hare once.*

hall means a passageway. *Ms. Tilly is coming down the hall.*
haul means to carry. *Brenda has to haul all her books home.*

halve means to cut in half. *It's hard to halve an apple by hand.*
have means to own. *No one can have more homework than this!*

hay means a dried grass. *We had to give hay to the horses.*
hey means an expression. *Shocked, my best friend yelled, "Hey!"*

heal means to make well. *Some people feel that herbs can heal an illness.*
he'll means he will. *He'll never want to do this again!*
heel means the back of the foot. *The shopping cart caught my heel.*

hear means to use ears. *Timothea likes to hear scary stories.*
here means this place. *It seems especially hot in here.*

k

heard is past tense of the verb *hear*. *Pilar heard about it first.*
herd means an animal group. *We ran down the road like a herd of buffaloes.*

hi means a greeting. *I was the first one to say, "Hi!"*
high means way up. *My parents have high hopes for me.*

higher means more high. *The temperature is higher than ever today.*
hire means to pay for work done. *I wish I could hire someone to do this.*

him is a pronoun. *It's all right if you tell him what I said.*
hymn means a religious song. *We practiced one hymn over and over.*

horse means an animal. *My best friend has her own horse.*
hoarse means a husky voice. *I was hoarse after cheering at the game.*

hole means an opening. *There's a hole in my favorite shirt.*
whole means all. *No one watched the whole movie.*

hour means sixty minutes. *Jillian leaves in an hour.*
our is a pronoun. *Our class is going on an overnight camping trip.*

in means inside of. *Just put it in my backpack.*
inn means a hotel. *My dad searched for a budget inn.*

knead means to mix with hands. *I will help you knead the yeast dough.*
need means to want badly. *Shelly may need some help too.*

knight means a warrior. *My little brother loves to pretend he's a knight.*
night means evening. *Our neighbor never goes out at night.*

knot means a tied loop. *We need to tie a square knot here.*
not means in no way. *Phoebe is not going with us.*

know means to be sure of. *Do you know when the concert begins?*
no means not so. *There is no way that can be true!*

lead means a heavy metal. *It feels like there's lead in my backpack.*
led means guided. *Mike led the team in goals scored.*

leased means paid to rent. *My parents leased a house for us.*
least means smallest. *Getting there is the least of my worries.*

lie means not the truth. *Leda didn't mean to lie to you.*
lye means a substance used in soap. *The smell of lye was sickening.*

made means created. *A committee made costumes for the play.*
maid means a hired person. *My sister seemed to think I was her maid.*

mail means letters. *I love to get mail.*
male means a man. *The paper said the male dancer stole the show.*

main means important. *Here's the main idea of the story.*
mane means horse's hair. *I got to comb Pauper's mane after the race.*
Maine means a state. *Augusta is the capital of Maine.*

maize means corn. *The farmer harvested the maize.*
maze means a confusing path. *The problem was like a maze.*

marry means to join in marriage. *Grandpa will marry his old friend.*
merry means happy. *The party seemed to be a merry time for all.*

meat means animal flesh. *Vegetarians prefer not to eat meat.*
meet means to come together. *Let's meet in the hall after school.*

might means likely to. *If June goes, I might sit with her.*
mite means an insect. *I saw only one mite on that plant.*

p

miner means a mine digger. *Uncle Ben is a coal miner.*
minor means under a particular age. *My brother is still a minor.*

missed means off target. *I'm glad you missed me!*
mist means a light rain. *The mist didn't affect the game.*

moan means a sound. *Did you hear someone moan?*
mown means having been cut. *The lawn was mown yesterday.*

morn means early in the day. *I woke up late this morn.*
mourn means to feel a loss. *We will mourn his loss forever.*

none means not any. *You have many, but I have none.*
nun means a religious person. *She is studying to become a nun.*

oar means a pole used to row. *Alex lost an oar in the river.*
or means you have a choice. *Do you want to see this movie or that one?*
ore means a mineral. *They hauled iron ore out of the canyon.*

one means a number. *Priscilla answered one question.*
won means succeeded. *The Sox won the game last night.*

pain means a lack of comfort. *Did Trish feel any pain in her leg?*
pane means a window glass. *Our dog smears every pane in the house.*

pair means two alike. *Dominie has a new pair of loafers.*
pare means to peel. *I'd like it if you would pare this apple.*
pear means a fruit. *That pear is bruised.*

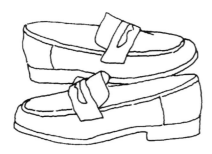

passed means moved on. *You passed my house on your way home.*
past means an earlier time. *It's already past nine o'clock.*

p

patience means willing to wait. *Mom says she needs more patience.*
patients means ill persons. *There were ten patients in the waiting room.*

pause means a short break. *Gavin's pause gave us time to think.*
paws means an animal's feet. *The tiger's paws were bandaged.*

peace means a quiet time. *Let's try for some peace in here.*
piece means a part. *May I have a piece of gum?*

peak means the top of. *We can hike to the peak of that mountain.*
peek means to sneak a look. *Don't you dare peek in that box!*

peddle means to sell. *We'll peddle cold drinks during the game.*
pedal means a part of a bike. *Nick's foot slipped off the pedal.*

peer means to look searchingly. *You may want to peer into the room.*
peer also means one equal in rank. *Tara wanted her peer to go along.*
pier means a dock. *The kids dove off the pier.*

plain means ordinary. *Let's add fruit to the plain yogurt.*
plane means a flat surface. *Tilt the plane a bit to see the ball roll.*

pore means a skin gland. *The doctor says it's a clogged pore.*
pour means to flow out of. *You may pour juice for all of us.*

pray means to worship. *I pray that doesn't happen.*
prey means the one being hunted. *The injured butterfly was anyone's prey.*

presents means gifts. *Please don't bring presents to the party.*
presence means to appear. *Your presence is all I need.*

principal means chief person. *The principal heads up our school.*
principle means a rule. *She has more than one principle we must follow.*

rain means wet weather. *It will surely rain today.*
reign means royal rule. *The king's reign lasted many years.*
rein means part of a horse's bit. *Pull back on the rein.*

read means to get meaning from print. *Elvira says she likes to read.*
reed means a plant. *That reed stands taller than any other.*

read means to have gotten meaning from print. *I read the best book!*
red means a color. *Our school colors are red and white.*

real means not pretend. *Nonfiction is about real things.*
reel means a part of a fishing pole. *Dad bought a new reel for his pole.*

right means correct. *It may not seem right, but it's the rule.*
rite means a special event. *A memorial rite was held last night.*
write means to form letters. *Don't forget to write me when you move.*

ring means jewelry worn on a finger. *Demetrius lost his class ring.*
wring means to squeeze. *Wring the rug to get the water out.*

road means a street. *That road goes nowhere.*
rode means moved along on. *Tom and Adrian rode their bikes.*
rowed means used oars. *Olivia said they rowed for hours.*

rose means a flower. *The rose bush is prickly.*
rows means in lines. *We'll have to line up in rows.*

sail means to go by boat. *My grandparents will sail to the Bahamas.*
sale means lowered prices. *We found a fantastic sale on shoes.*

scene means place and time. *They found a wig at the scene.*
seen means viewed. *I have seen every new movie.*

sea means a body of water. *Sea creatures fascinate me.*
see means to use eyes. *Did you see what happened?*

seam means where joined. *The seam in my shirt needs mending.*
seem means appear to be. *They didn't seem to notice anything.*

sew means to stitch. *We'll need to sew costumes next week.*
so means therefore. *I have to unlock the door so others can enter.*
sow means to plant. *Mom helped us sow grass seed.*

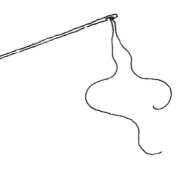

soar means to fly high. *An eagle can soar a long time.*
sore means painful. *I have a sore throat.*

some means an amount. *You might bring along some of your music.*
sum means the total when adding. *The sum is less than one hundred.*

son means a boy or man. *My aunt has a new son.*
sun means a hot star. *The sun hid behind the billowy clouds.*

stair means a step. *I thought I left my books on the stair.*
stare means to look at. *Everyone will stare at me!*

stationary means doesn't move. *Mom works out on a stationary bicycle.*
stationery means paper. *I need some stationery to write thank-you notes.*

tale means a story. *Sheila told a scary tale.*
tail means a body part. *He'll wag his tail as soon as he sees you.*

their means there is ownership. *The kids found their own props for the play.*
they're means they are. *They're about to open the curtain on Act I.*
there means that place. *If you put it there, it should be easy to find.*

theirs means there is ownership. *He and his friends think the room is theirs.*
there's means there is. *There's a reason why we did it this way.*

threw means having tossed. *Who threw this shirt in the laundry?*
through means by way of. *Po came through the back door.*

throne means a royal seat. *You must think your chair is a throne!*
thrown means tossed. *The referee had thrown a bad ball.*

thyme means an herb. *Thyme adds flavor to soup.*
time means a period when. *What time do we
    need to be home?*

to means toward. *Annette went to get more paper.*
two means a number. *Two heads are sometimes better than one.*
too means also. *I'd like to have one of those too.*

Y

toad means an animal. *I saw a toad on the sidewalk.*
towed means pulled. *Our van had to be towed.*

toe means a part of the foot. *Don't stub your toe on that brick.*
tow means to pull. *Who will tow the wrecked car?*

waist means a body part just above the hips. *My jeans are tight at the waist.*
waste means to destroy. *You'll waste time if you don't begin now.*

wait means to stop a while. *Please wait for me outside.*
weight means heaviness. *There's too much weight on one end.*

we is a pronoun. *We could stop now and finish this later.*
wee means very small. *My new niece is a wee thing.*

weak means not strong. *Your argument is weak.*
week means seven days. *Cecil had no homework at all last week.*

weave means to go through. *Could you weave that into your story?*
we've means we have. *Here's what we've been thinking.*

we'd means we had or we would. *We'd better get started.*
weed means a plant. *That weed is rather pretty.*

who's means who is. *Who's going to go first?*
whose means there is ownership. *Whose shoes are these?*

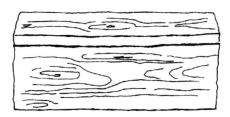

wood means a product from a tree. *This wood box is full.*
would means willing to. *Would you like to tell us
    what you think?*

yoke means a bar that joins oxen. *We have an antique yoke on our wall.*
yolk means part of an egg. *The yolk has all the cholesterol.*

you'll means you will. *You'll probably want to see this.*
Yule means Christmas. *It's a part of the Yule celebration.*

you're means you are. *You're not going to believe this!*
your is an adjective. *Your idea was clearly the best.*

Stuck with Each Other

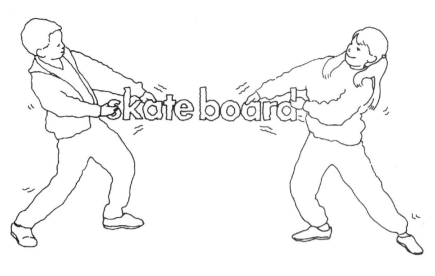

(Compound Words)

A *compound word* is formed when two smaller words are "glued" together. Compound words do not always join the meanings of the smaller words. For example, *understand* does not mean "to stand under something," and *brainstorm* is not truly "a storm inside of the brain."

Here is a list of compound words organized by topic. You may think of other words or topics to add to the list.

Animals

anteater
anthill
bluebird
butterfly
catfish
diamondback
dragonfly
earthworm
goldfish
greyhound
groundhog
hummingbird
jellyfish
longhorn
mayfly
meadowlark
rattlesnake
swordfish
watchdog
wildcat
woodpecker

Body

armpit
eyelid
jawbone
toenail
windpipe

Business

airline
drugstore
junkyard
lumberyard

newspaper
racetrack
supermarket

Celebrations

birthday
fanfare
honeymoon
noisemaker
peacetime
Thanksgiving

Clothing

cutoffs
earring
jumpsuit
necklace
nightgown
pantsuit
pullover
sweatshirt
turtleneck
underwear
waistband

Communication

brainstorm
folktale
goodbye
input
jokebook
loudspeaker
network
output
password
postcard
timetable
understand
videocassette
viewpoint

Descriptive Words

awesome
carefree
farsighted
ingrown
makeshift
masterpiece
nationwide
nearsighted
oddball
offbeat
outright
outspoken
outstanding

threadbare
trustworthy
waterproof
wholesale

Foods

applesauce
blueberry
breakfast
buttermilk
chestnut
coleslaw
doughnut
eggplant
eggshell
gingerbread
grapefruit
gumball
mealtime
meatball
mushroom
oatmeal
peanut
peppermint
pineapple
popcorn
strawberry
watermelon

Home

archway
bathroom
bedroom
bookshelf
carport
clothesline
cupboard
doorbell
doorknob
doorway
driveway
fireplace
headboard
keyhole

lampshade
rooftop
teapot
wallpaper

Music

bagpipe
earphones
keyboard

Nature

buttercup
cattail
earthquake
iceberg
landform
landslide
marshland
moonlight
overcast
quicksand
rainbow
rainfall
redwood
seashell
snowball
snowstorm

sunflower
sunlight
sunshine
thunderstorm
tumbleweed
vineyard
waterfall

offspring
oneself
roommate
somebody
sweetheart
themselves

Objects

anything
billfold
candlestick
clipboard
flashlight
floodlight
handcuff
handkerchief
haystack
nutcracker
padlock
passport
pocketbook
ponytail
something
suitcase
sunglasses
toothpaste
washcloth
wastebasket
windmill
windowpane
yardstick

People

anybody
anyone
everybody
everyone
gentlemen
godchild
grandchild
Irishmen
kinfolk
mankind
nickname

Places

airport
anywhere
crossroads
downstairs
downtown
fairgrounds
inland
inside
lighthouse
millpond
offshore
offstage
outdoors
outside
poolside
somewhere
thereabouts
treehouse
underground
upstairs
uptown

School

blackboard
classmate
classroom
homework
kindergarten
knapsack
notebook
playground
schoolteacher
textbook

Sports & Recreation

backboard
baseball
basketball
checkerboard
dugout
fieldhouse
football
fullback
goalkeeper
heavyweight
hopscotch
joystick
kickball
linebacker
paddleball
pinball
playoffs
quarterback
sandbox
scoreboard
skateboard
touchdown
volleyball
windup

Time

afternoon
daylight
daytime
lifelong
meanwhile
midnight
nightfall
nighttime
weekend
wristwatch

Compound Words

Tools

jigsaw
sandpaper
sawhorse
screwdriver
stepladder

Transportation

airplane
dashboard
drawbridge
freeway
gearshift
handlebar
hatchback
headlight
highway
motorcycle
overpass
railroad
rowboat
sailboat
turnpike
wheelchair
windshield

Work

cabinetmaker
cowboy
firefighters
goldsmith
housekeeper
landlord
lawmaker
lifeguard
redcap
ringmaster
undertaker

Other Words

another
goosebump
itself
loophole
madhouse
needlepoint
nightmare
otherwise
outcome
quicksilver
ringworm
runaway
runway
safeguard
tablespoon
teaspoon
undertake
upkeep
whirlpool

Trade Offs

(Contractions)

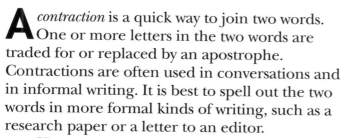

A *contraction* is a quick way to join two words. One or more letters in the two words are traded for or replaced by an apostrophe. Contractions are often used in conversations and in informal writing. It is best to spell out the two words in more formal kinds of writing, such as a research paper or a letter to an editor.

Here is a list of contractions you may want to use in informal writing, such as a note or letter to a friend.

am/are

I'm (I am)
you're (you are)
we're (we are)
they're (they are)

is/has

he's (he is; he has)
she's (she is; she has)
it's (it is; it has)

here's (here is)
one's (one is; one has)
that's (that is; that has)
there's (there is; there has)
what's (what is; what has)
who's (who is; who has)

would/had

I'd (I would; I had)
you'd (you would; you had)
he'd (he would; he had)
she'd (she would; she had)
it'd (it would; it had)
we'd (we would; we had)
you'd (you would; you had)
they'd (they would; they had)

that'd (that would; that had)
what'd (what would; what had)
who'd (who would; who had)

have

I've (I have)
you've (you have)
we've (we have)
they've (they have)

could've (could have)
might've (might have
should've (should have)
there've (there have)
who've (who have)
would've (would have)

will/shall

I'll (I will; I shall)
you'll (you will; you shall)
he'll (he will; he shall)
she'll (she will; she shall)
it'll (it will; it shall)
we'll (we will; we shall)
you'll (you will; you shall)
they'll (they will; they shall)

that'll (that will; that shall)
there'll (there will; there shall)
these'll (these will; these shall)
this'll (this will; this shall)
those'll (those will; those shall)
what'll (what will; what shall)
who'll (who will; who shall)

let

let's (let us)

not

can't (can not)
don't (do not)
isn't (is not)
won't (will not)
shouldn't (should not)
wouldn't (would not)
aren't (are not)
doesn't (does not)
wasn't (was not)
weren't (were not)
hasn't (has not)
haven't (have not)
hadn't (had not)
mustn't (must not)
didn't (did not)
mightn't (might not)
needn't (need not)

Word Play

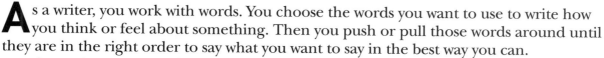

OINK
OINK

(Onomatopoeia, Palindromes, Hink-Pinks)

As a writer, you work with words. You choose the words you want to use to write how you think or feel about something. Then you push or pull those words around until they are in the right order to say what you want to say in the best way you can.

As a writer, you can also play with words. There are many ways to have fun with words. You can enjoy the funny or interesting sounds some words make when you say them aloud. You can join some words or just put words next to each other to suggest ridiculous or fascinating sounds or ideas. You can reverse the order of the letters in some words to make different words. And sometimes you get the same word in reverse! You can even make up, or "coin," new words whenever you want.

In this section, you will find lists of sound words, palindromes, and hink-pinks. You may want to simply play with the words and their sounds. Or you may want to use some of the fun words in your writing.

Onomatopoeia
(Sound Words)

Listen! What sounds do you hear around you? How might each of those sounds be spelled? *Onomatopoeia*, or sound words, are words that spell actual sounds. Sound words are often emphasized visually by using all capital letters, repeating the word, or spacing the letters to stretch the word.

The following list of words have been "coined," or made up, to identify sounds we hear around us. The words are organized under some general categories. You may want to add other sound words or sound-word categories to the list.

Animal Sounds

arf
baa
bark
bow-wow
buzz
cheep

chirp
clip-clop
clomp
cluck
cock-a-doodle-do
cuckoo
gr-r-r

growl
hee-haw
hiss
honk
howl
meow
moo

neigh
oink
purr
quack
ruff
squeak
squeal
tweet
woof

Breaking Sounds

crack
crunch
r-r-rip
snap

Bumping/Falling Sounds

bang
clang
clank
clink
clunk
crash
drip
flap
kerplop
kerplunk
ping
plop
plunk
pong
scrunch
slop
smack
splash
splat
tap
thump
whack
whomp
whop
zing
zonk

People Sounds

aack
ah
eek
giggle
ha-ha
hmmm
kerchoo
ooh
oomph
sigh
tee-hee
ugh
uh-huh
waa
whee
yuck

Machine Sounds

beep
bing
bleep
blip
boing
choo-choo
clack
clank
click
creak
ding-a-ling
ding-dong
grind
hum
ping
pop
r-r-ring
roar
sputter
squeak
tick-tock
whirr
zoom

Weather Sounds

bang
boom
crackle
crash
drip
ping
who-o-o-o
zing

Other Sounds

blink
bubble
crackle
crinkle
fizz
flip-flop
glug
gurgle
screech
sizzle
slurp
swish
whoosh
zap
zip
zoom

Palindromes

A *palindrome* is a word that is spelled the same way backward and forward. Check out the palindromes below. Then see if you can think of others.

Anna	level	pop
bob	ma'am	refer
dad	mom	rotor
did	noon	sees
eye	nun	toot
gag	peep	tot
kayak	Pip	

Some words can be arranged so that a whole phrase or sentence is a palindrome. Here are some samples.

A man–a plan–a canal–Panama
Now Dad won.
Ward did draw.
We sew.

Some word pairs are helpful when you want to create a phrase or sentence that is a palindrome. Can you think of more pairs of words to add to this list?

but	deer	evil
tub	reed	live
no	rats	parts
on	star	strap
saw	pets	pot
was	step	top
now	pals	
won	slap	
net	keep	
ten	peek	

Hink-Pinks, Hinky-Pinkys, and Hinkety-Pinketys

A *hink-pink* is two one-syllable words that rhyme. Hink-pinks are often humorous in sound or meaning. You'll find more hink-pinks among the one-syllable rhyming word lists beginning on page 97 of this book.

brain drain
dead bread
ham jam
hot spot
leaf thief

lone phone
mop top
nice mice
short sport
steer clear

mop top

A *hinky-pinky* is a two-syllable rhyme whose sound or meaning is often humorous. Hinky-pinkys sometimes even sound like "baby talk." You'll find more hinky-pinkys among the two-syllable rhyming word lists beginning on page 145 of this book.

boogie-woogie
eensy-weensy
even-Steven
fuzzy-wuzzy
hanky-panky
hocus-pocus
hokey-pokey
Humpty-Dumpty

itsy-bitsy
muscle tussle
piggly-wiggly
razzle-dazzle
super-duper
teensy-weensy
walkie-talkie

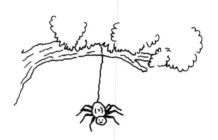

itsy-bitsy

A *hinkety-pinkety* is a three-syllable rhyme whose sound or meaning is often humorous. Hinkety-pinketys are harder to create, but you'll find "slobbery robbery" illustrated on page 167 in this book.

Rhyme It

(Rhyming Words)

field yield

What is a rhyme? Rhyming sounds are all around us. We hear rhyming words in nursery rhymes, poems, songs, greeting card verses, jump-rope jingles, and advertisements.

Rhyming sounds are word endings that sound alike. A rhyming sound begins with a vowel and can be shown by the letters that make the rhyming sound. For example, the rhyming sound at the ends of the words *freeze* and *please* can be represented by the letters *Ez.* The rhyming sound in *paste* and *waist* can be represented by *ast.*

Words can rhyme in different ways. Some writers use only *perfect* rhyme. Other writers like the freedom of also using *imperfect* or *slant* rhyme. Although homophones like *bear* and *bare* are not really rhyming words, some writers like to use them.

perfect rhyme	imperfect rhyme	slant rhyme
Rhyming words have different consonants before their rhyming sounds. Words such as *need* and *seed* are examples of perfect rhyme. The consonants are different before the rhyming sound *ed.*	Rhyming words have the same consonants before their rhyming sounds. Words such as *something* and *nothing* are examples of imperfect rhyme. The *th* comes before the rhyming sound *ing* in both words.	Rhyming words are pronounced as though their endings rhyme, even though spellings suggest different sounds. The *d* and *t* are pronounced alike in words like *waiting* and *wading* or *petal* and *medal.*

How do I find words that rhyme? A group of words that rhyme can be called a family. A family of rhyming words may have one, two, or three ending syllables that rhyme.

You will find more than 500 rhyming-word families in the lists below. One-syllable rhymes appear first, followed by lists of two-syllable and three-syllable rhymes. Rhyming sounds are listed alphabetically under the vowels A, E, I, O, and U. A sample word is given for each sound.

To find a family of words that rhyme with a particular word, look for the word's ending in the list below. For example, to find the family of words that rhyme with *neck*, think of the sound at the end of *neck*. That one-syllable rhyming sound can be spelled *ek*. Look in the alphabetical list of one-syllable rhymes for *ek*. Say the word *neck* and the sample word *deck*. The words rhyme, so all the words listed under "*ek* as in *deck*" rhyme with *neck*.

For a quick reference to all the rhyming-word families listed, refer to the *Index of Rhyming Sounds* found in the back of this book.

one-syllable rhyme	**two-syllable rhyme**	**three-syllable rhyme**
Rhyming words have one ending syllable that rhymes. The one-syllable rhyming sound heard in the words *cake* and *bake* can be represented by *ak*.	Rhyming words have two ending syllables that rhyme. The two-syllable rhyming sound heard in the words *hilly* and *chilly* can be represented by *il-e*. The rhyming syllables are separated by a hyphen.	Rhyming words have three ending syllables that rhyme. The three-syllable rhyming sound heard in the words *laboring* and *neighboring* can be represented by *a-bur-ing*. The rhyming syllables are separated by hyphens.

One-syllable rhyming-word pairs that present an interesting or humorous idea are called *hink-pinks*. Two- and three-syllable humorous rhymes are called *hinky-pinkys* and *hinkety-pinketys*, respectively. Look for some of these fun rhymes and their illustrations in the lists that follow.

brain drain

One-Syllable Rhymes

a as in *play*

A
bay
clay
day
gray
hay
hey
J
Jay
K
lay
May
neigh
pay
play
pray
prey
ray
say
slay
sleigh
spray
stay
stray
sway
they
tray
way
weigh

astray
away
ballet
betray
birthday
bouquet
decay

delay
display
essay
gourmet
halfway
hallway
highway
hooray
midway
obey
okay
payday
portray
relay
repay
runway
subway
Sunday
survey (verb)
today
toupee
x ray

Chevrolet
disobey
holiday
matinee
overpay
ricochet
runaway
USA
yesterday

a as in *spa*

ah
ha
ma
pa
spa

grandma
grandpa
hurrah

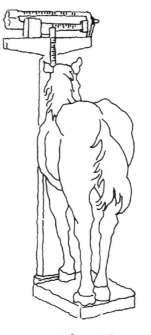

neigh weigh

algebra
camera
cinema
formula
gondola
opera
orchestra
retina

bacteria
peninsula
+ **aw** as in *straw*

ab as in *crab*

blab
cab
crab
dab
drab
gab
grab
jab
lab
nab
scab

a

crab gab

slab
stab
tab

ach as in *notch*

(see **och** as in *watch*)

ach as in *catch*

batch
catch
hatch
latch
match
patch
scratch
snatch

attach
dispatch
detach

ad as in *grade*

aid
aide
blade
braid
fade
grade
jade
laid
made
maid
paid
raid

shade
spade
suede
trade
wade

afraid
arcade
Band-aid
blockade
bridesmaid
brigade
charade
crusade
decade
evade
grenade
homemade
invade
lampshade
mermaid
parade
persuade
postpaid
prepaid
stockade
upgrade

barricade
centigrade
lemonade
marmalade
masquerade
overpaid
promenade
renegade
serenade
unafraid
+ **a** as in *play*: *played, stayed,* etc.

ad as in *dad*

ad
add
bad
brad
Chad
clad

dad
fad
glad
grad
had
lad
mad
pad
plaid
sad

comrade
granddad
nomad

ad as in *broad*

(see **od** as in *sod*)

af as in *safe*

chafe
safe
waif

unsafe

af as in *calf*

calf
graph
half
laugh
staff

decaf
giraffe

autograph
paragraph
phonograph
photograph
telegraph

aft as in *raft*

craft
draft
raft
shaft

aircraft

handicraft
+ **af** as in **calf:** *laughed, graphed,*
etc.

ag as in **snag**

bag
brag
drag
flag
gag
nag
rag
sag
shag
slag
snag
stag
swag
tag
wag

beanbag
handbag
sandbag
zigzag

saddlebag

aj as in **page**

age
cage
gauge
page
rage
sage
stage
wage
engage
offstage
rampage
teenage
upstage

ak as in **make**

ache
bake
brake
break
cake
drake
fake
flake
Jake
lake
make
quake
rake
sake

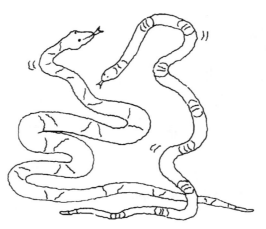

snake shake

shake
snake
stake
steak
take
wake

awake
cupcake
daybreak
earthquake
headache
heartache
heartbreak
keepsake

mistake
opaque
outbreak
pancake
snowflake
toothache

rattlesnake
undertake

ak as in **pack**

back
black
clack
crack
jack
knack
lack
pack
plaque
quack
rack
sack
shack
slack
smack
snack
stack
tack
track
whack
yak

attack
feedback
haystack
hijack
horseback
knapsack
soundtrack
thumbtack
Tic Tac
wisecrack
zwieback

almanac
Cadillac

a

cardiac
Pontiac

aks as in tax

ax
fax
lax
sax
tax
wax

beeswax
climax
earwax
lilacs
relax
+ ak as in pack: packs,
tacks, etc. and akt as
in fact: acts, facts, etc.

akt as in fact

act
fact
pact
tact

abstract
attract
compact
contact
contract
distract
exact
extract
react
subtract

counteract
+ ak as in pack: packed, sacked,
etc.

al as in sale

ail
ale
bail
bale
Braille

fail
frail
gale
hail
jail
kale
mail
male
nail
pail
pale
quail
rail

snail mail

sail
sale
scale
shale
snail
stale
tail
tale
they'll
trail
trail
veil
wail
whale

blackmail
detail
exhale
inhale

pigtail
retail
thumbnail
toenail
wholesale

monorail

al as in pal

Al
gal
pal
shall

canal
chorale
corral
decal
morale

rationale

al as in fall

(see ol as in fall)

am as in game

aim
blame
came
claim
dame
fame
flame
frame
game
lame
name
same
shame
tame

acclaim
became
exclaim
nickname
proclaim
reclaim

surname

overcame

am as in *jam*

am

clam

cram

dam

gram

ham

jam

lamb

ma'am

ram

Sam

scram

sham

slam

swam

tam

wham

yam

exam

program

diagram

hologram

kilogram

milligram

telegram

amp as in *stamp*

amp

camp

champ

clamp

cramp

damp

lamp

ramp

scamp

stamp

tramp

revamp

an as in *cane*

brain

cane

chain

crane

drain

gain

grain

lain

lane

main

Maine

mane

pain

pane

plain

plane

rain

reign

rein

sane

Seine

slain

Spain

sprain

stain

train

vain

vane

vein

Wayne

airplane

campaign

champagne

complain

contain

domain

explain

humane

insane

maintain

migraine

obtain

refrain

regain

remain

restrain

sustain

terrain

cellophane

entertain

hurricane

windowpane

an as in *can*

an

ban

bran

can

clan

fan

man

pan

plan

ran

scan

span

Stan

tan

than

van

began

Japan

outran

pecan

suntan

caravan

Pakistan

anch as in *ranch*

branch

ranch

avalanche

a

and as in *grand*

and
band
brand
gland
grand
hand
land
sand
stand

command
demand
expand
grandstand
headband
island
longhand
quicksand
shorthand

fairyland
reprimand
understand
+ **an** as in *can*: *canned, planned,* etc.

ang as in *rang*

bang
clang
fang
gang
rang
sang
slang
sprang
tang

meringue
mustang

boomerang
overhang

anj as in *range*

change
range
strange

arrange
exchange

rearrange

ank as in *thank*

bank
blank
clank
crank
drank
flank
frank
Hank
plank
prank
rank
sank
shrank
spank
tank
thank
yank

*Hank's pranks
earn him no thanks.*

ans as in *dance*

chance
dance
France
glance
prance
trance

advance
finance
romance

circumstance
+ **ant** as in *chant*: *chants, plants,* etc.

ant as in *paint*

faint
paint
quaint
saint

acquaint
complaint
restraint

ant as in *chant*

ant
aunt
can't
chant
grant
pant
plant
scant
slant

eggplant
enchant
implant
transplant

ap as in *shape*

ape
cape
crepe

102

drape
gape
grape
scrape
shape
tape

escape
landscape
seascape

ap as in *map*

cap
chap
clap
flap
gap
lap
map
nap
rap
sap
scrap
slap
snap
strap
tap
trap
wrap
zap

burlap
kidnap
kneecap
mishap

handicap
overlap

aps as in *perhaps*

collapse
perhaps
+ **ap** as in *map*: *maps, snaps,* etc.

ar as in *fair*

air
bare
bear
blare
care
chair
Claire
dare
fair
fare
flair
glare
hair
hare
heir
lair
mare
pair
pear
prayer
rare
scare
share
snare
spare
square
stair
stare
swear
tear
their
there
they're
wear
where

affair
airfare
aware
beware
compare
declare
despair
elsewhere
fanfare

impair
midair
nightmare
nowhere
prepare
repair
somewhere
unfair
welfare

anywhere
everywhere
millionaire
silverware
solitaire
unaware
underwear

ar as in *bar*

are
bar
car
czar
far
jar
mar
par
R
scar
star
tar

bazaar
boxcar
guitar
jaguar
memoir
streetcar

reservoir
seminar

arch as in *march*

arch
march
starch

a

ard as in *hard*

card
guard
hard
lard
yard

barnyard
bombard
discard
graveyard
leotard
lifeguard
postcard
regard
retard
vanguard

bodyguard
boulevard
disregard
+ **ar** as in **bar:** *barred, scarred,* etc.

arj as in *large*

barge
charge
large

enlarge
recharge

ark as in *park*

arc
ark
bark
dark
lark
mark
park
shark
spark
stark

aardvark
birthmark
bookmark

embark
landmark
monarch
postmark
remark

arm as in *farm*

arm
charm
farm
harm

alarm
disarm
firearm
forearm

arn as in *yarn*

barn
darn
yarn

arp as in *sharp*

carp
harp
sharp

heart part

art as in *smart*

art
cart
chart
dart
heart
part

smart
start
tart

depart
Mozart
pushcart
sweetheart

arv as in *starve*

carve
starve

as as in *chase*

ace
base
bass
brace
case
chase
face
Grace
lace
pace
place
race
space
trace
vase

briefcase
disgrace
embrace
erase
misplace
replace
shoelace
staircase
suitcase

as as in *gas*

ass
bass
brass
class

a

gas
glass
grass
lass
mass
pass

alas
bypass
harass
trespass

overpass
sassafras

ash as in *crash*

ash
bash
cash
cache
clash
crash
dash
flash
gash
hash
mash
rash
sash
slash
smash
splash
stash
thrash
trash

eyelash
mustache
whiplash

succotash

ask as in *mask*

ask
bask
cask
flask

mask
task

asp as in *grasp*

clasp
gasp
grasp

ast as in *paste*

baste
haste
paste
taste
waist
waste
+ **as** as in *chase: faced, laced,* etc.

ast as in *last*

blast
cast
fast
last
mast
passed
past
vast

aghast
broadcast
contrast
forecast
outlast
sandblast
steadfast

overcast

at as in *plate*

ate
bait
crate
date
eight
fate

gate
great
hate
late
mate
Nate
plate
rate
skate
slate
state
straight
strait
trait
wait
weight

await
checkmate
classmate
create
debate
dictate
donate
equate
estate
frustrate
inflate

late skate

a

locate
narrate
ornate
playmate
rebate
relate
rotate
translate
update
vacate
vibrate

amputate
calculate
candidate
celebrate
circulate
complicate
concentrate
cultivate
decorate
dedicate
demonstrate
dominate
duplicate
educate
elevate
emigrate
estimate (verb)
excavate
fascinate
formulate
generate
graduate (verb)
hesitate
hibernate
hyphenate
illustrate
imitate
indicate
innovate
irrigate
irritate
isolate
motivate
navigate
nominate

operate
overweight
populate
punctuate
regulate
separate
situate
suffocate
tolerate
violate

abbreviate
accumulate
anticipate
appreciate
associate (verb)
communicate
congratulate
cooperate
coordinate
eliminate
evaluate
evaporate
exaggerate
initiate
investigate
manipulate
negotiate
participate
recuperate

at as in *fat*

at
bat
brat
cat
chat
fat
flat
gnat
hat
mat
pat
rat
sat
scat

slat
spat
that
vat

combat
format
muskrat
wombat

acrobat
democrat
diplomat
habitat
laundromat
thermostat

at as in *what*

(see **ot** as in *hot*)

ath as in *path*

bath
lath
math
path
wrath

av as in *gave*

brave
cave
gave
grave
pave
rave
save
shave
slave
they've
wave

behave
engrave
forgave

microwave
misbehave

aw as in *straw*

awe
caw
claw
draw
flaw
gnaw
jaw
law
paw
raw
saw
slaw
squaw
straw
thaw

coleslaw
guffaw
in-law
jigsaw
macaw
outlaw
seesaw
Utah
withdraw

Arkansas
Omaha
Wichita
+ **a** as in *spa*

awd as in *sawed*

broad
fraud
gnawed
pawed
sawed
thawed

abroad
applaud

az as in *glaze*

blaze
chaise
craze
daze
faze
gaze
glaze
graze
haze
maize
maze
phase
phrase
praise
vase

always
amaze
cafes

mayonnaise
paraphrase
+ **a** as in *play: plays, weighs*, etc.

az as in *jazz*

as
has
jazz

topaz
whereas

e as in *fee*

B
be
bee
C
D
E
fee
flea
flee
free
G
gee
glee
he
key
knee
Lee
me
P
pea
plea
sea
see
she
ski
spree
T
tea
tee
three
tree

Said the flea to the bee,
"It's a mystery to me
how, with wings that are wee,
you can fly so easily."

Said the bee to the flea,
"I'm no curiosity!
Though my wings may be wee,
they are perfect for a bee."

e

V
we
wee
Z

A.D.
agree
B.C.
degree
easy
emcee
goatee
ID
M.D.
marry
monkey
peewee
teepee
trophy

absentee
addressee
agency
Annemarie
archery
bakery
bumblebee
C.O.D.
cavity
century
Cherokee
chimpanzee
colony
comedy
company
diary
disagree
easily
ebony
employee
energy
factory
family
fantasy
galaxy
Germany
guarantee

harmony
history
honesty
Italy
jamboree
liberty
loyalty
memory
mercury
mystery
nominee
nursery
oversee
parody
pedigree
Ph.D.
poetry
policy
privacy
recipe
referee
refugee
salary
secrecy
sesame
simile
sympathy
Tennessee

ability
accompany
activity
apostrophe
biography
biology
community
ecology
geography
January
mythology
necessity
photography
reality
Tallahassee

anniversary
curiosity

electricity
elementary
personality

ech as in *beach*

beach
beech
bleach
each
leech
peach
preach
reach
screech
speech
teach

impeach

ech as in *fetch*

etch
fetch
sketch
stretch

echd as in *stretched*

(see **ech** as in *fetch*)

ed as in *bead*

bead
bleed
breed
creed
deed
feed
greed
heed
knead
lead
need
plead
read
reed
seed

skied
speed
tweed
we'd
weed

agreed
exceed
indeed
mislead
precede
proceed
seaweed
secede
stampede
succeed

centipede
disagreed
guaranteed

ed as in *head*

bed
bled
bread
dead
dread
fed
fled
head
Jed
lead
led
read
red
said
shed
shred
sled
spread
thread
tread
wed

ahead
bedspread
behead
biped
bobsled
bunkbed
co-ed
forehead
homestead
instead
misread
moped
purebred
redhead
spearhead
widespread

copperhead
gingerbread
letterhead
overhead
thoroughbred
waterbed

leaf thief

ef as in *beef*

beef
brief
chief
grief

leaf
reef
thief

belief
motif
relief

handkerchief

ef as in *deaf*

chef
clef
deaf
Jeff
ref

eft as in *left*

cleft
left
theft

eg as in *league*

fatigue
league

eg as in *leg*

beg
egg
Greg
keg
leg
Peg

nutmeg

Winnipeg

ej as in *ledge*

edge
hedge
ledge
pledge
wedge

knowledge

e

ek as in *creek*

beak
bleak
cheek
chic
creak
creek
freak
Greek
leak
leek
meek
peak
peek
reek
seek
shriek
sleek
sneak
speak
squeak
streak
teak
weak
week

antique
critique
technique
unique

Chesapeake

ek as in *deck*

check
deck
neck
peck
speck
wreck
beck
fleck

Quebec
shipwreck

ekt as in *collect*

checked
pecked
wrecked

affect
bisect
collect
connect
correct
detect
direct
dissect
effect
eject
elect
erect
expect
infect
inject
insect
inspect
neglect
object (verb)
perfect
project
prospect
protect
reflect
reject
respect
select
subject (verb)
suspect (verb)

architect
dialect
disinfect
disrespect
incorrect
indirect
intellect
intersect

el as in *heal*

deal
eel
feel
he'll
heal
heel
kneel
meal
peel
real
reel
seal
she'll
squeal
steal
steel
veal
we'll
wheel
zeal

appeal
cartwheel
chenille
conceal
ideal
mobile
oatmeal
ordeal
reveal

automobile

el as in *fell*

bell
cell
dwell
fell
jell
L
sell
shell
smell
spell
swell

swell smell

tell
well
yell

compel
doorbell
dumbbell
eggshell
excel
expel
farewell
hotel
lapel
misspell
nutshell
pastel
pell-mell
rebel (verb)
repel
retell
seashell

carrousel
NFL
parallel
personnel

eld as in *field*

field
healed
peeled
sealed
shield
squealed
yield

appealed
concealed
repealed
revealed
windshield

battlefield

eld as in *weld*

held
weld
+ el as in *fell*: *smelled, yelled,* etc.

elf as in *self*

elf
self
shelf

bookshelf
herself
himself
itself
myself
yourself

elm as in *realm*

elm
helm
realm

overwhelm

elp as in *yelp*

help
yelp

elt as in *melt*

belt
dealt
felt
knelt
melt
pelt
smelt
welt

elth as in *wealth*

health
wealth

elv as in *twelve*

shelve
twelve

em as in *seam*

beam
cream
dream
gleam
ream
scheme
scream
seam
seem
steam
stream
team
theme

daydream
extreme
mainstream
moonbeam
redeem
regime
supreme

em as in *hem*

gem
hem
M
phlegm
stem
them

A.M.
condemn
P.M.

requiem

e

en as in *clean*

bean
clean
Dean
Gene
glean
green
keen
lean
mean
queen
scene
screen
seen
spleen
teen

between
caffeine
canteen
chlorine
Earleen
Eugene
hygiene
machine
marine
Marlene
obscene
preteen
protein
ravine
routine
sardine
sunscreen
thirteen
vaccine

gasoline
Halloween
kerosene
limousine
magazine
mezzanine
nicotine
quarantine
submarine

tambourine
tangerine
trampoline
velveteen

en as in *pen*

den
hen
men
N
pen
ten
then
when
wren

again
women

citizen
hydrogen
oxygen

comedienne

ench as in *trench*

bench
clench
drench
French
quench
stench
trench
wrench

end as in *friend*

bend
blend
end
fend
friend
lend
mend
penned
send

spend
tend
trend

amend
ascend
attend
befriend
commend
defend
depend
descend
extend
intend
offend
pretend
suspend

comprehend
dividend
recommend

ength as in *strength*

length
strength

ens as in *fence*

dense
fence
sense

condense
defense
expense
offense
presence
suspense

conference
confidence
consequence
difference
excellence
influence
innocence
reference

e

circumference
coincidence
convenience
experience
obedience
+ **ent** as in **sent**: *tents, events,* etc.

enst as in *sensed*

fenced
sensed

against
condensed
dispensed

ent as in *sent*

bent
cent
dent
gent
lent
meant
rent
scent
sent
spent
tent
vent
went

absent
cement
comment
consent
content
event
indent
intent
percent
present
prevent
resent
torment

accident
argument
compliment

confident
continent
document
element
government
monument
permanent
president
represent
resident
tournament

advertisement
embarrassment
encouragement
environment
experiment
intelligent
predicament

ep as in *keep*

beep
cheap
cheep
creep
deep
heap
jeep
keep
leap
peep
reap
sheep
sleep
steep
sweep
weep

asleep

ep as in *step*

pep
prep
step
strep

bicep
doorstep
footstep

ept as in *kept*

kept
pepped
slept
stepped
swept
wept

accept
except
windswept

intercept
overslept

er as in *dear*

cheer
clear
dear
deer
ear
fear
gear
hear
here
mere
near
peer
pier
rear
sheer
smear
spear
sphere
steer
tear
tier
year

adhere
appear
career

e

cashier
frontier
premier
reindeer
severe
sincere
atmosphere
chandelier
disappear
engineer
hemisphere
interfere
pioneer
souvenir
volunteer

erd as in *weird*

beard
weird
+ **er** as in *dear: feared, appeared,* etc.

es as in *geese*

cease
crease
fleece
geese
grease
Greece
lease
Nice
niece
peace
piece

decrease
increase
police
release

masterpiece

es as in *guess*

bless
chess

dress
guess
less
mess
press
S
stress
Tess
yes

access
address
confess
distress
excess
express
impress
possess
profess
progress
recess
success
unless

happiness
nonetheless
S.O.S.

geese peace

esh as in *fresh*

flesh
fresh
mesh

refresh

esk as in *desk*

desk

grotesque

picturesque

est as in *feast*

beast
ceased
east
feast
least
yeast

est as in *test*

best
blest
breast
chest
crest
guest
jest
nest
pest
quest
rest
test
vest
west
zest

arrest
conquest
detest
digest
invest
request
suggest

Budapest
+ **es** as in *guess: dressed, impressed,* etc.

et as in *feet*

beat
beet
cheat
cleat
eat
feat
feet
fleet
greet
heat
meat
meet
neat
seat
sheet
sleet
street
suite
sweet
treat
wheat

athlete
compete
complete
deceit
defeat
delete
elite
petite
receipt
repeat
retreat

incomplete
parakeet

et as in *jet*

bet
debt
fret
get
jet
let
met

wet pet

net
pet
set
sweat
threat
vet
wet
whet
yet

asset
brunette
cadet
cornet
Corvette
duet
forget
omelet
outlet
quartet
regret
reset
sextet
sunset
upset
vignette

alphabet
cabinet
clarinet
etiquette
majorette
silhouette
violet

eth as in *teeth*

teeth
wreath

beneath
underneath

eth as in *death*

breath
death

twentieth
Elizabeth

ev as in *sleeve*

eve
grieve
leave
sleeve
we've
weave

achieve
believe
deceive
naive
receive
relieve

ex as in *flex*

flex
sex
vex
X

annex
apex
complex
convex
duplex
index
+ **ek** as in *deck:* necks, wrecks, etc.
+ **ekt** as in *collect:* elects, selects, etc.

ext as in *text*

flexed
next
text

e

annexed
context
indexed

ez as in *these*

breeze
cheese
ease
freeze
frieze
he's
please
seize
she's
sneeze
squeeze
tease
these
wheeze

Chinese
disease
trapeze

expertise
Hercules
Japanese

isosceles
Vietnamese
+ **e** as in *fee:* *fees, keys,* etc.

i as in *cry*

buy
by
bye
cry
die
dry

dye
eye
fly
fry
guy
hi
high
I
lie
lye
my
pi
pie
rye
shy
sigh
sky
sly
spy
spry
sty
thigh
tie
try
why
Y

ally
apply
defy
deny
July
rabbi
rely
reply
Shanghai

alibi
amplify
butterfly
clarify
classify
dignify
dragonfly
FBI
horrify

justify
lullaby
magnify
multiply
notify
occupy
pacify
purify
qualify
samurai
satisfy
simplify
specify
underlie
verify

identify

ib as in *tribe*

bribe
scribe
tribe

describe
prescribe
subscribe

ib as in *rib*

bib
crib
fib
rib

ich as in *rich*

ditch
hitch
itch
niche
pitch
rich
snitch
stitch
switch
which

witch

bewitch

enrich

id as in *ride*

bride
chide
glide
guide
hide
I'd
pride
ride
side
slide
stride
tide
wide

beside
collide
decide
divide
fireside
inside
outside
provide
reside

peroxide
pesticide
+ **i** as in *cry: cried, sighed,* etc.

id as in *did*

bid
did
grid
hid
kid
lid
rid
skid
slid
squid

acid

candid
eyelid
forbid
Madrid
morbid
orchid
rancid
rapid
solid

katydid
pyramid

if as in *life*

knife
life
strife
wife

housewife
midwife
wildlife

if as in *sniff*

Cliff
if
sniff
stiff
whiff

mastiff
sheriff
tariff

ift as in *sift*

drift
gift
lift
shift
sift
sniffed
swift
thrift

shoplift
snowdrift

ig as in *fig*

big
dig
fig
gig
jig
pig
rig
sprig
swig
twig
wig

thingamajig

pig jig

ik as in *like*

bike
dike
hike
like
pike
spike
strike
trike
tyke

alike
dislike
hitchhike
turnpike

ik as in *lick*

brick
chick
click
flick
kick
lick
Nick
pick
prick
quick
sick
slick
stick

i

thick
tick
trick
wick

attic
basic
chopstick
classic
cosmic
cubic
cynic
epic
fabric
garlic
hectic
homesick
magic
metric
mimic
mystic
picnic
plastic
rustic
toothpick
toxic
tunic

domestic
candlestick
limerick
poetic

arithmetic
epidemic

iks as in *fix*

fix
mix
six

prefix

politics

acrobatics
mathematics
+ **ik** as in *lick:* licks, basics, etc.

ikt as in *strict*

strict

afflict
conflict
convict
depict
district
evict
predict
restrict
+ **ik** as in *lick:* kicked, tricked, etc.

il as in *mile*

aisle
dial
file
I'll
isle
mile
Nile
pile
smile
style
tile
trial
while

awhile
compile
exile
freestyle
meanwhile
profile
reptile
senile
worthwhile

crocodile
infantile
juvenile
reconcile

il as in *spill*

bill
chill
dill
drill
fill
frill
gill
grill
hill
ill
kill
mill
Phil
pill
quill
shrill
sill
skill
spill
still
thrill
till
twill
will

Brazil
downhill
fulfill
instill
treadmill
until
uphill
windmill

juvenile crocodile

daffodil
Evansville
whippoorwill
windowsill

ild as in *wild*

child
dialed
filed
mild
piled
smiled
styled
tiled
wild

ild as in *build*

build
+ **il** as in *spill: drilled, fulfilled,* etc.

ilk as in *silk*

milk
silk

ilt as in *quilt*

built
guilt
jilt
kilt
quilt
stilt
tilt
wilt

rebuilt

im as in *dime*

chime
climb
crime
dime
grime
I'm

lime
mime
prime
rhyme
slime
thyme
time

bedtime
daytime
enzyme
lifetime
mealtime
meantime
showtime
springtime
sublime

pantomime
wintertime

im as in *swim*

brim
dim
grim
gym
him
Kim
limb
prim
rim
skim
slim
swim
Tim
trim
whim

antonym
homonym
pseudonym
synonym

imp as in *shrimp*

blimp
chimp
crimp
imp
limp
primp
shrimp
skimp
wimp

in as in *line*

dine
fine
line
mine
nine
pine
Rhine
shine
shrine
sign
spine
swine
tine
twine
vine
whine

airline
assign
canine
combine
confine
decline
define
design
divine
feline
refine
resign

iodine
porcupine
underline
valentine

i

in as in *skin*

been
bin
chin
fin
grin
in
inn
kin
pin
shin
sin
skin
spin
thin
tin
twin
win

basin
begin
Berlin
cabin
coffin
goblin
margin
muffin
napkin
pigskin
raisin
snakeskin
tailspin
within

bulletin
discipline
feminine
gelatin
genuine
heroine
mandolin
masculine
moccasin
origin
violin

inch as in *pinch*

cinch
clinch
finch
flinch
inch
lynch
pinch

ind as in *kind*

bind
blind
find
grind
hind
kind
mind
rind
wind (verb)

behind
remind
unkind
unwind
+ **in** as in *line:* *signed, defined,* etc.

ind as in *pinned*

grinned
pinned
skinned
spinned
wind (noun)

disciplined
whirlwind
woodwind

ing as in *sing*

bring
cling
fling
king
ping
ring
sing

spring thing

sling
spring
sting
string
swing
thing
wing
wring
zing

earring
evening
nothing
offspring
Peking
something

anything
everything
Wyoming

inj as in *fringe*

cringe
fringe
hinge
singe
syringe
twinge

i

ink as in sink

blink
brink
clink
drink
fink
ink
kink
link
mink
pink
rink
shrink
sink
slink
stink
think
wink
zinc

inks as in lynx

jinx
lynx
sphinx
+ **ink** as in **sink:** *sinks, thinks,* etc.

inkt as in winked

distinct
extinct
instinct
precinct
+ **ink** as in **sink:** *blinked, winked,* etc.

ins as in since

chintz
mince
prince
rinse
since
wince

convince
province
+ **int** as in **print:** *mints, splints,* etc.

int as in print

glint
hint
lint
mint
print
splint
sprint
squint
stint
tint

blueprint
footprint
imprint
newsprint
spearmint

fingerprint

ip as in ripe

gripe
hype
pipe
ripe
stripe
swipe
type
wipe

bagpipe
sideswipe
tailpipe
windpipe

prototype

stereotype

ip as in drip

chip
clip
dip
drip
flip
grip
gyp

hip
lip
nip
quip
rip
ship
sip
skip
slip
snip
strip
tip
trip
whip
zip

catnip
courtship
equip
friendship
hardship
parsnip
spaceship
tulip
worship

battleship
championship
fingertip
membership
penmanship
scholarship
sportsmanship

citizenship
dictatorship
guardianship

ipt as in script

crypt
script

manuscript
+ **ip** as in **drip:** *dripped, skipped,* etc.

121

i

ir as in *hire*

choir
fire
hire
ire
lyre
mire
pyre
sire
spire
squire
tire
wire

acquire
admire
aspire
attire
bonfire
desire
empire
entire
expire
inquire
perspire
require
retire
sapphire
satire
umpire
vampire

is as in *rice*

dice
ice
lice
mice
nice
price
rice
slice
spice
splice
twice
vice

advice
concise
device
entice
precise
suffice

merchandise
paradise
sacrifice

is as in *miss*

bliss
hiss
kiss
miss
sis
Swiss
this

abyss
axis
crisis
dismiss
iris
justice
mantis
notice
novice
practice
tennis
thesis

apprentice
emphasis
hypnosis
prejudice

analysis
hypothesis
metropolis
parenthesis

ish as in *wish*

dish
fish
squish

fish dish

swish
wish

banish
finish
foolish
furnish
goldfish
lavish
radish
relish
selfish
tarnish

accomplish
admonish
establish
jellyfish

isk as in *risk*

brisk
disc
disk
frisk
risk
whisk

asterisk

isp as in *wisp*

crisp
lisp
wisp

ist as in *list*

cyst
fist
list
mist

twist
wrist

assist
checklist
consist
enlist
exist
insist
persist

motorist
optimist
pessimist
pianist
scientist
soloist

ecologist
+ **is** as in **miss:** *kissed, noticed,* etc.

it as in **kite**

bite
bright
byte
fight
flight
fright
height
kite
knight
light
might
mite
night
quite
right
rite
sight
site
slight
spite
tight
trite
white
write

daylight
delight
despite
excite
eyesight
frostbite
headlight
highlight
hindsight
ignite
invite
midnight
moonlight
polite
recite
spotlight
stoplight
sunlight
termite
tonight
twilight
unite

knight fright

appetite
copyright
dynamite
Fahrenheit
impolite
parasite
satellite

it as in **sit**

bit
fit
grit
hit
it
kit
knit
lit
mitt
pit
quit
sit
skit
slit
spit
split
wit
zit

acquit
admit
armpit
commit
exit
misfit
moonlit
omit
outfit
permit
submit
sunlit
unit

benefit
definite
favorite
opposite

i

ith as in *with*

myth
Smith
with

iv as in *drive*

chive
dive
drive
five
hive
I've
jive
live (adjective)
strive
thrive

alive
archive
arrive
beehive
contrive
deprive
revive
survive

iv as in *give*

give
live
sieve

forgive
outlive
relive

narrative
negative
positive
primitive
relative
sensitive
talkative

competitive
distributive
figurative

informative
preservative

representative

iz as in *prize*

guise
prize
rise
size
wise

advise
arise
baptize
capsize
chastise
comprise
despise
devise
disguise
franchise
likewise
revise
sunrise
surprise

advertise
agonize
analyze
authorize
burglarize
civilize
compromise
criticize
dramatize
emphasize
energize
enterprise
exercise
fantasize
fertilize
harmonize
hypnotize
idolize
improvise
jeopardize

legalize
magnetize
memorize
mesmerize
minimize
mobilize
modernize
naturalize
organize
otherwise
paralyze
pasteurize
penalize
publicize
realize
recognize
sensitize
socialize
specialize
sterilize
summarize
supervise
sympathize
televise
terrorize
tranquilize
utilize
verbalize

alphabetize
apologize
capitalize
categorize
characterize
deodorize
economize
familiarize
generalize
monopolize
+ **i** as in *cry: cries, sighs,* etc.

iz as in *quiz*

fizz
his
is
Ms.

quiz
whiz

o as in *sew*

beau
blow
bow
crow
doe
dough
floe
flow
fro
glow
go
grow
hoe
know
low
mow
no
O
oh
owe
Po
pro
row
sew
show
slow
snow
so
sow
though
throw
toe
tow
woe

aglow
ago

no dough

although
banjo
below
borrow
burro
burrow
depot
echo
elbow
hello
hero
hollow
info
lasso
meadow
oboe
pillow
plateau
rainbow
ratio
scarecrow
shadow
sorrow
Tokyo
widow
window
yoyo

buffalo
bungalow

o

calico
domino
embryo
Eskimo
Idaho
Mexico
mistletoe
potato
studio
tomato
video

Pinocchio
pistachio
portfolio

ob as in *robe*

globe
Job
lobe
probe
robe

bathrobe
earlobe

ob as in *job*

blob
Bob
cob
glob
gob
job
knob
lob
mob
rob
slob
snob
sob
swab
throb

o

och as in *coach*

brooch
coach
poach
roach

approach
reproach

och as in *watch*

blotch
notch
swatch
watch

hopscotch
wristwatch

od as in *road*

code
goad
load
mode
node
ode
road
rode
toad

abode
corrode
erode
explode
railroad

electrode
episode
overload
+ **o** as in *sew:* *sewed, snowed, etc.*

od as in *broad*

(see **awd** as in *sawed*)

od as in *sod*

clod
cod
God
mod
nod
odd
plod
pod
prod
quad
rod
shod
sod
squad
trod
wad

facade
tightwad
tripod

of as in *off*

cough
off
scoff
trough

cutoff

stroganoff

oft as in *soft*

coughed
loft
soft

og as in *fog*

clog
cog
dog
flog
fog

log hog

frog
hog
jog
log

bulldog
bullfrog
eggnog
groundhog
hotdog
leapfrog
prologue

catalog
dialogue
monologue
synagogue

oi as in *toy*

boy
buoy
Joy
ploy
soy
toy
Troy

ahoy
annoy
cowboy
decoy
destroy
employ
enjoy

corduroy
Illinois

o

oid as in **void**

Floyd
toyed
void

annoyed
avoid
destroyed
devoid
employed
tabloid

asteroid
celluloid
paranoid
trapezoid

oil as in **soil**

boil
broil
coil
foil
oil
soil
spoil
toil

embroil
gargoyle
loyal
recoil
royal
turmoil

oin as in **join**

coin
groin
join
loin

Des Moines
sirloin

oint as in **point**

joint
point

appoint
viewpoint

disappoint

ois as in **voice**

choice
Joyce
Royce
voice

invoice
rejoice

oist as in **moist**

hoist
moist
voiced

invoiced
rejoiced

oiz as in **noise**

noise
poise
+ **oi** as in **toy**: joys, cowboys, etc.

oj as in **lodge**

dodge
lodge

hodgepodge

ok as in **joke**

broke
choke
cloak
Coke
croak
folk
joke
oak
poke
smoke
soak

spoke
stoke
stroke
woke
yoke
yolk

awoke
baroque
evoke
kinfolk
provoke
revoke
slowpoke
sunstroke

artichoke

ok as in **knock**

Bach
block
clock
crock
dock
flock
frock
hock
knock
lock
pock
rock
shock
sock
stock
wok

headlock
hemlock
livestock
padlock
peacock
shamrock
wedlock
+ **ok** as in **walk**

o

oks as in *hoax*

coax
hoax
+ **ok** as in *joke: jokes, yolks, etc.*

oks as in *fox*

box
fox
lox
ox
phlox
pox

mailbox
smallpox

chickenpox
equinox
orthodox
paradox
+ **ok** as in *knock: clocks, knocks, etc.*
+ **olk** as in *walk: talks, walks, etc.*

ol as in *hole*

bowl
coal
foal
goal
hole
knoll
mole
pole
poll
role
roll
scroll
sole
soul
stole
stroll
toll
troll
whole

cajole
charcoal
console
control
eggroll
enroll
flagpole
loophole
patrol
pothole
tadpole

buttonhole
casserole
cubbyhole

ol as in *fall*

all
awl
ball
bawl
brawl
call
crawl
doll
drawl
fall
gall
Gaul
hall
haul
loll
mall
Paul
scrawl
shawl
small
sprawl
squall
stall
tall
wall
y'all

appall
baseball

downfall
eyeball
football
install
meatball
nightfall
overall
overhaul
parasol
rainfall
snowball
snowfall

alcohol
basketball
cannonball
Montreal
Taj Mahal
volleyball

old as in *bald*

bald
scald
+ **ol** as in *fall: hauled, installed, etc.*

old as in *fold*

bold
bowled
cold
fold
gold
hold
mold
old
rolled
scold
sold
strolled
told

behold
billfold
blindfold
controlled

enrolled
household
paroled
patrolled
retold
scaffold
unfold
untold
withhold

marigold
uncontrolled

olk as in *walk*

chalk
stalk
talk
walk

beanstalk
boardwalk
crosswalk
jaywalk
sidewalk
+ **ok** as in *knock*

olt as in *colt*

bolt
colt
jolt

deadbolt
revolt

olt as in *malt*

fault
halt
malt
salt
vault

asphalt
assault
default
exalt

somersault

oltz as in *waltz*

faults
halts
malts
waltz

assaults
exalts

somersaults

olv as in *solve*

solve

dissolve
involve
revolve

om as in *home*

chrome
comb
dome
foam
gnome
home
loam
Nome
roam

honeycomb
palindrome

om as in *mom*

bomb
calm
Guam
mom
palm
prom
psalm
qualm
Tom

embalm
sitcom
wigwam

intercom
Vietnam

omp as in *romp*

chomp
clomp
romp
stomp
swamp
tromp

ompt as in *romped*

prompt
+ **omp** as in *romp: stomped, tromped,* etc.

on as in *phone*

blown
bone
clone
cone
drone
flown
groan
grown
hone
known
loan
lone
moan
mown
own
phone
prone
scone
sewn
shone
shown
sown
stone
throne
thrown
tone
zone

o

alone
backbone
birthstone
cologne
condone
cyclone
disown
headphone
hormone
limestone
milestone
ozone
postpone
tombstone
trombone
unknown

baritone
chaperone
microphone
saxophone
telephone

on as in gone

con
Don
gone
John
Juan
on

coupon
icon
neuron
nylon
python
rayon
Szechwan
Tucson
upon
wonton

Amazon
electron
hexagon
leprechaun
liaison

marathon
octagon
Oregon
parmesan
pentagon
pentathlon
polygon
silicon
walkathon

phenomenon
Saskatchewan
+ **on** as in **lawn**

When Sean's account was overdrawn, he figured he might pawn a swan.

on as in lawn

dawn
drawn
fawn
lawn
pawn
Sean
spawn
swan
yawn

withdrawn

overdrawn
+ **on** as in **gone**

ond as in bond

blond
bond
fond
frond
pond
wand

beyond
respond

correspond
vagabond
+ **on** as in **lawn**: *pawned, yawned,*
etc.

ong as in long

gong
long
prong
song
strong
thong
throng
tong
wrong

along
belong
Hong Kong
King Kong
lifelong
oblong
ping-pong
prolong
sarong

ont as in won't

don't
won't

ont as in want

aunt
flaunt
gaunt

haunt
jaunt
taunt
want

onz as in *bronze*

bronze
Juan's
+ **on** as in *lawn*: *lawns, yawns*, etc.
+ **on** as in *gone*: *wontons*, *polygons*, etc.

ood as in *good*

could
good
hood
should
stood
wood
would

childhood
firewood

brotherhood
Hollywood
livelihood
motherhood
understood

ood as in *mood*

(see **ud** as in *mood*)

oof as in *proof*

(see **uf** as in *proof*)

ook as in *cook*

book
brook
cook
crook
hook
look

nook
rook
shook
took

checkbook
mistook
notebook
overlook
scrapbook

pocketbook

ook as in *spook*

(see **uk** as in *spook*)

ool as in *cool*

(see **ul** as in *cool*)

oom as in *room*

(see **um** as in *room*)

oon as in *moon*

(see **un** as in *moon*)

oop as in *soup*

(see **up** as in *soup*)

oos as in *juice*

(see **us** as in *juice*)

oost as in *roost*

(see **ust** as in *roost*)

oot as in *suit*

(see **ut** as in *suit*)

ooth as in *tooth*

(see **uth** as in *tooth*)

oov as in *move*

(see **uv** as in *move*)

ooz as in *choose*

(see **uz** as in *choose*)

op as in *soap*

cope
grope
hope
lope
mope
nope
pope
rope
scope
slope
soap
taupe

elope

antelope
cantaloupe
envelope
horoscope
microscope
periscope
telescope

kaleidoscope

op as in *shop*

bop
chop
cop
crop
drop
flop
hop
mop
plop
pop
prop
shop
slop
sop
stop

o

swap
top

eavesdrop
gumdrop
kerplop
raindrop
shortstop
teardrop
workshop

lollipop

or as in *pour*

boar
bore
chore
core
corps
door
drawer
floor
for
fore
four
gore
lore
more
nor
oar
or
ore
poor
pore
pour
roar
score
shore
snore
soar
sore
spore
store
swore
Thor
tore
war

wore
yore
your

adore
before
explore
folklore
galore
ignore
restore
seashore
therefore

bachelor
Baltimore
dinosaur
editor
furthermore
governor
Labrador
metaphor
senator
sophomore
sycamore
visitor
competitor

orch as in *torch*

porch
scorch
torch

ord as in *lord*

board
chord
cord
fjord
Ford
gourd
lord
sword
ward

afford
award

chalkboard
reward
scoreboard
skateboard
surfboard

checkerboard
harpsichord
smorgasbord
+ **or** as in *pour: bored, roared,* etc.

orf as in *wharf*

dwarf
wharf

ork as in *fork*

cork
fork
pork
stork
York

orm as in *storm*

dorm
form
norm
storm
swarm
warm

brainstorm
conform
inform
perform
reform
snowstorm

misinform
uniform

orn as in *corn*

born
corn
horn
morn

o

mourn
scorn
sworn
thorn
torn
warn
worn

acorn
adorn
airborne
bullhorn
foghorn
forewarn
forlorn
inborn
newborn
popcorn

Matterhorn
unicorn

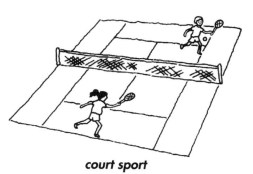

court sport

ors as in *horse*

coarse
course
force
hoarse
horse
source

divorce
endorse
enforce
remorse
resource

ort as in *fort*

court
fort
port
quart
short
snort
sort
sport
thwart
wart

airport
cohort
deport
distort
escort
export
import
passport
report
resort
support
transport

orth as in *fourth*

forth
fourth
north

os as in *gross*

close (adverb)
dose
gross

cosmos
engross
glucose

adios
diagnose
grandiose

os as in *loss*

boss
cross
floss

gloss
loss
moss
sauce
toss

across
crisscross
lacrosse

applesauce

osh as in *wash*

gosh
josh
posh
slosh
squash
wash

ost as in *most*

boast
coast
ghost
host
most
post
roast
toast

almost
utmost

diagnosed
innermost

ghost host

ost as in *cost*

bossed
cost
crossed
flossed
frost
glossed
lost
tossed

defrost
exhaust

holocaust

ot as in *goat*

boat
coat
float
goat
gloat
moat
note
oat
quote
rote
throat
tote
vote
wrote

devote
footnote
promote
remote
rowboat
sailboat

anecdote
antidote
motorboat
overcoat
petticoat
riverboat

ot as in *hot*

blot
clot
cot
dot
got
hot
jot
knot
lot
not
plot
pot
rot
shot
slot
spot
squat
swat
tot
trot
watt
what
yacht

boycott
forgot
jackpot
mascot
slingshot
snapshot
somewhat
teapot

apricot

forget-me-not
+ **ot** as in *taught*

ot as in *taught*

bought
brought
caught
fought
ought
sought

taught
taut
thought

astronaut
+ **ot** as in *hot*

oth as in *growth*

both
growth
oath

oth as in *moth*

broth
cloth
Goth
moth
sloth

ov as in *drove*

clove
cove
dove (verb)
drove
stove
wove

ow as in *cow*

bough
bow
brow
chow
cow
how
now
plow
sow
vow
wow

allow
endow
eyebrow
luau

meow
Moscow
snowplow
somehow

anyhow

owch as in *pouch*

couch
grouch
ouch
pouch
slouch

owd as in *loud*

bowed
cloud
crowd
loud
plowed
proud
vowed

allowed
aloud

owl as in *growl*

bowel
dowel
foul
fowl
growl
howl
jowl
owl
scowl
towel
trowel
vowel

own as in *down*

brown
clown
crown
down

clown frown

drown
frown
gown
noun
town

downtown
nightgown
renown
rundown
showdown
uptown

ownd as in *found*

bound
found
ground
hound
mound
pound
round
sound
wound (verb)

around
astound
background
compound
playground
profound
rebound
surround

battleground
underground

merry-go-round
+ **own** as in *down*: clowned,
frowned, etc.

owns as in *pounce*

bounce
flounce
ounce
pounce
trounce

announce
pronounce
renounce
+ **ownt** as in *mount*: mounts,
discounts, etc.

ownt as in *mount*

count
mount

account
amount
discount
recount

owr as in *sour*

cower
flour
flower
hour
our
power
scour
shower
sour
tower
devour
empower
Mayflower
sunflower
wildflower

cauliflower

ows as in *house*

blouse
douse
grouse
house
louse
mouse
spouse

*I poured it on and rubbed it through
before I read the label: GLUE!*

owt as in *pout*

bout
clout
doubt
drought
gout
out
pout
rout
scout
shout
snout
spout
sprout
stout
trout

about
blackout
campout
cookout
devout
dropout
layout
lookout
throughout
without

sauerkraut

owth as in *south*

mouth
south

oz as in *nose*

chose
close
clothes
doze
froze
hose
nose
pose
prose
rose
those

bulldoze
compose
dispose
enclose
expose
impose
oppose
propose
suppose
+ **o** as in *sew: sews, toes,* etc.

oz as in *cause*

cause
gauze
pause

applause
because

Santa Claus
+ **a** as in *spa: ahs, spas,* etc.
+ **aw** as in *straw: claws, straws,*
etc.

u as in *chew*

blew
blue
boo
brew
chew
clue
crew
dew
do
drew
due
flew
glue
gnu
grew
knew
moo
new
shoe
shoo
Sioux
stew
sue
threw
through
to
too
true

U

two
who
woo
you
zoo

bamboo
bayou
cashew
cuckoo
into
issue
kerchoo
Peru
pursue
renew
shampoo
unto
voodoo

avenue
caribou
kangaroo
overdue

u as in *few*

cue
few
mew
pew
Q
U
view
yew

curfew
IQ
preview
review

barbecue
I.O.U.
interview

ub as in *rub*

club
cub
dub
flub
grub
hub
nub
rub
scrub
shrub
snub
stub
sub
tub

uch as in *such*

clutch
crutch
Dutch
hutch
much
such
touch

ud as in *mood*

brood
brewed
chewed
clued
crude
dude
food
glued
mood
rude
shrewd
stewed
sued

viewed
you'd

include
pursued

renewed
altitude
attitude
latitude
longitude

ud as in *good*

(see **ood** as in *good*)

ud as in *flood*

blood
bud
cud
dud
flood
mud
spud
stud
thud

udj as in *fudge*

budge
drudge
fudge
grudge
judge
nudge
smudge

misjudge

uf as in *proof*

goof
hoof
poof
proof
roof
spoof
woof

aloof
childproof
fireproof
soundproof

U

uf as in *gruff*

bluff
buff
cuff
fluff
gruff
huff
muff
puff
rough
scuff
slough
snuff
stuff
tough

dandruff
enough
handcuff

ug as in *rug*

bug
chug
drug
dug
glug
hug
jug
lug
mug
plug
rug
shrug
slug
smug
snug
thug
tug
ugh

bedbug
earplug
fireplug
humbug

uk as in *spook*

duke
fluke
kook
spook

uk as in *duck*

buck
chuck
cluck
duck
luck
muck
pluck
puck
struck
stuck
suck
truck
tuck
yuck

awestruck
potluck
woodchuck

ukt as in *duct*

duct

conduct
construct
deduct
instruct
obstruct

aqueduct
+ **uk** as in **duck:** *clucked, tucked,* etc.

ul as in *cool*

cool
cruel
drool
fool
ghoul
gruel
pool
rule
school
spool
stool
tool

ul as in *fuel*

fuel
mule
yule

molecule
ridicule

ul as in *skull*

dull
gull
hull
cull
lull
skull

ul as in *full*

bull
full
pull
wool

powerful
wonderful

ulch as in *mulch*

gulch
mulch

ulk as in *sulk*

bulk
hulk
sulk

ulp as in *pulp*

gulp
pulp

ult as in *result*

cult

adult
consult
insult
occult
result

catapult
difficult

um as in *room*

bloom
boom
broom
doom
gloom
groom
loom
room
tomb
whom
womb
zoom

assume
costume

bloom groom

um as in *sum*

bum
chum
come
crumb
drum
dumb
from
glum
gum
hum
mum
numb
plum
plumb
scum
slum
some
strum
sum
thumb
yum

become
eardrum
kingdom
succumb
welcome

maximum
medium
minimum
overcome
premium

aquarium
chrysanthemum
geranium
gymnasium

auditorium

ump as in *jump*

bump
chump
clump
dump

grump
hump
jump
lump
plump
pump
rump
slump
stump
thump
trump
ump

un as in *moon*

dune
June
loon
moon
noon
prune
soon
spoon
strewn
swoon
tune

baboon
balloon
bassoon
cartoon
cocoon
commune
harpoon
immune
lagoon
lampoon
maroon
monsoon
raccoon
Rangoon
spittoon
teaspoon
tycoon
typhoon

afternoon

U

Cameroon
honeymoon
macaroon

un as in *fun*

bun
done
fun
gun
hon
Hun
none
one
pun
run
shun
son
spun
stun
sun
ton
won

begun
canyon
grandson
person
rerun
shotgun

everyone
skeleton

unch as in *lunch*

brunch
bunch
crunch
hunch
lunch
munch
punch
scrunch

ung as in *young*

clung
flung
hung
lung
rung
slung
sprung
strung
stung
sung
swung
tongue
wrung
young

among

unj as in *sponge*

lunge
plunge
sponge

unk as in *skunk*

bunk
chunk
clunk
drunk
dunk
flunk
gunk
hunk
junk
monk
plunk
shrunk
skunk
spunk
stunk
sunk
trunk

unts as in *hunts*

bunts
dunce
fronts
grunts
hunts
once
punts
runts
stunts

up as in *soup*

coop
coupe
croup
droop
goop
group
hoop
loop
scoop
sloop
snoop
soup
stoop
swoop
troop
troupe
whoop

up as in *pup*

cup
pup
up

hiccup
lineup
makeup
teacup

ur as in *her*

blur
burr
fir

fur
her
purr
sir
slur
spur
stir
were
whir

concur
confer
occur
prefer
transfer

computer
+ **ur** as in **tour**

ur as in **tour**

boor
cure
lure
poor
pure
sure
tour
you're
your

assure
brochure
chauffeur
detour
endure
future
insure
mature
secure
unsure

amateur
furniture
immature
premature
signature

literature
miniature
temperature
+ **ur** as in **her**

urb as in **verb**

blurb
curb
herb
Serb
verb

adverb
disturb
perturb
proverb
suburb
superb

urch as in **search**

birch
church
lurch
perch
search

research

urd as in **third**

bird
blurred
curd
heard
herd

bird word

purred
stirred
third
word

absurd
backward
blackbird
crossword
foreword
password

afterward
hummingbird
massacred
overheard

urf as in **surf**

serf
surf
turf

urj as in **urge**

merge
purge
splurge
surge
urge
verge

emerge
submerge

urk as in **work**

clerk
irk
jerk
lurk
perk
quirk
shirk
smirk
work

berserk
guesswork

U

url as in *girl*

curl
earl
girl
hurl
pearl
squirrel
swirl
twirl
whirl

urld as in *world*

curled
swirled
twirled
whirled
world

urm as in *germ*

firm
germ
perm
squirm
term
worm

affirm
confirm
earthworm

urn as in *learn*

burn
churn
earn
fern
learn
stern
turn
urn
yearn

adjourn
concern
return
sunburn

heartburn
overturn

urs as in *verse*

curse
hearse
nurse
purse
verse
worse

coerce
disperse
immerse
rehearse
reverse

reimburse
universe

urst as in *first*

burst
first
thirst
worst

outburst

liverwurst
+ **urs** as in *verse:* nursed,
rehearsed, etc.

urt as in *dirt*

blurt
curt
dirt
flirt
hurt
shirt
skirt
spurt
squirt

alert
assert
concert
convert

desert (verb)
dessert
exert
expert
insert
invert
revert
yogurt

urth as in *earth*

birth
earth
worth

urv as in *serve*

curve
nerve
serve
swerve

conserve
deserve
observe
preserve
reserve

us as in *juice*

deuce
goose
juice
loose
moose
noose
spruce
truce
use (noun)
Zeus

abuse (noun)
caboose
excuse (noun)
mongoose
obtuse
papoose
produce

recluse
reduce
vamoose

introduce

us as in *bus*

bus
cuss
fuss
muss
plus
pus
thus
us

discuss
famous
genius
rhombus
surplus

abacus
courteous
curious
dangerous
envious
fabulous
furious
generous
hazardous
hideous
humorous
mountainous
numerous
octopus
Pegasus
poisonous
rebellious
serious
stimulus
studious

adventurous
anonymous
continuous
deciduous

esophagus
mysterious
unanimous

hippopotamus
miscellaneous
simultaneous

ush as in *push*

bush
push
whoosh

ambush

ush as in *crush*

blush
brush
crush
flush
gush
hush
lush
plush
rush
slush

usk as in *tusk*

dusk
husk
musk
tusk

ust as in *roost*

boost
roost
+ **us** as in *juice: spruced, produced,* etc.

ust as in *must*

bust
crust
dust

just
must
rust
thrust
trust

adjust
disgust
distrust
robust
sawdust
+ **us** as in *bus: bussed, discussed,* etc.

ut as in *suit*

boot
brute
chute
flute
fruit
hoot
loot
lute
moot
newt
root
route
scoot
shoot
suit
toot

acute
commute
compute
dilute
dispute
minute (adjective)
pollute
pursuit
recruit
salute
tribute
uproot

absolute
institute

U

parachute
substitute

ut as in *cut*

but
butt
cut
hut
jut
mutt
nut
putt
rut
shut
strut

chestnut
doughnut
peanut
walnut

coconut
halibut

ut as in *put*

foot
put

uth as in *soothe*

smooth
soothe

uth as in *tooth*

booth
Ruth
sleuth
tooth
truth
youth

uv as in *move*

groove
move
prove
you've

improve
remove

disapprove

uv as in *love*

dove
glove
love
shove

above

uz as in *amuse*

fuse

abuse
accuse
amuse
confuse
excuse
refuse (verb)

uz as in *choose*

blues
boos
bruise
choose
cruise
lose
ooze
snooze
use (verb)
whose
+ **u** as in *chew: chews, shoes,* etc.

uz as in *fuzz*

buzz
does
fuzz
was

Earth Says
I'm giving you oodles of cues
to reduce, recycle, reuse.
It's time to refuse
the choice to abuse
or lose your freedom to choose.

Two-Syllable Rhymes

Words, such as *caring* and *sharing* or *edges* and *pledges* have two syllables that rhyme. Two-syllable rhymes are also called feminine rhymes. You may want to add more word families to this list.

a-bul as in *cable*

able
cable
fable
gable
label
Mabel
stable
table

disable
enable
unable

a-bur as in *labor*

labor
neighbor
saber

a-chur as in *scratcher*

catcher
hatcher
matcher
patcher
scratcher
snatcher
stature
thatcher

a-de as in *daddy*

batty
bratty

caddie
catty
chatty
daddy
fatty
laddie
Lattie
paddy
patty
ratty

Cincinnati

a-ded as in *shaded*

(see **a-dud** as in *shaded*)

a-dik as in *attic*

attic
static

dramatic
ecstatic
nomadic
sporadic

acrobatic
automatic
bureaucratic
democratic
diplomatic

a-ding as in *grading*

braiding
fading
grading
hating
raiding
shading

skating
spading
stating
trading
wading
waiting

charading
creating
debating
donating
frustrating
locating
parading
persuading
relating
rotating
translating

activating
celebrating
circulating
decorating
dedicating
duplicating
educating
fascinating
generating
hesitating
irrigating
irritating
moderating
motivating
relocating
stimulating
violating

abbreviating
accommodating
anticipating

a

associating
communicating
congratulating
consolidating
coordinating
discriminating
evaporating
exaggerating
investigating
negotiating
participating

differentiating
discombobulating
rehabilitating

ad-le as in *sadly*

badly
gladly
Hadley
madly
sadly

a-dud as in *shaded*

aided
baited
braided
crated
dated
faded
fated
freighted
gated
graded
grated
hated
mated
plaited
plated
raided
rated
shaded
skated
slated
spaded

stated
traded
waded
waited
weighted

belated
collated
created
cremated
crusaded
debated
deflated
dilated
donated
downgraded
elated
frustrated
inflated
invaded
located
migrated
outdated
paraded
persuaded
probated
related
rotated
translated
updated
upgraded
vacated

activated
advocated
aggravated
amputated
animated
annotated
barricaded
calculated
captivated
carbonated
celebrated
circulated
complicated
concentrated

contemplated
cultivated
decorated
dedicated
dehydrated
delegated
demonstrated
designated
desolated
devastated
deviated
dominated
duplicated
educated
elevated
elongated
emigrated
estimated
fabricated
fascinated
fluctuated
formulated
fumigated
generated
germinated
graduated
hesitated
hibernated
hyphenated
illustrated
imitated
immigrated
implicated
incubated
indicated
instigated
insulated
integrated
irrigated
irritated
isolated
laminated
legislated
liberated
liquidated
lubricated

masqueraded
medicated
moderated
motivated
nauseated
navigated
nominated
obligated
operated
penetrated
perforated
populated
radiated
regulated
relocated
renovated
saturated
segregated
separated
serenaded
simulated
situated
stimulated
suffocated
syndicated
tabulated
terminated
tolerated
understated
vaccinated
vacillated
validated
vindicated
violated

abbreviated
accelerated
accommodated
accumulated
alienated
alleviated
anticipated
appreciated
assassinated
associated
commemorated

communicated
congratulated
consolidated
contaminated
cooperated
coordinated
decaffeinated
dilapidated
discriminated
domesticated
elaborated
eliminated
enunciated
evacuated
evaporated
exaggerated
exasperated
exterminated
illuminated
impersonated
incriminated
indoctrinated
infatuated
inoculated
insinuated
interrogated
investigated
manipulated
miscalculated
negotiated
originated
participated
procrastinated
reciprocated
refrigerated
sophisticated

a-dul as in *saddle*

battle
cattle
faddle
paddle
prattle
rattle
saddle

straddle
tattle

embattle
Seattle
skedaddle
unsaddle

a-dur as in *grader*

braider
crater
freighter
gator
greater
hater
later
raider
skater
straighter
trader
traitor
wader
waiter

crusader
debater
dictator
equator
invader
narrator
persuader
spectator
translator

agitator
alligator
animator
aviator
calculator
decorator
demonstrator
duplicator
educator
elevator
escalator
generator
illustrator

imitator
indicator
innovator
legislator
masquerader
mediator
moderator
navigator
operator
radiator
serenader
terminator
ventilator

exaggerator
exterminator
impersonator
investigator
negotiator
refrigerator

a-dur as in *chatter*

adder
batter
bladder
chatter
clatter
fatter
flatter
ladder
latter
madder
matter
platter
sadder
shatter
splatter

af-tur as in *laughter*

after
drafter
laughter
rafter

a-juz as in *pages*

ages
cages
gauges
pages
rages
sages
stages
wages

engages
outrages
rampages

ak-tiv as in *active*

active

attractive
inactive
reactive

hyperactive
overactive
retroactive

radioactive

ak-tur as in *factor*

actor
factor
tractor

compactor
contractor
distracter
protractor

benefactor
chiropractor

a-kur as in *baker*

acre
baker
maker
Quaker
raker

shaker
staker
taker

caretaker
dressmaker
heartbreaker
homemaker
icemaker
jawbreaker
lawbreaker
lawmaker
matchmaker
noisemaker
tiebreaker
windbreaker

coffeemaker
moneymaker
undertaker

a-kur as in *stacker*

backer
clacker
cracker
lacquer
packer
quacker
sacker
smacker
stacker
tracker
whacker
yakker

attacker
backpacker
firecracker
hijacker
linebacker
lipsmacker
nutcracker
safecracker
skyjacker
wisecracker

a

a-le as in *daily*

daily
gaily
scaly

Israeli

ukulele

al-e as in *tally*

alley
dally
galley
rally
Sally
tally
valley

a-lur as in *sailor*

bailer
frailer
jailer
mailer
nailer
paler
sailor
scaler
tailor
trailer
whaler

exhaler
retailer
wholesaler

al-us as in *palace*

Alice
callous
chalice
Dallas
malice
palace

am-bul as in *scramble*

amble
gamble
gambol
ramble
scramble
shamble

preamble
unscramble

am-les as in *nameless*

aimless
blameless
flameless
frameless
nameless
shameless

am-pur as in *hamper*

camper
damper
hamper
pamper
scamper
stamper
tamper

a-mur as in *hammer*

clamor
glamour
grammar
hammer
slammer

stammer
jackhammer
programmer
sledgehammer

diagrammer
monogrammer

an-de as in *candy*

Andy
candy
dandy
handy
Mandy
sandy

an-ded as in *landed*

banded
branded
candid
handed
landed
stranded

demanded
disbanded
expanded

an-dul as in *handle*

candle
handle
sandal
scandal
vandal

damper camper

a

manhandle
mishandle
panhandle

an-e as in *nanny*

cranny
Danny
Frannie
Granny
nanny

ang-kur as in *tanker*

anchor
banker
canker
clanker
franker
hanker
spanker
tanker

ang-ul as in *tangle*

angle
bangle
dangle
jangle
mangle
strangle
tangle
wrangle

entangle
rectangle
quadrangle
triangle
untangle

a-nik as in *panic*

manic
panic

Hispanic
mechanic
organic

titanic
volcanic

an-jur as in *ranger*

changer
danger
ranger
stranger

arranger
endanger
exchanger

an-se as in *fancy*

antsy
chancy
fancy
Nancy

an-sez as in *dances*

chances
dances
glances
lances
prances
trances

advances
enhances
expanses
finances
romances

an-ted as in *planted*

chanted
granted
panted
planted
ranted
slanted

enchanted
implanted
transplanted

a-nur as in *manner*

banner
canner
fanner
manner
manor
planner
scanner
spanner
tanner

a-pur as in *shaper*

caper
draper
paper
scraper
shaper
taper
tapir

a-pur as in *rapper*

capper
clapper
dapper
flapper
mapper
napper
rapper
slapper
snapper
wrapper
yapper

ar-e as in *fairy*

airy
berry
bury
carry
cherry
dairy
fairy
ferry
hairy

very scary cemetery

Harry
marry
Mary
merry
prairie
scary
vary
very
wary

cemetery
culinary
customary
dictionary
dietary
dignitary
dromedary
February
honorary
January
legendary
literary
military
missionary
momentary
monastery
mortuary
necessary
ordinary
sanitary
secondary
secretary
solitary
stationary

stationery
temporary
voluntary

extraordinary
hereditary
imaginary
itinerary
obituary
preliminary
unnecessary
vocabulary

ar-o as in *narrow*

arrow
marrow
narrow
pharaoh
sparrow

bolero
sombrero

ar-ut as in *carrot*

carat
carrot
ferret
merit
parrot

inherit

a-sez as in *bases*

aces
bases
braces
cases
chases
faces
laces
paces
places
races
spaces
traces

disgraces
displaces
footraces
misplaces
replaces
unlaces

a-sez as in *glasses*

classes
gases
glasses
grasses
masses
passes

molasses
surpasses

ash-ez as in *crashes*

ashes
bashes
clashes
crashes
dashes
flashes
gashes
gnashes
lashes
mashes
rashes
sashes
slashes
smashes
splashes
stashes

mustaches

a-shun as in *nation*

nation
station

conversation
creation
dictation

a

donation
education
explanation
foundation
frustration
migration
operation
plantation
probation
quotation
relation
starvation
taxation
vacation
vibration

aggravation
application
aviation
calculation
cancellation
celebration
combination
complication
concentration
congregation
consolation
conversation
demonstration
decoration
declaration
desperation
duplication
expectation
explanation
exploration
fascination
generation
graduation
hesitation
illustration
imitation
immigration
information
innovation
integration
irritation

irrigation
motivation
legislation
limitation
nomination
perspiration
population
presentation
preparation
radiation
recreation
relaxation
segregation
separation
situation
stimulation
transportation
violation

abbreviation
anticipation
appreciation
assassination
communication
consideration
cooperation
coordination
determination
discrimination
evaluation
imagination
initiation
interpretation
intoxication
investigation
multiplication
notification
organization
participation
pronunciation
realization

a-ted as in *dated*

(see **a-dud** as in *shaded*)

a-tul as in *rattle*

(See **a-dul** as in *saddle*)

a-vur as in *saver*

braver
favor
flavor
paver
quaver
saver
savor
shaver
slaver
waiver
waver

a-zez as in *gazes*

blazes
crazes
dazes
gazes
glazes
grazes
hazes
mazes
phases
phrases
praises
raises

amazes

a-zur as in *blazer*

gazer
laser
praiser
raiser
razor

e-chez as in *peaches*

beaches
beeches
bleaches
breaches
breeches
leeches
peaches
preaches
reaches
screeches
speeches
teaches

e-chur as in *teacher*

bleacher
creature
feature
preacher
screecher
teacher

impeacher

e-de as in *greedy*

beady
greedy
needy
seedy
speedy

e-de as in *ready*

Eddie
ready
steady

already
unsteady

e-ded as in *needed*

beaded
cheated
deeded
greeted
heated
heeded
kneaded
needed
pleaded
pleated
seated
seeded
weeded

exceeded
preceded
proceeded
stampeded
succeeded

e-ded as in *headed*

dreaded
headed
leaded
shredded
threaded
wedded

e-ding as in *feeding*

bleeding
breeding
beating
cheating
eating
feeding
greeting
heating
leading
meeting
pleading
reading
speeding
treating

e-ding as in *getting*

bedding
betting
getting
heading
petting
shedding
spreading
sweating
threading
wedding
wetting

e-dul as in *pedal*

kettle
medal
meddle
metal
pedal
peddle
petal
settle
treadle

e-dur as in *reader*

beater
breeder
cedar
cheater
eater
feeder
greeter
heater
leader
liter
meter
neater
Peter
pleader
pleater
reader
speeder
sweeter
weeder

e

e-dur as in *spreader*

better
cheddar
getter
header
letter
redder
setter
shredder
spreader
threader
treader
wetter

e-ing as in *seeing*

being
fleeing
freeing
seeing

agreeing

guaranteeing

e-jez as in *pledges*

edges
hedges
ledges
pledges
wedges

e-king as in *leaking*

creaking
leaking
peeking
seeking
shrieking
sneaking
speaking

e-king as in *pecking*

checking
decking

pecking
wrecking

ek-shun as in *section*

section

affection
collection
connection
correction
dejection
direction
election
infection
inflection
injection
objection
perfection
protection
reflection
selection

e-kur as in *weaker*

beaker
bleaker
meeker
seeker
sneaker
speaker
weaker

e-kur as in *wrecker*

checker
wrecker

e-ling as in *feeling*

ceiling
dealing
feeling
healing
kneeling
peeling
sealing
squealing

stealing
appealing
revealing

el-ling as in *selling*

dwelling
selling
shelling
smelling
spelling
telling
yelling

compelling
excelling
expelling
misspelling
rebelling
repelling

el-lo as in *hello*

bellow
cello
fellow
hello
mellow
yellow

el-lur as in *speller*

cellar
dweller
seller
smeller
speller
stellar
teller

em-bur as in *member*

ember
member

December
November
September

e

e-mur as in *screamer*

dreamer
femur
schemer
screamer
steamer
streamer

en-ded as in *blended*

blended
ended
mended
splendid
tended

en-ding as in *sending*

bending
blending
ending
fending
lending
mending
pending
sending
spending
tending
vending

amending
attending
commending
contending
depending
extending
intending
offending
pretending
suspending
unending

en-dur as in *fender*

bender
blender
fender

fender bender

gender
lender
mender
sender
slender
spender
splendor
tender
vendor

contender
defender
goaltender
offender
pretender
surrender
suspender

e-ne as in *genie*

beanie
genie
Jeanie
meany
teeny
weeny

bikini
Houdini
linguine
zucchini

e-ning as in *meaning*

cleaning
gleaning
leaning
meaning
preening
screening
weaning

en-shun as in *tension*

mention
tension

attention
convention
detention
dimension
dissension
extension
intention
invention
retention
suspension

comprehension
intervention

en-tal as in *rental*

dental
gentle
lentil
mental
rental

parental

accidental
continental
departmental
detrimental
fundamental
incidental
monumental
regimental
sentimental
supplemental

developmental
experimental

en-ted as in *rented*

dented
rented
scented
vented

e

accented
assented
cemented
consented
dissented
fermented
indented
invented
lamented
presented
prevented
relented
repented
resented
tormented

e-pe as in *sleepy*

creepy
sleepy
teepee
weepy

er-e as in *cheery*

bleary
cheery
dreary
eerie
Erie
leery
query
smeary
teary
weary

e-shun as in *session*

freshen
session

aggression
compression
concession
confession
depression
expression
obsession

oppression
possession
profession
progression
regression

e-sing as in *guessing*

blessing
dressing
guessing
messing
pressing

addressing
assessing
caressing
confessing
depressing
distressing
impressing
progressing

e-sted as in *tested*

breasted
crested
jested
nested
rested
tested
wrested

arrested
detested
digested
infested
invested
protested
suggested

e-ted as in *sweated*

fetid
fretted
netted
sweated
whetted

e-thing as in *teething*

breathing
seething
teething

e-ting as in *meeting*

beating
bleating
cheating
eating
greeting
heating
meeting
seating
treating

competing
completing
defeating
repeating
retreating

e-tul as in *petal*

(see **e-dul** as in *pedal*)

e-tur as in *meter*

(see **e-dur** as in *reader*)

e-vur as in *never*

clever
ever
lever
never

endeavor
forever
however
whatever
wherever
whichever
whoever

i

e-zhur as in *pleasure*

measure
pleasure
treasure

e-zing as in *teasing*

breezing
easing
freezing
pleasing
seizing
sneezing
squeezing
teasing
wheezing

e-zur as in *freezer*

Caesar
freezer
pleaser
sneezer
squeezer
teaser
tweezer
wheezer

sneezer teaser

i-bul as in *nibble*

dribble
nibble
quibble
scribble

i-chez as in *riches*

britches
ditches
hitches
itches
niches
pitches
riches
stitches
switches
twitches
witches

i-ded as in *guided*

chided
glided
guided
prided
sided

collided
confided
decided
divided
lopsided
misguided
provided
resided

i-dul as in *bridal*

bridal
bridle
idle

idol
tidal

i-dul as in *middle*

fiddle
griddle
middle
riddle
twiddle

i-dur as in *spider*

cider
glider
rider
slider
spider
wider

divider
insider
outsider
provider

if-te as in *thrifty*

fifty
nifty
shifty
thrifty

if-tur as in *sifter*

differ
sniffer
stiffer

i-ful as in *rifle*

Eiffel
rifle
stifle
trifle

i

i-gul as in *jiggle*

giggle
jiggle
squiggle
wiggle
wriggle

i-ing as in *drying*

buying
crying
drying
dyeing
dying
eyeing
frying
lying
plying
prying
sighing
spying
trying
tying
vying

applying
implying
relying
replying
untying

clarifying
crucifying
dignifying
falsifying
gratifying
justifying
magnifying
multiplying
notifying
qualifying
satisfying
simplifying
terrifying
unifying

dissatisfying
identifying

i-jit as in *midget*

digit
fidget
midget

i-ke as in *sticky*

dickey
Ricky
sticky
tricky

i-ket as in *ticket*

cricket
picket
thicket
ticket
wicket

i-king as in *striking*

biking
hiking
liking
spiking
striking
Viking

disliking

ik-li as in *sickly*

prickly
quickly
sickly

ik-shun as in *fiction*

diction
fiction
friction

addiction
affliction

conviction
eviction
prediction
restriction

i-kur as in *quicker*

bicker
clicker
flicker
kicker
licker
liquor
quicker
sicker
slicker
snicker
sticker
thicker
ticker
tricker
vicar
wicker

il-e as in *chili*

Billy
Chile
chili
chilly
dilly
filly
frilly
hilly
lily
silly

il-nes as in *stillness*

illness
shrillness
stillness

il-yun as in *million*

billion
million

trillion
zillion

Brazilian
pavilion
reptilian
sextillion

im-bul as in *symbol*

cymbal
nimble
symbol
thimble

i-ming as in *rhyming*

chiming
climbing
miming
priming
rhyming
timing

i-ming as in *swimming*

brimming
dimming
skimming
slimming
swimming
trimming

im-ping as in *limping*

crimping
limping
primping
scrimping
shrimping
skimping

im-pul as in *pimple*

dimple
pimple
simple

in-ding as in *finding*

binding
blinding
finding
grinding
minding
winding

in-e as in *skinny*

Ginny
mini
ninny
skinny
whinny

ing-ing as in *singing*

bringing
clinging
dinging
flinging
ringing
singing
slinging
springing
stinging
stringing
swinging
wringing

ing-ke as in *slinky*

blinky
dinky
hinky
inky
kinky
pinky
slinky
stinky
Twinkie

ing-kul as in *twinkle*

crinkle
sprinkle

tinkle
twinkle
wrinkle

i-nur as in *winner*

dinner
inner
sinner
skinner
spinner
thinner
winner

beginner
breadwinner

i-pe as in *drippy*

dippy
drippy
flippy
hippie
lippy
nippy
snippy
tippy
yippee
zippy

i-pur as in *wiper*

diaper
griper
piper
sniper
striper
swiper
viper
wiper

i-pur as in *shipper*

chipper
clipper
dipper
dripper
flipper

gripper
nipper
ripper
shipper
sipper
skipper
slipper
snipper
stripper
tripper
zipper

ir-ing as in *wiring*

firing
hiring
tiring
wiring

acquiring
admiring
aspiring
desiring
expiring
inquiring
inspiring
perspiring
retiring
transpiring
untiring

i-shun as in *mission*

fission
mission

addition
admission
ambition
audition
condition
edition
ignition
magician
musician
nutrition
omission
physician

position
technician
tradition
tuition

ammunition
competition
composition
definition
disposition
electrician
politician
preposition
proposition

i-sing as in *pricing*

dicing
icing
pricing
spicing
splicing

enticing
sufficing

sacrificing

is-tic as in *artistic*

mystic

artistic
simplistic
statistic

realistic
characteristic
idealistic
unrealistic

is-tur as in *sister*

blister
mister
sister
twister

transistor

i-sul as in *missile*

bristle
gristle
missile
thistle
whistle

dismissal

it-le as in *nightly*

brightly
knightly
lightly
nightly
slightly
sprightly
tightly

politely
unsightly

i-tur as in *sitter*

bitter
fritter
glitter
hitter
knitter
litter
quitter
sitter
spitter
splitter
twitter

i-vur as in *shiver*

giver
liver
quiver
river
shiver
sliver

deliver

O

i-ze as in *dizzy*

busy
dizzy
frizzy
Lizzie

i-zul as in *sizzle*

chisel
drizzle
fizzle
sizzle
swizzle

o-be as in *hobby*

Bobbie
hobby
knobby
lobby
snobby

o-bing as in *sobbing*

bobbing
lobbing
mobbing
robbing
sobbing
swabbing
throbbing

o-bul as in *gobble*

bauble
cobble
gobble
hobble
squabble
wobble

o-ching as in *coaching*

broaching
coaching
poaching

approaching
reproaching

spotty body

o-de as in *spotty*

body
haughty
knotty
naughty
potty
Scottie
snotty
spotty

karate
nobody

o-ding as in *prodding*

nodding
plodding
prodding
wadding

o-dul as in *waddle*

coddle
model
swaddle
toddle
waddle

o-dur as in *totter*

(see **o-tur** as in *totter*)

o-ing as in *rowing*

blowing
crowing
flowing
glowing
going
growing
hoeing
knowing
mowing
owing
rowing
sewing
showing
snowing
sowing
stowing
throwing
toeing
towing

o-ken as in *spoken*

broken
spoken
token

o-ket as in *pocket*

docket
locket
pocket
rocket
socket
sprocket

o-kur as in *soccer*

blocker
cocker
docker
knocker
locker

rocker
shocker
soccer

ol-dur as in *colder*

bolder
boulder
colder
folder
holder
molder
older
scolder
shoulder
smolder

ol-le as in *jolly*

collie
dolly
folly
golly
holly
jolly
Molly
trolley
volley

o-ne as in *pony*

bony
crony
phony
pony
stony
Tony

baloney

macaroni

o-nik as in *tonic*

chronic
phonic
sonic
tonic

o-pur as in *shopper*

bopper
chopper
cropper
dropper
hopper
popper
proper
shopper
stopper
swapper
topper
whopper

floppy poppy

o-pe as in *poppy*

choppy
copy
floppy
poppy
sloppy

or-dur as in *porter*

boarder
border
hoarder
mortar
order
porter
quarter
shorter
warder

disorder
exporter
importer
recorder
reporter

or-e as in *story*

Cory
glory
gory
quarry
story

category
lavatory
mandatory
territory

conservatory
explanatory
observatory
reformatory

or-mur as in *warmer*

dormer
former
warmer

informer
performer
transformer

or-ul as in *floral*

choral
coral
floral
moral
oral
quarrel

o-se as in *glossy*

bossy
glossy
mossy

posse
saucy

o-shun as in *motion*

Goshen
lotion
motion
notion
ocean
potion

commotion
emotion
promotion

o-shus as in *ferocious*

atrocious
ferocious
precocious

o-tur as in *totter*

fodder
hotter
otter
plotter
potter
totter
trotter
water

ow-dur as in *louder*

chowder
doubter
louder
pouter
powder
prouder
shouter

u-be as in *hubby*

chubby
grubby
hubby
stubby
tubby

double trouble

u-bul as in *trouble*

bubble
double
rubble
stubble
trouble

u-de as in *study*

bloody
buddy
cruddy
muddy
nutty
putty
ruddy
study

u-dul as in *puddle*

cuddle
huddle
muddle
puddle
shuttle
subtle

u-dur as in *tutor*

cuter
looter
neuter
rooter
scooter
shooter
suitor
tutor

u-dur as in *shutter*

butter
clutter
cutter
flutter
mutter
putter
rudder
shudder
shutter
sputter
stutter
udder
utter

u-fing as in *puffing*

bluffing
cuffing
fluffing
huffing
puffing
roughing
stuffing

ug-lur as in *struggler*

juggler
smuggler
snuggler
struggler

u-ke as in *lucky*

ducky
lucky
plucky

Kentucky

uk-tiv as in *destructive*

constructive
destructive
instructive
productive

u-kul as in *chuckle*

buckle
chuckle
knuckle

u-le as in *truly*

coolly
duly
newly
truly

u-lur as in *ruler*

cooler
ruler

um-bul as in *stumble*

crumble
fumble
grumble
humble
jumble
mumble
rumble

stumble
tumble

u-me as in *tummy*

chummy
crummy
dummy
gummy
mummy
rummy
scummy
tummy
yummy

um-pe as in *lumpy*

bumpy
clumpy
dumpy
frumpy
jumpy
lumpy
stumpy

u-mur as in *rumor*

bloomer
groomer
rumor
tumor

consumer

u-mur as in *summer*

bummer
drummer
dumber
hummer
plumber
strummer
summer

un-dur as in *wonder*

blunder
plunder

thunder
under
wonder

u-ne as in *money*

bunny
funny
honey
money
runny
sonny
sunny

ung-ur as in *younger*

hunger
younger

un-ke as in *monkey*

chunky
clunky
funky
junky
monkey
spunky

u-nur as in *tuner*

crooner
lunar
pruner
schooner
sooner
tuner

u-pur as in *super*

scooper
snooper
stupor
super
trooper
trouper

ur-dul as in *turtle*

fertile
girdle
myrtle
turtle

ur-e as in *worry*

blurry
flurry
furry
hurry
scurry
worry

ur-le as in *surely*

curly
early
pearly
surely
surly
swirly
twirly
whirly

u-shun as in *solution*

dilution
pollution
solution

constitution
contribution
distribution
evolution

execution
institution
prosecution
resolution
revolution
substitution

u-siv as in *exclusive*

abusive
allusive
conclusive
conducive
exclusive
intrusive
obtrusive

u-ste as in *dusty*

crusty
dusty
gusty
musty
rusty
trusty

u-sul as in *muscle*

bustle
hustle
muscle
mussel
rustle
tussle

u-thur as in *mother*

brother
mother
other
smother

another

u-zez as in *chooses*

bruises
chooses
cruises
loses
oozes
uses

u-zul as in *nuzzle*

guzzle
muzzle
nuzzle
puzzle

u-zur as in *loser*

chooser
cruiser
loser
snoozer
user

Three-Syllable Rhymes

Words, such as *ability* and *utility* or *pottery* and *watery* have three syllables that rhyme. Here is a sampling of three-syllable rhymes. Can you add others to the list?

a-be-est as in *crabbiest*

blabbiest
crabbiest
flabbiest
gabbiest
shabbiest

a-bur-ing as in *neighboring*

laboring
neighboring

ach-u-bul as in *patchable*

matchable
patchable
scratchable

attachable
detachable
unpatchable

a-de-um as in *stadium*

radium
stadium

palladium

al-i-te as in *legality*

brutality
finality
formality
frugality
legality

locality
mentality
modality
mortality
reality
vitality

hospitality
immortality
partiality

confidentiality
individuality

al-ur-e as in *salary*

calorie
gallery
salary
Valerie

a-ze-nes as in *laziness*

craziness
haziness
laziness

e-di-kat as in *medicate*

dedicate
medicate

e-di-tor as in *editor*

creditor
editor
predator

e-de-ur as in *speedier*

greedier
needier
seedier
speedier

ek-tiv-le as in *objectively*

collectively
deceptively
effectively
objectively
protectively
respectively
selectively
subjectively

e-pi-le as in *sleepily*

creepily
sleepily
weepily

i-e-ting as in *quieting*

dieting
quieting
rioting

il-i-te as in *mobility*

ability
agility
facility
hostility

humility
mobility
nobility
senility
stability
tranquillity
utility

capability
disability
durability
inability
legibility
liability
movability
possibility
probability
readability
sensibility
visibility

availability
compatibility
desirability
eligibility
excitability
flexibility
irritability
reliability
respectability
responsibility

i-se-ning as in *glistening*

christening
glistening
listening

i-si-kul as in *icicle*

bicycle
icicle
tricycle

unicycle

is-tur-e as in *mystery*

history
mystery

slobbery robbery

o-bur-e as in *snobbery*

robbery
slobbery
snobbery

o-ji-kul as in *logical*

logical

illogical

astrological
biological
chronological
geological
mythological
neurological
psychological
technological
theological

anthropological
archaeological
sociological

o-me-tur as in *thermometer*

barometer
micrometer
odometer
spectrometer
speedometer
tachometer
thermometer

audiometer

or-i-te as in *majority*

authority
majority
minority
seniority
sorority

inferiority
superiority

o-si-te as in *curiosity*

atrocity
ferocity
monstrosity
velocity

animosity
curiosity
generosity

o-tur-e as in *pottery*

lottery
pottery
watery

o-ze-est as in *nosiest*

coziest
nosiest
rosiest

un-dur-ing as in *wondering*

blundering
thundering
wondering

ur-e-us as in *furious*

curious
furious

luxurious

ur-i-te as in *maturity*

purity

impurity
maturity
obscurity
security

immaturity
insecurity

ur-u-bul as in *durable*

curable
durable

endurable
incurable
insurable
securable

u-ste-est as in *dustiest*

crustiest
dustiest

gustiest
mustiest
rustiest
trustiest

uth-ful-nes as in *youthfulness*

truthfulness
youthfulness

u-tur-ing as in *muttering*

buttering
fluttering
muttering
sputtering
stuttering
uttering

Making Words Count

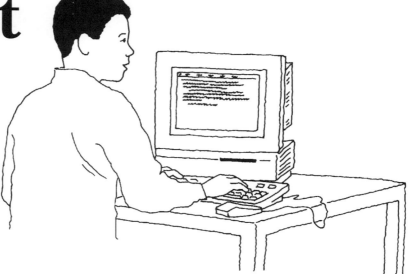

Write It Right
(Common Spelling Errors)

How do you find a word's spelling in the dictionary if you are not sure how to spell the word? In this mini-dictionary, words are listed in alphabetical order. Correct spellings are printed in **darker** or **boldface** type.

Look up a word (however you think it is spelled) in the left-hand column. If you have spelled the word correctly, it will appear in boldface type. If your spelling is incorrect, you will find the correct spelling in boldface type to the right.

abcents	**absence**	**all right**	
abot	**about**	allright	**all right**
about		alltho	**although**
abowt	**about**	allways	**always**
absence		**already**	
absense	**absence**	alredy	**already**
absents	**absence**	alright	**all right**
accurate		altho	**although**
ackshun	**action**	**although**	
acros	**across**	alwaize	**always**
across		**always**	
acshun	**action**	alwaze	**always**
action		amatchur	**amateur**
acurate	**accurate**	**amateur**	
acurut	**accurate**	**among**	
address		amuchur	**amateur**
adres	**address**	amung	**among**
adress	**address**	**angle**	
again		angol	**angle**
agen	**again**	angul	**angle**
akshun	**action**	**ant**	

a

ant	**aunt**	**awhile**	
apearance	**appearance**	awile	**awhile**
apologize		**balloon**	
appearance		ballune	**balloon**
appearence	**appearance**	baloon	**balloon**
appologize	**apologize**	bawt	**bought**
appreciate		**because**	
appresheate	**appreciate**	becaws	**because**
Apral	**April**	becus	**because**
apreciate	**appreciate**	**been**	
April		befor	**before**
Aprul	**April**	**before**	
Arcktic	**Arctic**	befour	**before**
Arctic		ben	**been**
arguement	**argument**	berthday	**birthday**
argument		bi	**buy**
arithmatic	**arithmetic**	bi	**by**
arithmetic		**bicycle**	
Artic	**Arctic**	bilt	**built**
ateth	**eighth**	bin	**been**
ath	**eighth**	**birthday**	
athelete	**athlete**	bisy	**busy**
atheletic	**athletic**	bizy	**busy**
athlete		**blew**	
		blew	**blue**
		blue	
		blue	**blew**
		boal	**bowl**
		bole	**bowl**
		bought	
		bowl	
		breathe	
		breth	**breathe**
		brethe	**breathe**
		built	
		bullatin	**bulletin**
		bulletin	
		bullitin	**bulletin**
		bullutin	**bulletin**
		burthday	**birthday**
athletic		**busy**	
audience		**buy**	
audiense	**audience**	**by**	
aunt		**calendar**	
		calender	**calendar**
		canceled	

172

cancelled	**canceled**	Christmos	**Christmas**
canseled	**canceled**	Christmus	**Christmas**
carear	**career**	chuse	**choose**
career		chuze	**choose**
carreer	**career**	cloaze	**close**
cawf	**cough**	cloaze	**clothes**
cematery	**cemetery**	**close**	
cemetery		**clothes**	
cemitery	**cemetery**	cloze	**close**
cemutery	**cemetery**	cloze	**clothes**

		cof	**cough**
		colar	**color**
		colom	**column**
		color	
		colum	**column**
		column	
		colur	**color**
		come	
certain		comeing	**coming**
certan	**certain**	comfert	**comfort**
certen	**certain**	comfirt	**comfort**
certin	**certain**	**comfort**	
certon	**certain**	comfurt	**comfort**
certun	**certain**	**coming**	
cheef	**chief**	comittee	**committee**
chews	**choose**	commitee	**committee**
chief		**committee**	
childran	**children**	cood	**could**
children		**correspondence**	
childrin	**children**	corrispondence	**correspondence**
childron	**children**	corrospondence	**correspondence**
childrun	**children**	corruspondence	**correspondence**
chocalate	**chocolate**	**cough**	
chockolate	**chocolate**	**could**	
choclate	**chocolate**	**country**	
chocolate		**county**	
choculate	**chocolate**	**courteous**	
chokolate	**chocolate**	courtious	**courteous**
choose		**cousin**	
Christmas		cownty	**county**
Christmes	**Christmas**	**criticize**	
Christmis	**Christmas**	critisize	**criticize**
		cuboard	**cupboard**
		cud	**could**
		culor	**color**
		cum	**come**

d

cumfurt	**comfort**
cuntry	**country**
cupboard	
curiosity	
curiousity	**curiosity**
cuzin	**cousin**
cuzun	**cousin**
dairy	
darey	**dairy**

dear	
decision	
deckorate	**decorate**
decorate	
deer	
defanitely	**definitely**
definately	**definitely**
definitely	
dere	**dear**
dere	**deer**
desision	**decision**
diference	**difference**
difference	
disappear	
disappoint	
discipline	
disease	
diseppear	**disappear**
disterb	**disturb**
distirb	**disturb**
disturb	

disupline	**discipline**
disuppear	**disappear**
disuppoint	**disappoint**
division	
divition	**division**
divizion	**division**
dizease	**disease**
dizeaze	**disease**
doctar	**doctor**
docter	**doctor**
doctir	**doctor**
doctor	
does	
doz	**does**
duz	**does**
early	
easy	
eaze	**easy**
eazy	**easy**
eighth	
embarass	**embarrass**
embarrass	
embearass	**embarrass**
eneek	**unique**
enough	
enuf	**enough**
enviornment	**environment**
environment	
especially	
espeshally	**especially**
evary	**every**
every	
evry	**every**
exagerate	**exaggerate**
exaggerate	
exajerate	**exaggerate**
excelent	**excellent**
excellent	
experiance	**experience**
experience	
experiunce	**experience**
extreemly	**extremely**
extremely	
extremly	**extremely**
familar	**familiar**
familiar	

fascinate
fasinate   **fascinate**
favarite   **favorite**
faverite   **favorite**
favorite
favrite   **favorite**
favurite   **favorite**
fearce   **fierce**
February
Febuary   **February**
Feburary   **February**
feerce   **fierce**
ferst   **first**
fierce
finally
finaly   **finally**
finly   **finally**
first
football
foreign
foren   **foreign**
forth
forth   **fourth**
forty

fourth
fourty   **forty**
freind   **friend**
frend   **friend**
Friday

friend
Fryday   **Friday**
fuel
fule   **fuel**
fulfill
fullfil   **fulfill**
furst   **first**
futball   **football**
garantee   **guarantee**
gard   **guard**
garintee   **guarantee**
garontee   **guarantee**
garuntee   **guarantee**
gess   **guess**
geting   **getting**
getting
goes
government
govornment   **government**
govurnment   **government**
goze   **goes**
grade
graid   **grade**
grate   **great**
grayed   **grade**
great
greef   **grief**
grefe   **grief**
greif   **grief**
grewp   **group**
grief
groop   **group**
group
guarantee
guard
guess
haf   **half**
half
handkerchief
handsome
handsum   **handsome**
hangerchief   **handkerchief**
hankerchief   **handkerchief**
hansome   **handsome**
haveing   **having**
having

h

hear		**interesting**	
heard		**interrupt**	
hearos	**heroes**	intiresting	**interesting**
heer	**hear**	intirrupt	**interrupt**
heer	**here**	intoresting	**interesting**
height		inturesting	**interesting**
heit	**height**	inturrupt	**interrupt**
hello		**it's**	
helo	**hello**	**its**	
helow	**hello**	jealos	**jealous**
herd	**heard**	**jealous**	
here		jealus	**jealous**
heroes		jellous	**jealous**
hight	**height**	jelous	**jealous**
hite	**height**	jewalry	**jewelry**
hole		**jewelry**	
hopeing	**hoping**	**journal**	
hoping		journel	**journal**
hopping	**hoping**	**journey**	
hospital		journil	**journal**
hospitle	**hospital**	journol	**journal**
houer	**hour**	journul	**journal**
hour			
house			
howse	**house**		
huemorous	**humorous**		
humorous			
humourous	**humorous**		
hurd	**heard**		
illastrate	**illustrate**		
illestrate	**illustrate**		
illistrate	**illustrate**		
illostrate	**illustrate**		
illustrate			
ilustrate	**illustrate**		
imaginary			
imajinary	**imaginary**		
imediately	**immediately**	journy	**journey**
immediately		judgement	**judgment**
immeediately	**immediately**	**judgment**	
instead		jurney	**journey**
insted	**instead**	kindagarten	**kindergarten**
intaresting	**interesting**	kindargarten	**kindergarten**
intarrupt	**interrupt**	kindegarten	**kindergarten**
inteligence	**intelligence**	kindergarden	**kindergarten**
intelligence		**kindergarten**	

kindigarten	**kindergarten**	lesans	**lessons**
kindirgarten	**kindergarten**	lesins	**lessons**
kindogarten	**kindergarten**	lesons	**lessons**
kindorgarten	**kindergarten**	lessans	**lessons**
kindugarten	**kindergarten**	lessens	**lessons**
kindurgarten	**kindergarten**	lessins	**lessons**
knew		**lessons**	
know		lessuns	**lessons**
knowledge		lesuns	**lessons**
knowlege	**knowledge**	letar	**letter**
knowlidge	**knowledge**	leter	**letter**
knowlige	**knowledge**	letir	**letter**
kwantity	**quantity**	lettar	**letter**
kwarrel	**quarrel**	**letter**	
kwit	**quit**	lettir	**letter**
kwite	**quite**	lettor	**letter**
kworter	**quarter**	lettur	**letter**
labaratory	**laboratory**	letur	**letter**
laberatory	**laboratory**	**library**	
labiratory	**laboratory**	librerry	**library**
laboratory		librery	**library**
		licence	**license**
		license	
		licince	**license**
		licinse	**license**
		lightening	**lightning**
		lightning	
		lisin	**listen**
		lison	**listen**
		lissan	**listen**
		lissen	**listen**
		lissin	**listen**
		lisson	**listen**
		lissun	**listen**
labratory	**laboratory**	**listen**	
laburatory	**laboratory**	lital	**little**
lad	**laid**	litel	**little**
lade	**laid**	litil	**little**
laid		litle	**little**
lator	**latter**	litol	**little**
lattar	**latter**	litor	**letter**
latter		littal	**little**
lattir	**latter**	littel	**little**
lattor	**latter**	littil	**little**
lattur	**latter**	**little**	
		littol	**little**

I

littul   **little**
litul   **little**
loose
luse   **loose**
makeing   **making**
making
many
mathamatics   **mathematics**
mathematics
mathimatics   **mathematics**
mathomatics   **mathematics**
mathumatics   **mathematics**
maybe
mayby   **maybe**

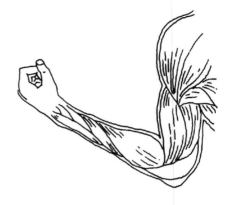

meny   **many**   **muscle**
milage   **mileage**   musel   **muscle**
mileage   musil   **muscle**
milege   **mileage**   musle   **muscle**
milige   **mileage**   mussal   **muscle**
mineature   **miniature**   mussel   **muscle**
miniature   mussil   **muscle**
minit   **minute**   mussol   **muscle**
minute   mussul   **muscle**
misaleneous   **miscellaneous**   muthar   **mother**
miscelaneous   **miscellaneous**   muthor   **mother**
miscellaneous   muthur   **mother**
mischiefous   **mischievous**   naim   **name**
mischievious   **mischievous**   **name**
mischievous   natchurally   **naturally**
miselaneous   **miscellaneous**   **naturally**
misilaneous   **miscellaneous**   nease   **niece**
misolaneous   **miscellaneous**   nece   **niece**
mispell   **misspell**   necesary   **necessary**
missalaneous   **miscellaneous**   **necessary**
misselaneous   **miscellaneous**   neece   **niece**
missolaneous   **miscellaneous**   neese   **niece**
misspell   neice   **niece**
missulaneous   **miscellaneous**   neise   **niece**
misulaneous   **miscellaneous**   **neither**
morening   **morning**   nese   **niece**
morning   nesesary   **necessary**
mothar   **mother**   nesessary   **necessary**
mother   nethar   **neither**
mothir   **mother**   nether   **neither**
mothor   **mother**   nethir   **neither**
mothur   **mother**   nethor   **neither**
                                     nethur   **neither**

new		**off**	
nice		offan	**often**
nickal	**nickel**	offen	**often**
nickel		offin	**often**
nickil	**nickel**	offon	**often**
nickol	**nickel**	offun	**often**
nickul	**nickel**	ofin	**often**
niece		ofon	**often**
niese	**niece**	**often**	
nikal	**nickel**	oftun	**often**
nikel	**nickel**	ofun	**often**
nikil	**nickel**	**once**	
nikol	**nickel**	onese	**once**
nikul	**nickel**	opartunity	**opportunity**
nineth	**ninth**	opertunity	**opportunity**
ninety		**opinion**	
ninth		opinon	**opinion**
ninty	**ninety**	opinyun	**opinion**
nise	**nice**	opirtunity	**opportunity**
no	**know**	oportunity	**opportunity**
none		oppartunity	**opportunity**
noticable	**noticeable**	oppasite	**opposite**
noticeable		oppazite	**opposite**
notisable	**noticeable**	oppertunity	**opportunity**
now		oppesite	**opposite**
now	**know**	oppexite	**opposite**
nu	**knew**	oppirtunity	**opportunity**
nu	**new**	oppisite	**opposite**
nue	**knew**	oppizite	**opposite**
nue	**new**	**opportunity**	
nuesance	**nuisance**	**opposite**	
nuisance		oppozite	**opposite**
nuisanse	**nuisance**	oppurtunity	**opportunity**
nun	**none**	opurtunity	**opportunity**
o'clock		opusite	**opposite**
o'clok	**o'clock**	opuzite	**opposite**
ocasion	**occasion**	oreginal	**original**
ocassion	**occasion**	orejinal	**original**
occaision	**occasion**	**original**	
occasion		otside	**outside**
occassion	**occasion**	**our**	
occur		**outside**	
ocurr	**occur**	owr	**hour**
of	**off**	owr	**our**
ofan	**often**	owtside	**outside**
ofen	**often**	paralel	**parallel**

179

p

parallel

parelel	**parallel**
parilel	**parallel**
parillel	**parallel**
parte	**party**

particular

partie	**party**
partikular	**particular**

party

parulel	**parallel**
parullel	**parallel**

peace

peece	**peace**
peece	**piece**

peepal	**people**
peepel	**people**
peeple	**people**
peepol	**people**
peepul	**people**
peopal	**people**
peopel	**people**
peopil	**people**

people

peopol	**people**
peopul	**people**
peple	**people**
pepol	**people**

performance

permanent

personal

personall	**personal**
personil	**personal**

persuade

perswade	**persuade**
perticular	**particular**
pertikular	**particular**
pese	**peace**
pese	**piece**

piece

pirformance	**performance**
pirmanent	**permanent**
pirsonal	**personal**
pirsuade	**persuade**
pirticular	**particular**
pirtikular	**particular**
plade	**played**
plase	**plays**
playd	**played**

played

plays

plaze	**plays**

pleasant

please

pleaze	**please**
pleese	**please**
pleeze	**please**
plesant	**pleasant**
poisan	**poison**
poisen	**poison**
poisin	**poison**

poison

poisun	**poison**
poizen	**poison**
porticular	**particular**
portikular	**particular**
posession	**possession**

possession

pozession	**possession**
practice	**practice**
pracktice	**practice**
pracktis	**practice**

practice

practis	**practice**
praktice	**practice**
praktis	**practice**

precede

preceed	**precede**
presede	**precede**

pretty

prononciation	**pronunciation**
pronounciation	**pronunciation**
pronunciation	
pumkin	**pumpkin**
pumpkin	
purformance	**performance**
purmanent	**permanent**
pursonal	**personal**
pursuade	**persuade**
purticular	**particular**
purtikular	**particular**
quantaty	**quantity**
quantety	**quantity**
quantity	
quantoty	**quantity**
quantuty	**quantity**
quarel	**quarrel**
quaril	**quarrel**
quarol	**quarrel**
quarral	**quarrel**
quarrel	
quarril	**quarrel**
quarrol	**quarrel**
quarrul	**quarrel**
quartar	**quarter**
quarter	
quartir	**quarter**
quartor	**quarter**
quartur	**quarter**
quarul	**quarrel**
quit	
quite	
quontity	**quantity**
quorrel	**quarrel**
quortar	**quarter**
quorter	**quarter**
quortir	**quarter**
quortor	**quarter**
quortur	**quarter**
raise	
rase	**raise**
rayze	**raise**
raze	**raise**
read	
realeyes	**realize**
realise	**realize**

princepal	**principal**
princeple	**principle**
principal	
principle	
prinsepal	**principal**
prinseple	**principle**
prinsipal	**principal**
prinsiple	**principle**
prinsopal	**principal**
prinsople	**principle**
prinsupal	**principal**
prinsuple	**principle**
pritty	**pretty**
prity	**pretty**
privalege	**privilege**
privelege	**privilege**
privilege	
privulege	**privilege**
probably	
probebly	**probably**
probibly	**probably**
procede	**proceed**
procedure	
proceed	
proceedure	**procedure**
profesor	**professor**
professir	**professor**
professor	
professur	**professor**

r

realize

receave	**receive**
receeve	**receive**
receive	
receve	**receive**
recieve	**receive**
reckagnize	**recognize**
reckegnize	**recognize**
reckignize	**recognize**
reckognize	**recognize**
reckommend	**recommend**
reckugnize	**recognize**
recognize	
recomend	**recommend**
recommend	
rede	**read**

rediculous	**ridiculous**
reed	**read**
rehearse	
reherse	**rehearse**
rehirse	**rehearse**
rehurse	**rehearse**
reilize	**realize**
rekagnize	**recognize**
rekegnize	**recognize**
rekignize	**recognize**
rekognize	**recognize**
rekommend	**recommend**
rekugnize	**recognize**
releaf	**relief**
releef	**relief**

releif	**relief**
relief	
relife	**relief**
religious	
religous	**religious**
relijous	**religious**
remember	
remembir	**remember**
remembor	**remember**
remembur	**remember**
reseave	**receive**
reseive	**receive**
reseve	**receive**
resieve	**receive**
restarant	**restaurant**
restaurant	
resterant	**restaurant**
restirant	**restaurant**
resturant	**restaurant**
rhythm	
ridickulous	**ridiculous**
ridiculous	
ridikulous	**ridiculous**
right	
rite	**right**
rite	**write**
riteing	**writing**
rithem	**rhythm**
rithim	**rhythm**
rithm	**rhythm**
rithom	**rhythm**
rithum	**rhythm**
rote	**wrote**
rough	
rout	**route**
route	
rowt	**route**
ruf	**rough**
rytham	**rhythm**
rythem	**rhythm**
rythim	**rhythm**
rythm	**rhythm**
rythom	**rhythm**
rythum	**rhythm**
safety	
safty	**safety**

said		siround	**surround**
Saterday	**Saturday**	sirprize	**surprise**
Satirday	**Saturday**	sirround	**surround**
Satorday	**Saturday**	sirtun	**certain**
Saturday		sisors	**scissors**
says		sissors	**scissors**
scedjule	**schedule**	sizors	**scissors**
scedule	**schedule**	sizurs	**scissors**
scejule	**schedule**	sizzors	**scissors**
schedule		skeeing	**skiing**
school		**skiing**	
scissors		sking	**skiing**
scool	**school**		
sed	**said**		
sees			
seez	**sees**		
seez	**seize**		
seeze	**sees**		
seeze	**seize**		
seize			
semetery	**cemetery**		
sevaral	**several**		
sevearly	**severely**		
seveerly	**severely**		
several			
severely			
seviral	**several**	skool	**school**
sevoral	**several**	**some**	
sevral	**several**	sommer	**summer**
sevural	**several**	**soon**	
sez	**says**	**souvenir**	
shews	**shoes**	stor	**store**
shoes		**store**	
shoor	**sure**	**straight**	
shues	**shoes**	strate	**straight**
shugar	**sugar**	**strength**	
shugur	**sugar**	strenth	**strength**
shur	**sure**	studeing	**studying**
simalar	**similar**	**studying**	
simelar	**similar**	succead	**succeed**
similar		succede	**succeed**
similiar	**similar**	**succeed**	
simolar	**similar**	suckceed	**succeed**
simular	**similar**	**sugar**	
since		**sum**	
sinse	**since**		

S

sum	**some**
sumer	**summer**
summer	
summir	**summer**
summur	**summer**
Sunday	
Sundy	**Sunday**
sune	**soon**
supose	**suppose**
suppose	
suppoze	**suppose**
sure	
suround	**surround**
surownd	**surround**
surprise	
surprize	**surprise**
surround	
surrownd	**surround**
suvenir	**souvenir**
swiming	**swimming**
swimming	
teacher	
teachur	**teacher**
techer	**teacher**
teecher	**teacher**
temparature	**temperature**
temperature	
tempirature	**temperature**
temprature	**temperature**
tempurature	**temperature**
terable	**terrible**
tereble	**terrible**
terible	**terrible**
teroble	**terrible**
terrable	**terrible**
terreble	**terrible**
terrible	
terruble	**terrible**
tha	**they**
thair	**their**
thair	**there**
thair	**they're**
thare	**their**
thare	**there**
thare	**they're**
tharefore	**therefore**

thawt	**thought**
their	
theirfore	**therefore**
there	
therefor	**therefore**
therefore	
therefour	**therefore**
Thersday	**Thursday**
thay	**they**
they	
they're	
thiro	**thorough**
Thirsday	**Thursday**
tho	**though**
thorough	
thot	**thought**
though	
thought	
through	
thru	**threw**

thru	**through**
thuro	**thorough**
Thursday	
Thurzday	**Thursday**
tird	**tired**
tired	
to	

together		**usually**	
tois	toys	usualy	usually
tomorrow		uzed	used
tongue		vacashon	vacation
tonight		**vacation**	
too		**vegetable**	
Toosday	Tuesday	vegitable	vegetable
toys		vegtable	vegetable
toyz	toys	vejatable	vegetable
train		vejetable	vegetable
trane	train	vejitable	vegetable
traveling		vejotable	vegetable
travelling	traveling	vejtable	vegetable
traviling	traveling	vejutable	vegetable
troubal	trouble		
troubel	trouble		
troubil	trouble		
trouble			
troubol	trouble		
troubul	trouble		
trubal	trouble		
trubel	trouble		
trubil	trouble		
truble	trouble		
trubol	trouble		
trubul	trouble		
truely	truly		
truly		verry	very
tu	to	**very**	
tu	too	volewm	volume
tu	two	**volume**	
Tuesday		volyume	volume
Tuezday	Tuesday	wa	way
tugether	together	wa	weigh
tumorrow	tomorrow	wants	once
tung	tongue	**ware**	
tunight	tonight	ware	wear
two		ware	where
uneak	unique	**way**	
uneque	unique	**wear**	
unique		weathar	weather
until		**weather**	
untill	until	weathir	weather
urly	early	weathor	weather
usally	usually	weathur	weather
used		**Wednesday**	

w

weerd	**weird**
weigh	
weird	
Wendsday	**Wednesday**
were	
wethar	**weather**
wether	**weather**
wether	**whether**
wethir	**weather**
wethor	**weather**
wethur	**weather**

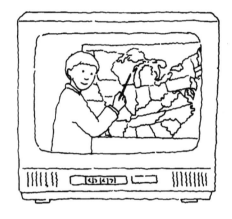

whair	**where**
when	
where	
whether	
whethir	**whether**
whethor	**whether**
whethur	**whether**
which	
whin	**when**
whitch	**which**
white	
who's	

whoal	**hole**
whoal	**whole**
whole	
whoos	**who's**
whoos	**whose**
whooz	**who's**
whooz	**whose**
whose	
wich	**which**
wierd	**weird**
wimen	**women**
wimin	**women**
wimon	**women**
wimun	**women**
Winsday	**Wednesday**
wir	**were**
witch	**which**
wite	**white**
women	
wonse	**once**
wood	**would**
would	
write	
writeing	**writing**
writing	
wrote	
wur	**were**
yeild	**yield**
yield	
yore	**your**
you	
you're	
your	
your	**you're**
yu	**you**
yue	**you**

VIP Letters
(Capitalization)

AVery Important Person stands out in a crowd. A capital letter might be thought of as a VIP Letter. It helps an important word stand out among other words. The first word of a sentence always begins with a VIP Letter.

> **T**he fans swarmed the rock star.
>
> **W**hat was the star's name?

If you are not sure whether to use a capital letter or a small letter, try asking yourself each of the following questions:

- Is the word *I?* If so, write the word as a capital letter, regardless of where it appears in the sentence. Here are some examples:

  > **I** couldn't find my roller blades.
  >
  > My roller blades turned up when **I** cleaned my room.
  >
  > None of my friends can roller blade as well as **I**.

- Does the word name a special person, place, group, or thing? If so, begin the word with a capital letter. Here are some examples:

person	**month**	**day of the week**
Dad	**J**uly	**S**aturday
Grandma	**S**eptember	**T**uesday
Sophie		

pet	**special place**	**company**
Fido	**A**dopt-a-**P**et **S**helter	**M**icrosoft
Hector	**N**atural **S**cience	**S**ears
Snakey	**M**useum	**P**epsi **C**ola
	Yorktown **M**all	

product name

Guess
Kleenex
Macintosh

organization

United Way
Girl Scouts of America

state, city, country, continent

Asia
Charleston
Kentucky
Quebec

race, language, religion

African American
Judaism
Spanish

document

Declaration of
   Independence
Ten Commandments

- Is the word an initial or acronym that stands for one or more longer words? If so, use a capital letter. Here are some examples:

  J. T. Smith
  Phyllis M. James
  UNESCO
  USA

- Is the word a specific person's title? If so, begin the word or abbreviated word with a capital letter. Here are some examples:

  Calvin Walker, Attorney
  Ms. Steig
  Professor Avery

- Is the word the first word or an important word in the title of a book, a magazine, a painting, a movie, a song, or a story? If so, begin the word with a capital letter. Here are some examples:

  Mona Lisa
  Star Trek
  The Black Cat

Mona Lisa

- Does the word begin the exact words spoken or written by someone? If so, begin the word with a capital letter. Here are some examples:

  "Help me find my skates," my brother pleaded.
  The reporter wrote, "The crowd swelled into the gymnasium."

Does That Make Sense?

(Commonly Confused Words)

Would you write the word *picture* or *pitcher* to tell about your position on a softball team? When you write *theirs,* do you need to put an apostrophe before the *s?* If you make a mistake, are you acting *human* or *humane?*

Sometimes (like Mrs. Malaprop in Richard Sheridan's 1775 comedy *The Rivals*) we confuse words that are similar in sound. Other times, we may use two words when one word will do the job. The following examples will help you choose the right word to make all your words count.

accept or except

I *accept* the award. (take what is offered)

I'd like all of these *except* the blue one. (excluding)

access or excess

The ramp provides *access* for everyone. (permission to approach or enter)

We have an *excess* of cake and ice cream. (extra)

adapt or adopt

My dog had to *adapt* to a tiny yard. (adjust)

We'll *adopt* a kitten from the shelter. (take as one's own)

affect or effect

The radio does not *affect* my studying. (influence)

The computer had an *effect* on my grades. (the result)

a

all ready or already

> We're *all ready* to go. (prepared)
>
> I *already* told my Dad. (by this time)

all right (*alright* is not an accepted spelling)

> I think his idea is *all right.* (okay)

all together or altogether.

> We were *all together* at the movie. (everyone at one time)
>
> I was *altogether* wrong about what happened. (completely)

alley or ally

> There's an *alley* behind our house. (a roadway)
>
> My best friend is a good *ally.* (one who agrees with)

already (see *all ready*)

altogether (see *all together* or *altogether*)

Is it "Andy and I" or "Andy and me?" If I leave "Andy" out, it's easy to see!

and I or and me

> Don't: *Dad and me* played hockey.
>
> > (Leave out *Dad and: Me played hockey* doesn't make sense.)
>
> **Do:** **Dad and I** **played hockey.**
>
> > (Leave out *Dad and: I played hockey* makes sense.)

> Don't: Shirley played ball with *Tal and I.*
>
> > (Leave out *Tal and: Shirley played ball with I* doesn't make sense.)
>
> **Do:** **Shirley played ball with** **Tal and me.**
>
> > (Leave out *Tal and: Shirley played ball with me* makes sense.)

> Don't: Shirley tackled *Tal and I.*
>
> > (Leave out *Tal and: Shirley tackled I* doesn't make sense.)
>
> **Do:** **Shirley tackled** **Tal and me.**
>
> > (Leave out *Tal and: Shirley tackled me* makes sense.)

anecdote or **antidote**

 His *anecdote* helped me understand. (a short story)

 The *antidote* saved my life. (something that acts against a poison)

any way or **anyway**

 I can't find *any way* to make this work. (in any manner)

 I'll do it *anyway*. (however or regardless)

at or **with**

 Use *at* for things or situations and *with* for people.

 Do: **I am angry *at* my homework.**

 Do: **I am angry *with* my sister.**

aural or **oral**

 I like it when there's *aural* information. (listening)

 I have to give an *oral* report. (spoken)

bazaar or **bizarre**

 Dad took us to the *bazaar*. (a market place)

 I saw a *bizarre* movie. (strange or odd)

biannual or **biennial**

 We publish a *biannual* newspaper. (two times each year)

 They have a *biennial* celebration. (once every other year)

bibliography or **biography**

 My report has a *bibliography*. (a list of written resources)

 I just read a good *biography*. (the story of a person's life)

biennial (see *biannual* or *biennial*)

big or **bigger** or **biggest**

 Jonas is *big*.

 Jonas is *bigger* than Derrick.
  (compares two persons or things)

 Jonas is the *biggest* of all the boys.
  (compares three or more)

b

biography (see *bibliography* or *biography*)

bizarre (see *bazaar* or *bizarre*)

breath or breathe

I'll just take a deep *breath.* (inhaling and exhaling one time)

I can't *breathe.* (inhale and exhale air)

calendar or colander

The *calendar* shows five Mondays this month. (a chart of months and days)

Put the spaghetti in the *colander.* (a container with holes for draining)

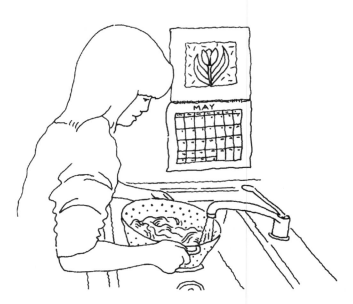

can or may

I *can* do my homework. (having the ability)

May I go the movie tonight? (suggests permission)

can't help or can't help but

Can't help but is not accepted usage.

Don't: I *can't help but* think you did it.

Do: I *can't help* **thinking you did it.**

cannot or can not

Don't: I *can not* go tonight.

Do: I *cannot* **go tonight.**

cease or seize

I wish you'd *cease* whistling! (stop)

Our team will *seize* this chance to win. (grab)

click or clique

I heard a *click,* and then the lights went out. (a quick sound)

That *clique* does not interest me. (a select group)

d

colander (see *calendar* or *colander*)

coma or comma

He was in a *coma* for two days. (a state of unconsciousness)

I forgot to put a *comma* after the date. (a punctuation mark)

command or commend

I *command* you to laugh at my jokes! (give an order)

I like to hear my parents *commend* my friends. (praise)

commend (see *command* or *commend*)

confidant or confident

My best friend is my *confidant*. (a trusted listener)

I'm *confident* she won't tell my secret. (sure)

conscience or conscious

My *conscience* tells me not to do it. (knowing right and wrong)

I am *conscious* of what I must do. (aware)

continually or continuously

We have asked for help *continually*. (happening over and over)

They ran *continuously* for five miles. (ongoing without interruptions)

cooperation or corporation

Your *cooperation* will help us all. (working together)

My mom works for an energy *corporation*. (a business group)

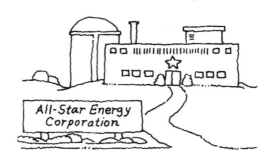

could of or could have

Could of is not accepted usage. Use *could have*.

Don't: We *could of* picked peaches today.

Do: We *could have* picked peaches today.

deceased or diseased

My great-grandpa is *deceased*. (dead)

The cattle are *diseased*. (ill)

d

decent or descent or dissent

> This is a *decent* suggestion. (proper)
> I'll help you on the *descent*. (way down)
> There was no *dissent*. (disagreement)

detract or distract

> This color will *detract* from the others. (take away from)
> Please don't *distract* me! (take attention away)

device or devise

> A can opener is a useful *device*. (something to do a job)
> Let's *devise* a way to make it happen! (make a plan)

different from or different than

> *Different than* is not accepted usage. Use *different from*.
> My hairstyle is *different from* hers.

diseased (see *deceased* or *diseased*)

disinterested or uninterested

> I am rather *disinterested* in politics. (having no strong feelings either way)
> I am *uninterested* in swimming. (having no interest)

dissent (see *decent* or *descent* or *dissent*)

distract (see *detract* or *distract*)

divide or divide up

> *Up* is unnecessary.
> Don't: Let's *divide* up the baseball cards.
> **Do: Let's *divide* the baseball cards.**
>
> Don't: We *drank up* all the juice.
> **Do: We *drank* all the juice.**

e

don't ever or **don't never** (double negative)

>Use one negative to express a negative idea.
>
>Don't: I *don't never* want to do it again. (*not never* is a double negative)
>
>**Do:**   **I *don't ever* want to do it again.** (*not* is one negative)

don't or **doesn't**

>Tran and Jerry *don't* want to play with us.
>   (The subject *Tran and Jerry* is plural, so the verb *don't* must be plural.)
>He *doesn't* want to play with us.
>   (The subject *He* is singular, so the verb *doesn't* must be singular.)

effect (see *affect* or *effect*)

either . . . or and **neither . . . nor**

>*Either* goes with *or; neither* goes with *nor.* Both sets of words are used with only
>   two persons or ideas.
>
>Don't: *Either* Opra, Sammi, *or* Thea will help you. (one person too many)
>
>**Do:**   **Opra, Sammi, *or* Thea will help you.** (three persons—use *or*)
>
>**Do:**   ***Either* Opra *or* Sammi will help you.** (two persons)
>
>**Do:**   ***Neither* Opra *nor* Sammi will help you.** (two persons)

elicit or **illicit**

>I need to *elicit* ideas from all of you. (pull from)
>What they want to do is *illicit.* (not legal)

emerge or **immerge** or **immerse**

>Some good ideas will *emerge* when we brainstorm. (rise up)
>Let's *immerge* ourselves and get this job done. (plunge into)
>Here, I will *immerse* you in a new idea. (surround)

emigrate or **immigrate**

>The people will *emigrate* as soon as they can.
>   (leave one country for another)
>Grandma hopes to *immigrate* soon. (enter a
>   country with plans to live there)

envelop or **envelope**

>This music will *envelop* you. (surround)
>Put the letter in the *envelope.* (mailing wrapper)

e

except (see *accept* or *except*)

excess (see *access* or *excess*)

expand or **expend**

>We need to *expand* our circle. (make larger)
>I'll *expend* whatever it takes. (spend)

expect or **suspect**

>I *expect* they will arrive in an hour or so. (look forward to)
>Surely you don't *suspect* me! (think of as guilty)

expend (see *expand* or *expend*)

farther or **further**

>My house is *farther* away. (a distance that can be measured)
>I will think on it *further.* (a distance that cannot be measured)

finale or **finally** or **finely**

>It's almost time for the grand *finale.* (end)
>*Finally* you'll get to see what I mean! (at last)
>My dad keeps our car *finely* tuned. (in a good way)

formally or **formerly**

>We'll invite you *formally* next month. (in a formal way)
>My mom worked there *formerly.* (at an earlier time)

former or **latter**

>Of math and science, I prefer the *former.* (the first one of two)
>Of math and science, he prefers the *latter.* (the last one of two)

formerly (see *formally* or *formerly*)

further (see *farther* or *further*)

good or **well**

>You are a *good* friend. (an adjective that describes)
>You hit the ball *well.* (an adverb that tells how)

I

human or **humane**

It's *human* to be fearful now and then. (like a person)

You acted *humane* about the whole thing. (kind)

If . . . was or **if . . . were**

If always requires the use of *were*. *Was* is not accepted usage.

If I *were* going, I'd take a raincoat.

He would probably agree *if* he *were* here.

illicit (see *elicit* or *illicit*)

imitate or **intimate**

Can you *imitate* a hyena? (act like)

I guess I did *intimate* I would go. (hint or suggest)

immerge (see *emerge* or *immerge* or *immerse*)

immerse (see *emerge* or *immerge* or *immerse*)

immigrate (see *emigrate* or *immigrate*)

intimate (see *imitate* or *intimate*)

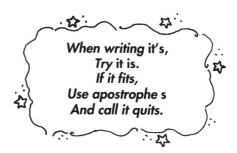

When writing it's,
Try it is.
If it fits,
Use apostrophe s
And call it quits.

it's or **its**

It's good that you're here. (contraction for *it is)*

The kitten licked *its* paws. (shows that something is owned)

later or **latter**

Something will probably happen *later*. (more late)

Jamie likes the *latter* of the two movies. (last of two things)

latter (see *former* or *latter*)

latter (see *later* or *latter*)

lay or **lie**

I'll *lay* my book on the table. (to place something)

I'll *lie* down for a nap. (to rest)

I

lend or loan

I'll *lend* you a dollar. (to give for temporary use)

I need a $5 *loan*. (something given for temporary use)

lie (see *lay* or *lie*)

loose or lose

The geese are *loose* in the yard. (free or not contained)

I'm afraid I'll *lose* my place in line. (not have)

massage or message

Dad says to *massage* a sore muscle. (rub soothingly)

They have a funny *message* on their answering machine. (communication)

may (see *can* or *may*)

may or might

I may go to Chicago. (future possibility)

When he gets here, we might go to Chicago. (future possibility that is dependent on something else)

message (see *massage* or *message*)

might (see *may* or *might*)

moral or morale

A fable has a *moral*. (lesson to be learned)

Our team lost its *morale*. (feeling of confidence)

my mother or my mother she

A sentence can have only one subject. Either use *my mother* or *she*.

Don't: *My mother she* told me to go to bed.

Do: *My mother* **told me to go to bed.**

Do: *She* **told me to go to bed.**

of or off

The purpose *of* the meeting is to elect officers. (shows possession)

My mom gets *off* work at six. (opposite of on)

oral (see *aural* or *oral*)

ours or **our's**

Possessive pronouns such as *ours, his, hers, its, yours, theirs,* and *whose* do not need an apostrophe.

Don't: This room is *our's.*

Do: This room is *ours.*

Don't: I thought this book was *your's.*

Do: I thought this book was *yours.*

out or **out of**

Try to avoid using the double preposition.

Don't: I looked *out of* the window.

Do: I looked *out* the window.

Don't: The puppy jumped *off of* the porch.

Do: The puppy jumped *off* the porch.

Don't: Gary reached *up under* the shelf.

Do: Gary reached *under* the shelf.

pastor or **pasture**

The *pastor* spoke to all of us. (minister)

The horses are in the *pasture.* (a grassy field)

persecute or **prosecute**

Please don't *persecute* me! (harass or annoy)

They must *prosecute* the criminal. (act toward punishment for a crime)

personal or **personnel**

I'd like to have a *personal* trainer. (private)

The store's *personnel* ran outside to help. (employees)

picture or **pitcher**

I'll make a *picture* for you. (a drawing or photograph)

Here's a *pitcher* of juice. (a container for liquid)

precede or **proceed**

The parade will *precede* the bazaar. (go in front of)

Let's *proceed* to the front of the line. (move forward)

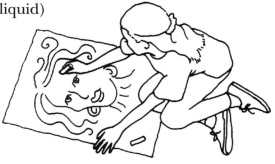

p

preposition or **proposition**

This sentence needs a different *preposition*. (word that is a part of speech)

I have an interesting *proposition* for you! (suggestion)

principal or **principle**

Our *principal* told us the good news. (the main one)

We have a *principle* we must follow. (a rule or law)

proceed (see *precede* or *proceed*)

proposition (see *preposition* or *proposition*)

prosecute (see *persecute* or *prosecute*)

proved or **proven**

We had *proved* we were right. (supported as a fact)

It's a *proven* solution. (factual)

quiet or **quit** or **quite**

It's awfully *quiet* in here. (not loud)

I don't want to *quit* soccer. (stop)

This is *quite* nice. (very)

raise or **rear**

We will *raise* rabbits and vegetables. (cause things to grow)

Parents *rear* children. (help people to grow)

raise or **rise**

We can *raise* the flag. (cause something to move upward)

The bread will not *rise*. (move upward)

rear (see *raise* or *rear*)

reason is that or reason is because

Don't: The *reason* I'm going *is because* I need some new clothes.

Do: **The *reason* I'm going *is that* I need some new clothes.**

Do: **I am going *because* I need some new clothes.**

Don't: The *reason* I'm angry *is because* you lied to me.

Do: **The *reason* I'm angry *is that* you lied to me.**

Do: **I'm angry *because* you lied to me.**

rise (see *raise* or *rise*)

seize (see *cease* or *seize*)

set or sit (see also Verb Tenses)

I *set* the cups on the table. (place something)

I can *sit* at the table. (bend at the knee)

suspect (see *expect* or *suspect*)

that or who

Use *who* to refer to people.

The boy *who* owns these computer games is my friend.

Use *that* to refer to things or animals.

I have a new coat *that* has a warm hood.

their or there or they're

Here is *their* house. (shows ownership)

There aren't any chips left. (used to introduce a sentence)

They're nowhere to be seen. (contraction for *they are*)

themselves (*theirselves* is not accepted usage)

Cats lick their fur to clean *themselves*.

there (see *their* or *there* or *they're*)

t

there is or there are

If the subject of the sentence is singular, use *is*.

There is no reason to be sad. (both *is* and *reason* are singular)

There is someone I'd like to see. (both *is* and *someone* are singular)

If the subject is plural, use *are*.

There are empty boxes in here. (both *are* and *boxes* are plural)

There are many that would work. (both *are* and *many* are plural)

they're (see *their* or *there* or *they're*)

thorough or through

I gave my bike a *thorough* cleaning. (complete)

We go *through* the city to get to the zoo. (by way of)

try to or try and

And is a conjunction; it connects two equal words or phrases.

Don't: I will *try and* be there on time.

Do: I will *try to* be there on time.

turned on the TV or turned the TV on

Try to keep the verb and preposition together.

Don't: I *turned* the TV *on*.

Do: I *turned on* the TV.

two or to or too

I bought *two* new shirts. (a number)

We need *to* go now. (a preposition showing motion toward)

I want to do that *too*. (also)

uninterested (see *disinterested* or *uninterested*)

way or **ways**

> Maine is a long *way* from Utah. (one path)
>
> There are many *ways* to get to the ocean. (two or more paths)

well (see *good* or *well*)

what for or **why**

> *What for* is not accepted usage. Use *why*.
>
> Don't: *What* did you do that *for*?
>
> **Do: *Why* did you do that?**

where or **where at**

> *At* is not needed at the end of a sentence that begins with *where*.
>
> Don't: *Where* is your house *at*?
>
> **Do: *Where* is your house?**
>
> Don't: I don't know *where* it is *at*.
>
> **Do: I don't know *where* it is.**

which or **in which**

> Use *which* to ask a question.
>
> *Which* CD has my favorite song?
>
> Use *in which* to mean one thing is inside another.
>
> Is this the case *in which* I put that CD?

who's or **whose**

> *Who's* going to the park with us? (contraction for *who is*)
>
> *Whose* notebook was lost? (shows ownership)

why or **what for** (see *what for* or *why*)

with or **at** (see *at* or *with*)

your or **you're**

> *Your* coat is handsome. (shows ownership)
>
> *You're* looking handsome! (contraction for *you are*)

More Tips to Help Make Your Words Count

active voice or passive voice

Active voice is preferred when possible. In active voice, the subject of the sentence does the action:

Tom Sawyer painted the fence.

The subject is acted upon in passive voice:

The fence was painted by Tom Sawyer.

adjectives in series

Arrange adjectives in order from the shortest word to the longest:

Fred found a *tiny, hungry, abandoned* bird.

verbs in series

Arrange verbs in the order the actions would naturally happen:

I've finished *washing, drying,* and *putting* away the dishes.

When a word or phrase is in the wrong place, the meaning of a sentence can be confusing. The following examples can help you avoid confusing your readers.

misplaced word

Don't: Keegan's team almost won every game. (The meaning is not clear. Did the team lose every game? Or did the team win most of the games?)

Do: **Keegan's team won almost every game.** (The meaning is clear—the team won many, but not all, of the games.)

misplaced phrase

Don't: Before her game, Connie's mom served dinner. (Was it Connie's game or her mom's game?)

Do: **Before Connie's game, her mom served dinner.**

dangling modifier

Don't: While eating, the news came on. (Was the news eating?)

Do: **While I was eating, the news came on.**

Do: **While eating, I heard the news.**

Don't: When doing homework, the dog chewed my book. (Was the dog doing homework?)

Do: **When I was doing homework, the dog chewed my book.**

The Cast of Characters

(Parts of Speech)

Just as actors play roles in a play, every word plays a particular role in a sentence. A word can play one of the eight roles, or *parts of speech.*

Noun
Pronoun
Adjective
Verb
Adverb
Conjunction
Preposition
Interjection

It is helpful to know something about each of these parts of speech. For example, every sentence has a subject which includes a noun or pronoun. Every sentence also has a verb, a word or words that show action or being.

Like actors who play different roles in different plays, some words can play different roles in different sentences. A word's role, or part of speech, depends on how the word is being used in the sentence.

Sometimes I like to take a long *walk.* (*walk* used as a noun)
Sometimes I *walk* across town. (*walk* used as a verb)

A dictionary not only gives a word's meaning; it also tells the word's part of speech.

A **noun** names a person, place, or thing.

> **Pete** jogged. (person)
>
> **Pete** jogged to the **park.** (person; place)
>
> **Pete** jogged to the **park** to play **tennis.** (person; place; thing)

There are too many nouns to ever list them all. Can you tell which of these nouns names *a person?* Which names *a place?* Which names *a thing?* Which nouns could name *a place* or *a thing?*

> skate, movie, Africa, pencil, picture, Dr. Philips, bicycle, happiness, people, towel, guide, pain, video, seat, rainfall, space, Hawaiian Islands

A **pronoun** takes the place of a noun.

> Shawna played basketball.
>
> **She** played basketball. (takes the place of *Shawna*)

Each of these pronouns can be used in place of a noun:

all	his	ours	whatever
any	I	ourselves	which
anybody	it	several	whichever
anything	its	she	who
both	itself	some	whoever
each	many	somebody	whom
either	me	someone	whomever
everybody	mine	something	whose
everything	my	that	you (singular)
few	neither	their	you (plural)
he	nobody	theirs	your
her	none	themselves	yours
hers	nothing	they	yourself
herself	one	us	yourselves
him	oneself	we	
himself	our	what	

An **adjective** describes a noun or pronoun to tell *which one, how many,* or *what kind.*

> I bought **these** flags. (which ones)
>
> I bought **these two** flags. (which ones; how many)
>
> I bought **these two American** flags. (which ones; how many; what kind)

It would take thousands of pages to list every adjective in the English language! Which of these adjectives tells *how many?* Which adjectives tell *what kind?* Which words tell *which one?*

> beautiful, American, middle, silly, broken, this, twenty-five, those, first, huge, yellow, lovely, Jamaican, short, last, noisy, awesome, handmade

A **verb** shows action.

> The light **flickered.**

A **verb** can also show a state of being.

> The light **had been** out for two days.

Which of these verbs shows *action?* Which show a *state of being?*

> dance, were, feel, has, watch, been, drive, move, blink, will be, touch, become, imagine, could, race, clean, is, admire, seem, are, write, had, read, run, can

An **adverb** describes a verb to tell *how, when,* or *where.*

> Monty drove **slowly.** (*how* he drove)
>
> Monty drove **late** into the night. (*when* he drove)
>
> Monty drove **past** my house. (*where* he drove)

Which of these adverbs could be used to tell *how* something happened? Which words could tell *when* something happened? Which adverbs might tell *where* something happened?

> swiftly, there, always, perfectly, secretly, beside, never, hopefully, very, sometime, still, nicely, here, anytime, wisely, around, off, out, maybe

A **conjunction** is like a bridge—it connects words or groups of words.

His shirt **and** pants look new. (connects two words)

He is sad **because** his pet is missing. (connects two sentences)

I would like to go; **however,** I must do homework. (connects two sentences)

More conjunctions:

but, since, for, while, as, either . . . or, neither . . . nor

A **preposition** is a word that shows how one word relates to another word.

He stayed **on** base. (shows relationship between *stayed* and *base*)

Some bears hibernate **during** the wintertime. (shows relationship between *hibernate* and *wintertime*)

More prepositions:

above, up, under, over, around, at, into, of, until, from, to, after

An **interjection** is a word that shows strong feeling.
An **interjection** usually stands alone and is followed by an exclamation mark.

Oh! That was a scary movie.

That tastes awful. Yuck!

More words that may be used as interjections:

No! Help! Awesome! Ouch! Fantastic! Stop! Quick! Super! Stay!

Teams at Work

(Collective Nouns and Subject-Verb Agreement)

We think of a team as a group that works together to accomplish a goal. The team may try to win a game, create a project, or perform some other task. When a team works together, its members act as one.

Like a team, a collective noun includes or names a group of persons, ideas, or objects. A collective noun usually requires the use of a singular verb. When in doubt about whether to use a singular or plural verb, you might omit the word *of* and any plural noun that follows or is suggested—then ask yourself, "Does the sentence make sense?"

> Don't: The *batch* of cookies *are* still hot. (*Batch* is a collective noun, but *are* is a plural verb. *The batch are still hot* does not make sense.)
>
> **Do:**   The **batch** of cookies **is** still hot. (*Batch* and *is* are both singular.)

Notice how each collective noun in the following sentences requires a singular verb.

> The **audience** (of people) **loves** to applaud.
>
> The **band** (of musicians) **likes** to play outside.
>
> This **batch** of biscuits **tastes** sour.
>
> Jerry's **bundle** of matches **is** wet.
>
> My **chest** of drawers **holds** all my clothes.
>
> The **class** of students **is** in the auditorium.
>
> A **colony** of ants **was** under the shelf.
>
> This year's **committee** of workers **has done** a fine job.

Here are more collective nouns that require singular verbs:

company of soldiers	**group** of authors	**pride** of lions
corps of drummers	**herd** of elephants	**roll** of stamps
crew of workers	**host** of ideas	**row** of seats
crowd of people	**league** of bowlers	**school** of fish
deck of cards	**line** of buyers	**set** of silverware
fleet of ships	**list** of rules	**squad** of officers
flock of sheep	**litter** of piglets	**stack** of books
flood of orders	**nest** of birds	**swarm** of bees
flotilla of ships	**pack** of gum	**team** of players
gaggle of goslings	**pile** of sticks	**troop** of hikers
galaxy of stars	**portfolio** of stories	

b

It's No Lie!
(Verb Forms)

*Things **lay** all around,
but people **lie** on the ground.*

I t's true that you *lay* things down, while you lie down. But, you might say, "*Lay* down your things before you *lie* on the ground." So when do you write *lie* and when do you write *lay*? And what about *laid* and *lain*?

It helps to know the present, past, and past participle forms of verbs. Then you'll know the right word to use.

Verbs in present tense, such as *play* or *look,* are called regular verbs. You merely add *d* or *ed* to form the past and past participle forms:

Present: Tony, *look* all around the room.

Past: Tony *looked* all around the room.

Past Participle: Tony *has looked* all around the room. (Notice how the past participle always has a "helping" verb, such as *had, has, is, was,* or *were.*)

Irregular verbs do not follow the pattern. The following sentences illustrate the present, past, and past participle forms of many irregular verbs you will use as you speak and write.

am   I *am* happier than ever.
            I *was* full of joy.
            I *had been* laughing.

are   Marcos and Jed *are* here today.
            They *were* not late.
            The boys *had been* here for hours.

begin   We can *begin* at seven o'clock.
            We *began* at seven o'clock.
            We *had begun* at seven o'clock.

211

b

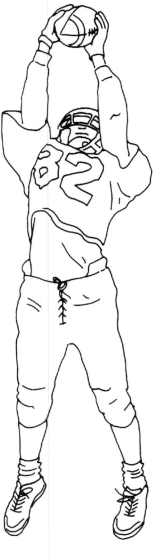

blow I like to feel the wind *blow* through my hair.
The wind *blew* for hours.
The wind *has blown* all day long.

bring Caitlin *brings* her sister with her.
She *brought* her brother last time.
No one *had brought* friends before this year.

build My uncle *builds* houses.
He *built* the house where I live now.
My uncle *has built* hundreds of houses.

burst What if that balloon *bursts!*
The twigs *burst* the other balloons.
All the balloons *had burst* before the parade began.

catch I hope you *catch* the ball.
We *caught* all the balls that came our way.
Kao *has caught* every ball thrown to him.

choose Let's *choose* teams.
We already *chose* teams.
No one had *chosen* teams before we arrived.

come Please *come* to my house.
I *came* to your house, but you weren't home.
I didn't think you *had come.*

cost These shoes *cost* more than I want to spend.
My old shoes *cost* nearly half this much.
With the tax, my shoes *had cost* more than my allowance.

cut Wayne, *cut* the pizza into four pieces.
He carefully *cut* the pizza.
Wayne *has cut* pizzas many times.

dig My dog *digs* holes in our yard.
She *dug* two new holes yesterday.
She *has dug* several holes every day.

dive
My grandma *dives* like a fish.
She *dove* (or *dived*) for her college team.
She *has dived* for years.

do
Look what I *do* for you!
I *did* this painting all by myself.
I *have done* it before, but it was never this easy.

draw
This illustrator *draws* fabulously.
She *drew* herself in one of the pictures.
She *has drawn* thousands of pictures.

drink
I *drink* eight glasses of water every day.
I *drank* more than eight glasses of water yesterday.
I *have drunk* eight glasses of water already.

drive
My mom *drives* us today.
Your dad *drove* us to the movie.
We *had driven* too far and became lost.

eat
I *eat* breakfast with my sister every morning.
Yesterday, we *ate* cereal and bagels.
We *have eaten* all the cereal.

fall
I *fall* if I'm not careful.
He *fell* the last time he did that trick.
He *has fallen* more than the others have.

feed
Please *feed* the dog and take him for a walk.
I just *fed* the dog and walked him.
I *have fed* the dog twice today.

feel
I *feel* all right now.
I *felt* as if I were going to faint.
I *have felt* like this for several minutes.

fight
They *fight* too much!
They *fought* about something silly.
They *have fought* about this before.

f

fly
I *fly* with my mom.
She *flew* with him to Greece last year.
She *has flown* all over the world.

forget
I *forget* what I was planning to do.
I *forgot* how to tie a square knot.
Have you *forgotten* what I said?

forgive
Please *forgive* my tardiness.
My teacher *forgave* my being late to class.
He already *had forgiven* others for being late.

freeze
Mom *freezes* the extra grapes.
I *froze* some strawberries, and they were a good snack.
I *have* never *frozen* grapes before.

get
Fred and Mazie *get* into the cupboards.
Mom was not happy when they *got* rice all over!
Now my hamsters *have gotten* into the pantry!

give
I hope you *give* good advice.
You *gave* me good suggestions the other day.
I'm grateful for all the help you *have given* me.

go
I *go* to the movies on weekends.
Dad *went* with me last weekend.
My mom *has gone* to see my favorite movie.

grow
I sure hope I *grow* over the summer.
I *grew* three inches last summer.
Over the past two years, I *have grown* about four inches.

has
Sydnie *has* a new brother.
Her mom *had* the baby last week.
Sydnie *has had* the flu for two days.

hear
I *hear* music coming from somewhere.
Roy says he *heard* the music this morning.
No one else *has heard* the music.

hide   Some people *hide* money in strange places.
I heard about one woman who *hid* money in the freezer!
My money *is hidden* in my room.

hold   Please *hold* this for me.
Shawna *held* my place in line.
Nedra *has held* my backpack as a favor to me.

hurt   The elbow *hurts*.
It *hurt* like this once before.
It *has hurt* for nearly a week.

is   Monty *is* my best friend.
He *was* new to our school last year.
He *has been* my best friend since his first day here.

keep   I *keep* a book until I finish it.
I *kept* one book for nearly two weeks.
I *have kept* some books for as long as three weeks.

lay   Please *lay* your clothes on my bed.
I think you *laid* your books on the sofa.
You *have laid* your papers in the water!

leave   *Leave* your backpacks here.
We *left* our bikes in the driveway.
Dad *has left* us a note to move our bikes.

let   Robin, *let* us help you!
She *let* us help her the other day.
She *has let* her friends help her.

lie   I *lie* down for a few minutes every day.
I *lay* in the nurse's office until my dad came.
I *had lain* on the cot all morning.

lose   I *lose* things sometimes.
I *lost* my wallet one time.
Lissie looked as though she *had lost* her best friend.

m

make You *make* something out of nothing!
One time she *made* a sculpture from toothpicks.
She *has made* many art treasures.

put We *put* our warm clothes away for the summer.
One year we *put* them away too early.
Most years we *have put* them away in April.

read *Read* this book to me.
You already *read* that book!
You *have read* that book many times.

ride We *ride* down to the lake.
We *rode* there yesterday.
We *have ridden* there many times this week.

ring When the bell *rings,* we'll change classes.
The bell just *rang!*
No, I don't think it *has rung* yet.

rise I watch the sun *rise.*
This morning it *rose* before six o'clock.
Most days I am up before the sun *has risen.*

run Nellie *runs* faster than anyone in our class.
She *ran* the mile in record time.
She *has run* in every event this year.

say Lamar *says* Tiffany is shy.
Someone *said* that the other day.
Tiffany *has said* she would rather listen to others.

saw

We *saw* the boards by ourselves.

We *sawed* many boards to build our clubhouse.

By now each of us *has sawed* (or *has sawn*) our share.

see

Rhonda *sees* well without her glasses.

Her friends *saw* the dog first.

They *have seen* that dog act mean.

sell

Students *sell* cookies at the school fair.

We *sold* dozens last year and earned money for our library.

We *have sold* other baked goods too.

sew

Grandpa *sews* anything!

He *sewed* an incredible monster costume when I was little.

He *has sewed* (or *has sewn*) most of my family's clothing.

set

We *set* some goals for our new club.

Last week we *set* a time and place to meet each week.

By next week, we hope to *have set* membership rules.

shake

Watch Dingo *shake* his head!

He *shook* his head as if to say he doesn't want to go outside!

Dingo *has shaken* his head like that since he was a puppy.

shine

Shine that flashlight over here!

You *shined* (or *shone*) the light in the wrong place!

You *have shined* (or *have shone*) that light everywhere but here!

sing

My cousin *sings* at weddings.

She *sang* at her brother's wedding.

She *has sung* for hundreds of weddings.

sink

Did you see the cotton ball *sink* in water?

The pebbles *sank* immediately.

What things *have sunk* to the bottom?

sit
Rachel, *sit* in the back of the room.
She says she *sat* there last week.
She says she has done better work when she *has sat* in the back.

sleep
Grandma *sleeps* till daybreak.
I *slept* until noon today!
During the summer, I *have slept* until two o'clock!

speak
Please *speak* to my parents about increasing my allowance.
They and I *spoke* about it this time last year.
We already *have spoken* about chores.

spend
Hillary *spends* all her allowance every week.
Two weeks ago she even *spent* her sister's allowance!
I *have spent* less since I opened a savings account.

spread
Spread this blanket for all of us.
Deidre *spread* another blanket on the ground.
Don't lie down until we *have spread* the blankets fully.

spring
Watch the clowns *spring* from the music box.
The door *sprang* open, and clowns bounced onto the table.
A different clown *has sprung* from the box each time.

stand
Sometimes I *stand* during the bus ride home.
My friends *stood* and stated their opinions.
My actions *have stood* for what I believe.

steal
I don't think someone ever *steals* one shoe.
Surely someone would know who *stole* it.
My friends and I doubt that my shoe *was stolen*.

sting
A frightened bee *stings* anyone within its reach.
It hurts where the bee *stung* me.
Bees *have stung* some of our neighbors.

strike
When I *strike* the ball, it barely moves.
Raime *struck* the ball like a pro.
Mandy *has struck* out twice so far this year.

sweep
Sweep your room!
I *swept* it this morning before I left for school.
Mom was surprised that I *had swept* the floor before school.

swim
I *swim* the length of the pool and back.
The lifeguard *swam* over to help someone.
Nearly every swimmer *has swum* here before.

swing
Swing this rope across the road.
We *swung* the rope, but it got tangled in a shrub.
We didn't succeed until we *had swung* the rope four times.

take
Take these props backstage.
Leesa *took* some of the props with her.
Who *has taken* the costumes from the closet?

teach
Please *teach* me how to set a volleyball.
The coach *taught* that skill when I was absent.
The same coach *has taught* baseball every
  season.

tell
Tell me what you would like to me to do.
No one *told* me these chores had to be done so
  soon.
If someone *had told* me, I would have done
  them sooner.

think
Ruthie, *think* about what your mom suggested.
As she *thought* about it, Ruthie admitted she
  had to agree.
At first she *had thought* her mom's words were
  useless.

throw
I need to watch how you *throw* the ball.
You *threw* a curve ball!
Never could I *have thrown* her out at third.

understand
Baby Carl *understands* anything!
He *understood* every word we were saying!
He *has understood* us since he was only a few months old.

w

wake   I *wake* up and get going!

My alarm *woke* (or *waked*) me in the middle of the night.

This is not the first time it *has waked* (or *has woken*) me at the wrong time.

wear   Delby *wears* jeans to every party.

We *wore* skirts last time.

It's true that we *have worn* jeans before.

wet   That little baby sure *wets* a lot of diapers!

She *wet* three diapers in one hour.

I think she *has wet* every diaper in the house!

win   If we *win* one more game, we'll be in the finals.

We *won* our first two games.

Everyone knows we *should have won* that last game.

write   I get new ideas every time I *write*.

Just now I *wrote* a few sentences about peace in the world.

I *may have written* the beginning of a poem!

What's More Than One?

(Plural Forms)

A singular noun names one person, place, or thing, while a plural noun names two or more people, places, or things.

For most plural nouns, you'll simply add *s*, as in *dogs, computers,* or *desks,* but some plural nouns can be tricky to spell. If you are not sure of a word's plural form, follow these four steps:

1. Look for the word in the alphabetically arranged list of *Irregular Plural Forms.*

2. If the word is *not* in the list, chances are the word's plural form is *regular.* That means it probably follows one of the six "rules" listed below.

3. Using the six rules, test the word.

4. Look up the word in a dictionary. It's always a good idea to check a word's plural spelling in a dictionary. Then you can be sure you have spelled it correctly.

Irregular Plural Forms

auto–autos	crisis–crises	focus–foci
axis–axes	datum–data	foot–feet
bacterium–bacteria	deer–deer	goose–geese
cactus–cacti or cactuses	die–dice	gross–gross
child–children	dozen–dozen	index–indices
corps–corps	fish–fish	louse–lice

Plural Forms

man–men   ox–oxen   solo–solos
medium–media   parenthesis–parentheses   stimulus–stimuli
mouse–mice   piano–pianos   tooth–teeth
oasis–oases   radius–radii   woman–women

Words That Are Singular *or* Plural

corps   dozen   series
deer   fish   sheep
                   perch

Rules for Words with Regular Plural Forms

Rule 1 Does the word end in *ch, s, ss, sh, x,* or *zz?* If so, add *es.*
   Examples:

       ch   beach–beaches
               inch–inches

       s   bus–buses
               gas–gases

       ss   glass–glasses
               mess–messes

       sh   crash–crashes
               dish–dishes

       x   box–boxes
               six–sixes

       z   buzz–buzzes
               quiz–quizzes

Rule 2 Does the word end in a consonant followed by *o?* If so, add *es.*
   Examples:

     echo–echoes
     potato–potatoes

Rule 3 Does the word end in a vowel followed by *o*? If so, add *s*.

> *Examples:*

>> radio–radios
>> video–videos

Rule 4 Does the word end in a consonant followed by *y*? If so, change the *y* to *i* and add *es*.

> *Examples:*

>> baby–babies
>> country–countries

Rule 5 Does the word end in *f* or *fe*? If so, be careful!

> For the plurals of some words, simply add *s*:
> *Examples:*

>> belief–beliefs
>> cliff–cliffs
>> roof–roofs
>> dwarf–dwarfs
>> gulf–gulfs

> For the plurals of other words, change the *f* to *v* and then add *es*:
> *Examples:*

>> calf–calves
>> elf–elves
>> knife–knives
>> leaf–leaves
>> loaf–loaves
>> wife–wives
>> yourself–yourselves

Remember: The safest way to be absolutely sure is to check the word's plural form in a dictionary. Then you'll know your word will count!

Word Accessories
(Prefixes and Suffixes)

You're getting dressed for school. You pull on the basics, a shirt and some pants or a skirt. Now what, if any, accessories will you add to the basic "look"? Will you choose to create a "unique you" with a belt, a tie or scarf, or some jewelry?

Like dressing yourself, you can also "dress up" your bedroom at home. You may choose accessories or special touches, such as posters, pictures, or a bulletin board, to change an ordinary bedroom into a room that is uniquely yours.

Like people and rooms, words too can be "dressed up." Special accessories called *prefixes* and *suffixes* change the meanings of basic words or root words. A *prefix* is a letter or group of letters that "dresses up" a word's beginning. A *suffix* is a group of letters added to the end of a word. Here are some common prefixes and their meanings, followed by a list of common suffixes and their meanings. At the end of the lists, you will find some spelling tips to help you use suffixes to dress up your words.

Prefixes

The prefix *pre* means *before* or *in front of,* so a prefix is "fixed" in front of a base, or root word. Here are some common prefixes and their meanings:

ac- and **ad-** mean *to* or *toward*

> To *ac*knowledge something is to know it is true or real.
>
> An *ad*equate amount of food is equal to what is expected.

ambi- and **amphi-** mean *both* or *on both sides*

> An *ambi*dextrous person can do things easily with both hands.
>
> An *amphi*theater has seats all around a center area.

ante- means *before* or *in front of*

> An *ante*chamber is an entrance or a room in front of another.

a

anti- means *against*

> An *anti*depressant is a medication that works against depression.

auto- means *same* or *self*

> A person writes his own life story in an *auto*biography.

bene- means *good*

> A *bene*fit is anything that is a good fit or is good for a person or thing.

bi- means *two*

> A *bi*monthly magazine is published every two months.

by- means *near* or *next to*

> A *by*stander stands near the scene but is not involved.

centi- means *hundred* or *hundredth*

> A *centi*meter is one hundredth of a meter.

circum- means *around*

> You *circum*scribe a correct answer by drawing a circle around it.

co- and **com-** and **con-** mean *with* or *together*

> To *co*operate is to work together.
> To *com*miserate is to feel sad for or sympathize with someone.
> You *con*tribute by giving something along with others.

contra- and **counter-** mean *against* or *the opposite of*

> You *contra*dict when you say the opposite.
> *Counter*act is to act in an opposite way.

de- means *away* or *down*

> To *de*hydrate is to take water away.
> You *de*press a button when you push it down.

deca- means *ten*

> A *deca*meter is ten meters.

dis- means *not* or *the opposite of*

> A *dis*organized person does not have things
> in order.

em- and **en-** mean *in* or *on*

> To *em*bed is to place something in a bed or area.
>
> To *en*danger is to place in danger.

ex- means *out of* or *from*

> When you *ex*hale, you push air out.

extra- means *beyond* or *besides*

> An *extra*terrestrial is a being from beyond the Earth.

fore- means *front* or *before*

> To *fore*warn is to give a warning before the event.

hyper- means *more than usual*

> A *hyper*active person is more active than usual.

hypo- means *under*

> A person with *hypo*tension has low blood pressure.

im- means *in* or *on* or *not*

> Something that is *im*proper is not acceptable.
>
> An *im*migrant is someone who moves into a country.

in- means *not* or *into*

> An *in*correct answer is not correct.
>
> An *in*laid tabletop has pieces laid into the surface.

ir- means *not*

> An *ir*responsible person cannot be trusted to do what is asked.

inter- means *together* or *between*

> An *inter*national airport welcomes flights to and from other nations.

intra- means *in* or *within*

> An *intra*venous feeding is when liquid nourishment is injected into the veins.

mal- means *bad* or *badly*

> Fortunately, my *mal*functioning radio is under warranty.

mid- means *the middle*

> A *mid*day meal is eaten in the middle of the day.

m

mis- means *bad* or *wrong*

> I *mis*read that sentence and got the wrong idea.

mono- means *one*

> It was scary to hang from one rail on the *mono*rail.

non- means *not*

> The book is a true story, so it should be on the *non*fiction shelf.

out- means *greater* or *better*

> Her better running meant she *out*distanced us all.

over- means *too* or *too much*

> The car *over*heated, or became too hot.

post- means *after*

> A *post*script, or P.S., is a note that comes after the letter.

pro- means *before* or *move ahead*

> My *pro*motion means I get moved ahead.

re- means *again* or *back*

> The company announced a *re*call to have the bad CDs sent back.

retro- means *back*

> A *retro*active pay raise means I'll get more money for last week's work.

sub- means *under* or *not quite*

> A *sub*marine moves under the water.

trans- means *across*

> The ferry will *trans*port us across the bay.

tri- means *three*

> I entered all three events in the *tri*athlon.

un- means *not*

> An *un*caring person simply does not care.

Suffixes

A suffix is a letter or group of letters that "dresses up" the end of a word—giving you choices in expressing an idea. For example, you can add different suffixes to the word *help* to express an idea in a number of ways:

> That lady help*ed* me.
>
> That help*ful* lady saved me.
>
> That lady's help*fulness* saved me.
>
> That lady was my help*er*.
>
> I was help*less* until that lady came along.

Adding a suffix to the end of a base, or root word, changes the word's meaning somewhat. A suffix can also change a word's part of speech. Below are some common suffixes and their meanings, followed by some spelling tips you may find useful when adding suffixes.

-able and **-ible** mean *able to* or *full of.* When you add one of these suffixes to a verb, it changes the verb to an adjective or a noun.

> My parents say I am reli*able* and depend*able.*
>
> I wonder if that means I'll get a convert*ible* when I turn sixteen!

-al means *belonging to* or *acting on.*

> The music*al* began with the arriv*al* of the roy*al* guests.

-ance and **-ence** and **-ency** and **-ancy** mean *the quality of* or *act of being.*

> I found all these clothes on the clear*ance* rack!
>
> There's a big differ*ence* between the regular and sale prices.
>
> I like this store's frequ*ency* of sales!
>
> This shopping mall has more than one vac*ancy.*

-ant and **-ee** and **-ent** mean *someone who* or *that which.*

> Which merch*ant* sells deodor*ant?*
>
> Yesterday I was an interview*ee;* today I am an employ*ee!*
>
> I am a resid*ent* so I can repres*ent* our group.

-ate means *the result of* or *to provide with.*

> I felt desper*ate* when the ground began to vib*rate.*
>
> Let's refriger*ate* the cake until it's time to celeb*rate.*

a

-ation and **-ion** and **-ition** mean *the result of* or *the condition of*. When you add one of these suffixes to a verb, it changes the verb to a noun or an adjective.

> I learned about a contest during a conver*sation* at school.
> I got a reject*ion* letter when I entered the contest.
> There was too much compet*ition*!

-d or **-ed** added to a word changes the word to past tense.

> We rak*ed* and gather*ed* leaves all day long.

-dom means *the state of*.

> Free*dom* sometimes involves martyr*dom*.

-ed (see **-d**)

-ee (see **-ant**)

-eer and **-ist** and **-or** mean *someone who* or *something that*.

> The auction*eer* looked for a volunt*eer* to begin the bidding.
> A scient*ist* is sometimes a real*ist* and sometimes an ideal*ist*.
> We borrowed this project*or* from the supervis*or*.

-en and **-ize** mean *to make*.

> This may fright*en* you, but I think you need to length*en* your paper.
> We might real*ize* success when we computer*ize* this project.

-ence (see **-ance**)

-ency (see **-ance**)

-ent (see **-ant**)

-er means *someone who* or *something that*. This suffix can also be added to a word to compare two things.

> The shipp*er* paid my postage to return the comput*er*.
> No one could say a nic*er* thing than what you just said!

-es and **-s** change a word to its plural form.

> Box*es* of pizza*s* were delivered to our school just now!

-ess means *a female who*.

> That lion*ess* is quite an actr*ess*!

i

-est added to a word compares three or more things.

> I may not be the strong*est* person in my class, but I try to be the healthi*est*.

-ful means *full of.*

> The Pilgrims were thank*ful* for a bounti*ful* harvest.

-fy means *to make.*

> I have to classify rocks to satis*fy* my science assignment.

-hood and **-ment** and **-ship** mean *the act of, the condition of,* or *membership in.* When you add one of these suffixes to a word, the word becomes a noun.

> Our neighbor*hood* has many teenagers.
> The teenagers started a club to provide entertain*ment* for younger children.
> I applied for member*ship* in the teen club.

-ible (see **-able**)

-ic and **-ish** mean *relating to.*

> The publ*ic* seems to like that poet*ic* com*ic* strip.
> I may be fool*ish* and child*ish,* but this movie makes me feel squeam*ish.*

-ics means *the practice of.*

> I like athlet*ics,* especially gymnast*ics.*

-ing means *a quantity* or *the action of.*

> Mom is stuff*ing* frosting between the layers of cake.
> We were jogg*ing* when we smelled the burn*ing* rubbish.

-ion (see **-ation**)

-ish (see **-ic**)

-ist (see **-eer**)

-ition (see **-ation**)

-ity and **-ty** mean *quality* or *state of.*

> It's important to consider legal*ity* and safe*ty.*

-ive means *having to do with.*

> My teacher says my story is act*ive,* impress*ive,* and imaginat*ive.*

i

-ize (see **-en**)

-let means *small in size.*

> A pig*let* is pictured on this farm leaf*let.*

-like means *similar to.*

> This puppet is child*like.*

-ly means *how* or *in a certain way.* This suffix changes a word to an adverb or an adjective.

> Third*ly,* I am definite*ly* responsible for my dai*ly* chores.

-ment (see **-hood**)

-ness means *state of* or *quality of.*

> His friendli*ness* and good*ness* bring happi*ness* to all!

-or (see **-eer**)

-ous means *full of.*

> It may seem monstr*ous* to you, but I think it's a wondr*ous* thing!

-phobia means *fear of.*

> I get claustro*phobia* in this tiny space.

-s (see **-es**)

-ship (see **-hood**)

-ty (see **-ity**)

-ward means *a direction toward.*

> We went for*ward* and back*ward* trying to get here!

-wise means *in the direction of* or *in respect to.*

> Time*wise,* I think this job is impossible.

-wright means *one who works with.*

> That play*wright* wrote one fantastic play!

-y means *state* or *quality of.*

> This has been a rain*y,* mudd*y,* funn*y* day!

Spelling Tips for Adding Suffixes

Generally, you will just add the suffix to the word.

    go—goes, going
    soft—softly, softer, softest
    box—boxes, boxing, boxer
    help—helpful, helper, helping

There are a few exceptions. Spelling can get tricky when you are adding a suffix to a word ending in *c, e,* or *y.* You may also be unsure about when to double a final consonant before adding a suffix. Here are some tips to help you spell every word correctly.

If a word ends in *c:* Add *k* when the suffix begins with an *e, i,* or *y.*

    panicked
    panicking
    panicky
    picnicked
    picnicking

If a word ends in *e:* Drop the final *e* when the first letter of the suffix is a vowel.

    safe—safer, safest
    erase—eraser, erasing, erasable
    take—taken, taking

If a word ends in *le:* Drop *le* when adding the suffix *ly.*

    whole—wholly
    cuddle—cuddly

If a word ends in a consonant followed by *y:* Change the *y* to *i* before adding a suffix.

    marry (consonant *r* followed by *y*)—married, marries
    Exception—If the suffix begins with *i:* marrying

Double the final consonant when adding a suffix if

 The word has one syllable: sun—sunny

 The word has more than one syllable and the final syllable is accented: admit—admitting

 The word has one vowel letter: can—canned

 The word has one consonant other than *x* at the end: mad—maddest

On Your Mark . . .

(Punctuation)

?   **A question mark** ends a sentence that asks a question.

> Do you know me?
> What kind of pasta is this?

!   **An exclamation point** follows words that express a strong feeling.

> Stop that!
> My book is overdue!
> Crash!

●   A **period** ends a sentence or an abbreviation.

> Today is my mom's birthday.
> etc. (abbreviation for *et cetera* meaning "and so on")
> Mon. (abbreviation for *Monday)*

/   A **comma**:

Separates two complete sentences joined by a conjunction.

> I don't want to do that, and I'm not going to.
> Uncle Elmer is eighty, but he still works out every day.

Follows the day's number in a date.

> May 16, 1912
> September 4, 1944

Separates a speaker from the speaker's words.

Luis yelled, "I don't agree!"
"Come home before dinnertime," my dad reminded.

Separates words or phrases in a series.

We ate hot dogs, peanuts, and popcorn at the All-Star game.
We watched movies, played games, and ate pizza at my sleepover.

Separates two or more adjectives that describe a noun.

I can't wait to see that new, exciting, adventure movie.
My sister wants a red, sporty car.

Separates a person's name and title.

Joan Lowery Nixon, Author
George R. Bush, President

Follows the salutation in an informal letter.

Dear Aunt Stella,
Dear Dad,

Follows the closing in a letter.

Sincerely,
Best regards,

Follows an introductory clause.

Although she's short, Chelsea jumps well.
Once he put his mind to it, Evan began making good grades.

Sets off a word or phrase that renames or explains another word.

My sister, Marcie, runs five miles every day.
Everyone likes Billy, the class clown.

Separates the names of a city and state or a nation and continent.

Fort Wayne, Indiana
Kenya, Africa

Follows a person's last name in an index entry.

Bird, Larry
Parks, Rosa

● A **semicolon**:

Separates and emphasizes equal clauses.

Homework is hard; history takes forever.
We can't eat this food; it's spoiled.

Substitutes for a comma when there are other commas in the sentence.

I have to go now; however, I'll be back shortly.
I just learned about it; therefore, I haven't had time to tell you.

● A **colon**:
●

Precedes a series.

Next summer I'll do these things: work for my dad, take swim lessons, play softball, and go to camp.

Separates a book's main title from its subtitle.

No More Chores: Every Kid's Wish Come True
Dinosaurs: Are They Really Extinct?

An **apostrophe**:

Shows ownership.

Tawanda's house is on the next block. (singular possessive)
I have to clean out the cats' litterbox. (plural possessive)

Substitutes for missing letters in a contraction.

I won't be going if Roddy doesn't.

Parentheses:

Set off an explanatory word, phrase, or number in a sentence.

> How much (money) can I expect to earn for the job?
> He took Pilar (my sister) to the movies.
> Please bring all ten (10) things on the list.

Emphasize a word or phrase in a sentence.

> I think someone (you) should do something about this.
> I have something (you won't believe it) to tell you!

Enclose numbers in a list.

> (1) Clean my room.
> (2) Do homework.
> (3) Feed the dog.
> (4) Call Matty.

" " Quotation Marks:

Enclose the exact words spoken by someone.

> I said, "Dad, I promise."
> "Help!" screamed my mom. "That snake of yours is in my closet!"

Enclose slang words, made-up words, or emphasized words.

> Grandma's probably going to "nix" our plans.
> My brother thinks he's the "super-duperest" kid around.
> Maybe you just "think" you saw a ghost.

Enclose the title of a story, article, poem or song.

> Be sure to read "Silly Things to Think About" in that magazine.
> I can sing all the words of "Gotta Have a Friend."

A **dash** (also called "en dash"):

Connects words or numbers to indicate a range.

> pen–people (as in guide words at the top of dictionary pages)
> 47–50 (includes 47, 48, 49, and 50)
> 1984–88 (includes 1984, 1985, 1986, 1987, and 1988)

Separates syllables in a word.

> con-cert
> com-pu-ter
> ba-by

A **long dash** (also called "em dash") acts like a comma or colon to separate and emphasize words or phrases in a sentence.

> We want to see that movie—regardless of the reviews.

An **ellipsis** notes that one or more words have been omitted from a sentence. An ellipsis is often used to omit unnecessary or irrelevant words when quoting someone's actual words. For example:

> Suppose you took a survey to find out how your classmates feel about repairing or replacing a statue in front of your school. You then decide to write a letter to share with your school's principal how students want to keep the statue. To keep your letter brief and to-the-point, you quote the most important words of some classmates. You write: *One student said, "That statue . . . reminds me of a character in my favorite book." Another said, "The statue . . . welcomed me when I first came to this school."*

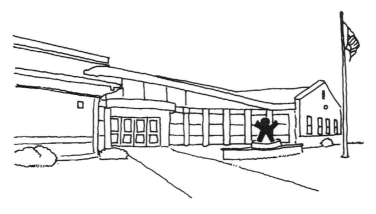

Making Your Words Stand Out

Sometimes you want certain words to stand out from other words in a sentence. When writing with a pencil or pen, you can emphasize a word by CAPITALIZING it, by s t r e t c h i n g it, or by <u>underlining</u> it.

When using a word processing program, you have several more options to emphasize a word:

boldface

italics

larger size type

different font

Tip: The titles of books and periodicals are always underlined when writing in longhand, but in italics when typed.

<u>People Magazine</u>　　　　　*People Magazine*

<u>The Chronicles of Narnia</u>　　　*The Chronicles of Narnia*

Putting Knowledge to Work

(Activities)

Antonyms
Compound Words
Homophones and Homographs
Onomatopoeia, Palindromes, Hink-Pinks
Parts of Speech
Plurals
Prefixes and Suffixes
Punctuation
Rhyming Words
Spelling
Synonyms, Metaphors, Similes

Opposites Attract (Antonyms)

A Friendly Disagreement

Invite a friend to join you in a friendly disagreement. Take turns, with one of you saying a word and the other saying its antonym. For example, if one of you says "open," the other should say "close" or "shut." How long can you and your friend agree to disagree?

Just Checking

How well do others listen to what you say? Take a few minutes to check it out, *and* have some fun with antonyms. Try saying just the opposite of what a friend or family member says. For example, if the person says, "It's hot outside," you would say something like, "Yes, it's really cold outside." Continue "disagreeing" to see how long it takes before someone stops to check *you* out!

"Read My Mind!"

Invite a friend to play this "mind-reading" game. Decide on an antonym pair such as *in* and *out*. Then name two things that could be described by one of the words. For example, a baseball diamond and stars go with the word *out*. Your friend must "read your mind" and name two *in* things, such as a sofa and refrigerator. Try associating words with other antonym pairs from the list beginning on page 47.

There's More Than One Right Answer

See how many different antonyms you can name for one word. For example, the opposite of *ugly* could be *pretty* or *lovely* or *beautiful* or *handsome* or—well, it's your turn now!

The Flip Side

Draw or cut from magazines two pictures that could illustrate a word and its antonym. Attach the pictures to opposite sides of a note card. Similarly prepare additional cards. Challenge a friend or family member to view the front and flip side of a card and then guess your antonym pair.

Stuck with Each Other (Compound Words)

Threesomes

Here are a few compound words made up of three smaller words. Can you think of more "threesomes"?

faraway

hereinafter

heretofore

inasmuch

notwithstanding

Things Are Not Always as They Seem

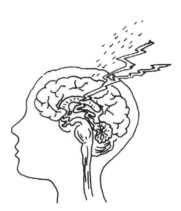

The meaning of a compound word is sometimes very different from the meanings of its smaller words. For example, a *billfold* is not paper money that is folded. Nor does *brainstorm* mean there is lightning and thunder in someone's brain. How might you illustrate words such as *dragonfly* or *rainbow*?

A Common Bond

The compound words *armload, armrest, armband,* and *armhole* all begin with *arm.* Can you think of two or more compound words that begin with each of these words?

back	life
door	news
eye	play
fire	some

Try naming two or more compound words that *end* with each of these words:

ball	thing
body	time
light	way

They Look the Same, but . . . (Homographs)
They Sound the Same, but . . . (Homophones)

What's That You Say?

Coin a homograph by inventing a new meaning for an existing word. For example, suppose you decide that *cap* means "happy." Try out your homograph with friends and family members. You might say, "This music makes me so cap!" or "I'm not at all cap about this homework assignment." Keep using your new word to see how long it takes others to understand your meaning.

Word Play

Illustrate some of the following ideas that play with homographs and homophones.

a patient patient   a tail tale

a bat bat   arms in arms

Wait, Weight!   one won

the whole hole   a hoarse horse

pitchers' pitchers   cents sense

He heals heels.   a new gnu

a Sunday sundae

Doubletalk?

Might the crook of your elbow get tossed into jail? Is there a troll under the bridge of your nose? Read the following poem to learn more "doubletalk."

Two girls were quarreling one day
With garden tools, and so
I said, "My dears, let Mary rake
And just let Idaho."

Anonymous

Try your hand at creating some playful language with words like *penny* (coin or girl's name), *pupil* (student or part of the eye), or *a Ford* (make of car) and *afford* (to be able to buy).

Word Play (Onomatopoeia, Palindromes, Hink-Pinks)

Travel Partners

The words *lightning* and *thunder* go together. So do *comb* and *brush, left* and *right, king* and *queen,* and *girls* and *boys.* Can you think of more words that travel in pairs?

How about words that travel in threesomes, such as *bacon, lettuce,* and *tomato* or *ready, set, go?* Can you think of more?

Palindromes That Count

The numbers 77 and 363 are palindromes since the numbers read the same backwards and forwards. How many two or three-digit palindromes can you list? How about palindromes with four or more digits?

Sound Off!

Listen to sounds around you. Write each sound as a word. See if a friend can "read" your sound words. Add any new words to the list of sound words beginning on page 91.

Picture It!

A rebus is a picture that represents a word or idea. Sometimes letters are added to complete an idea. Read each of these rebus words or phrases and then create some of your own.

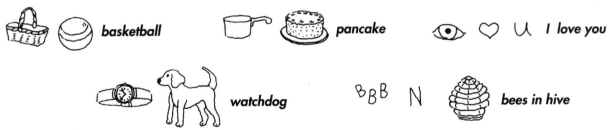

Riddle in Rhyme

Play this Hink-Pink/Hinky-Pinky Riddle Game with a friend or family member. Ask a question whose answer is two words that rhyme. For example, you might ask riddles such as the following:

What do you call a crowd of pigs at a barnyard trough? (ham jam)

What do you call a ladder from the ground to the sky? (air stair)

What do you call an angry father? (mad dad)

What do you call a robber who steals candles? (candle vandal)

What do you call the slimmer of two thiefs? (thinner sinner)

What do you call a lightweight boxer? (lighter fighter)

The Cast of Characters (Parts of Speech)

Uncovering Gossip

An adjective "gossips" about a noun by telling which, what kind, or how many. An adverb "gossips" about a verb by telling how, when, or where. Take turns with a friend or family member to "uncover the gossip" told by each of the boldfaced words in these sentences. Then make up some of your own sentences that contain "gossipy" adjectives and adverbs.

Victoria plays the tuba **majestically.**

My uncle farms **three hundred** acres in Nebraska.

We jogged to the park **yesterday.**

After Sean arrived, everyone went **downstairs.**

That movie is one of my favorites.

Casting Talented Characters

Some words might be thought of as "talented," since they can play more than one role, or be used as more than one part of speech. For example, the word *park* is "cast" first as a verb and then as a noun in this sentence: *My brother will park his car in the park.* Can you name the role in which each of the boldfaced words is "cast" in these sentences?

What did that **mean** witch **mean** when she said that the kids were gone?

This **shade** will not **shade** us from the sun.

What Words Go Together?

Name an adjective, or descriptive word, such as *outstanding* and ask a friend to name a noun your word might describe. Take turns naming adjectives that describe nouns, nouns that could go with verbs, or adverbs that could tell about verbs.

Challenge yourselves to name words that begin with the same sound. Examples might be a *befuddled baboon* (adjective describing noun), *donkeys dashing* (noun and verb), or *walked wearily* (adverb telling how something walked).

Bridging the Gap

A conjunction acts like a bridge to connect sentences. Can you "build bridges" using the conjunctions *but, so,* or *since* to connect each of these pairs of sentences?

I'd like to go with you. I've already seen that movie.

No one is at my house. Everyone went to the airport.

My uncle won the lottery. He's buying a new sports car.

What's More Than One? (Plurals)

I Say One, You Say More

Invite friends or family members to see how quickly they can say the plural form of any singular word you say. Then increase the difficulty by saying two or more singular words in succession. For example, if you say, "ox, sheep, candle, peach," another person would say, "oxen, sheep, candles, peaches."

It Says in the Paper

Select any page from a newspaper. Circle all plural words found on the page. Can you name the singular form of each word?

At another time, challenge a friend to see who can find a newspaper page with the most plural words.

What Am I Saying?

Ask a friend or family member to find your mistakes as you tell a story in which you use a singular word in place of a plural word or vice versa. For example, your story might begin like this: "I went skating at the ices rinks today. Three of my friend went with me. None of us had our own skate, so we had to rent skate. It was so cold that our toe and finger felt frozen after only a few minute on the ice. . . ."

Word Accessories (Prefixes and Suffixes)

"Well-Dressed" Words

Challenge a partner to name "well-dressed" words, such as *helpfulness, disappointedly,* or *unmistakenly.* Score one point for each prefix or suffix. Double the value for a word with two or more prefixes or suffixes. A word with a prefix *and* a suffix earns triple value. Consult a dictionary when in doubt about a word's accessories.

Same but Different

Using the same prefix or suffix, see how many different words you can name. For example, what other words could be added to these lists?

unable	delightful
uneasy	graceful
uninterested	helpful

They Begin and End the Same

Use prefixes and suffixes to name more word pairs in which one word begins as the other word ends.

likely	dislike
army	disarm
viewing	preview

What's My Word?

Invite a friend or family member to play "What's My Word?" Name a word with a prefix or suffix. Give clues to your word by saying its prefix or suffix and the word's meaning. For example, for the word *venomous,* say, "The suffix is *-ous* and the word means *full of poison.*" A correct response earns a turn to present the next mystery word.

Pairing Opposites

Since the prefixes *non-* and *dis-* mean *not,* you can use the prefixes to create many antonyms, or words that mean the opposite. And some prefixes, such as *pre-* and *post-, over-* and *under-, in-* and *out-, up-* and *down-,* or *pro-* and *anti-* can be paired as antonyms. See how many pairs of antonyms you can add to this list.

like	dislike
violence	nonviolence
pregame	postgame

On Your Mark . . . (Punctuation)

Who's on Vacation?

Send punctuation on a vacation! Omit all punctuation as you write a paragraph about the adventures of a made-up character during an imaginary vacation. Title your story "Whos on Vacation" leaving out all marks of punctuation. Share your story with a friend and then ask, "Who's on vacation?" Does the answer focus on the character in your story? Or is your friend's answer, "Punctuation"?

All About Me

Is there a mark of punctuation you seldom use in your writing? Try using that mark two or more times in a short paragraph about yourself.

On Your Mark . . . Get Set . . . Go!

Challenge a friend to find marks of punctuation in newspaper articles. Who can find an article that includes three different marks of punctuation? Four? Five? More?

Quotable Quotes

Invite friends or family members to help you punctuate a friendly conversation to show how a person's actual words go inside of quotation marks. Two of you can be "quotation marks" who run to "pose in front of someone's words" and then run to pose at the end of that person's words. Whew! "Quotation marks" do a lot of work, don't they?

Conversation Punctuation

Invite friends to discuss a movie or video game you've enjoyed. Record the conversation. Then replay the conversation as each of you stands to role-play the part of a "period," "question mark," or an "exclamation mark" when the appropriate type of sentence is heard. Is any one punctuation mark used more often? Replay the conversation and reverse roles.

Are You Telling or Asking?

Have a friend or family member ask you a question. Change as few of the person's words as possible to make the question a statement. For example, if your friend asks, "Do you like to fish?" you might answer, "I do like to fish." Try rewording statements to create questions. For example, note how the same words are used in the statement, "The computer is turned on." and the question, "Is the computer turned on?"

Rhyme It (Rhyming Words)

Being a Sleuth

Listen for rhyming words in conversations around you. Look for rhymes in advertisements in stores, and in newspaper and magazine ads. Are your "heard" words included in the rhyming-word lists beginning on page 97? If not, add them! Your detective work may also lead you to add more rhyming-word families to the lists.

With a Hink-Pink Here and a Hinky-Pinky There . . .

A hink-pink is two one-syllable rhyming words that suggest an unusual and often humorous way of viewing an idea. For example, a "ham jam" could describe several hungry pigs at one small hog trough. Similarly, a hinky-pinky is a two-syllable rhyme, such as "fender bender" or "Steady Eddie."

Look for illustrated hink-pinks and hinky-pinkys in the rhyming-word lists beginning on page 97. Then create some of your own hink-pinks and hinky-pinkys.

All in the Family

Write a poem using words from one word family in the rhyming-word lists beginning on page 97. How might two or more of the words be related? For example, the words *feet, heat, beat,* and *greet* might be used to write a poem about a police officer whose feet walk a beat and who pours on the heat to greet anyone who disobeys the law.

Coin a Word

Create and name a character, such as a "Stiggle" or a "Grop." From the list beginning on page 97, which rhyming-word family would welcome your new word? Can you make up some words that rhyme with your character's name? Using words from the list and your own coined words, write a rhyme such as those below about *your* character.

To sniggle some Stiggles,
just wiggle some biggles,
and hope that the Stiggles
don't give you the giggles!

His soda shop became a flop
when Grounchy Grop refused to mop.

Writing Parodies

A parody is a humorous rewrite of another author's words:

> Old Mother Hubbard went to her cupboard
> to get her poor doggie a bone.
> But when she got there,
> the cupboard was bare—
> because her dog had hosted a party.

Write a parody based on one of *your* favorite poems or songs.

Picking Them Out of the Lineup

A *perfect,* or *true,* rhyme is when two words have different consonants preceding their rhyming sounds. Here are some examples of *perfect* rhyme:

> *pill* and *hill* (Different consonants, *p* and *h,* come before the rhyming sound *il.*)
> *keep* and *cheap* (Different consonants *k* and *ch* come before the rhyming sound *ep.*)
> *click* and *pick* (Different consonants *cl* and *p* come before the rhyming sound *ik.*)

An *imperfect rhyme* or *repetition* is when two words have the same consonants preceding their rhyming sounds. Here are some examples of *imperfect rhyme:*

creak and *creek* (The same consonant blend *cr* is repeated before the rhyming sound *ek.*)

highway and *halfway* (The same consonant *w* is repeated before the rhyming sound *a.*)

heel and *heal* (The same consonant *h* is repeated before the rhyming sound *el.*)

Choose a rhyming-word family from the lists beginning on page 97. How many perfect and imperfect rhyming pairs can you identify?

Singles Club

Some words can be paired with many rhyming words. For example, the word *air* is part of a very large rhyming-word family. *Air* rhymes with more than sixty other words, including *bear, there, where,* and *stare.* The word *safe* is part of a small rhyming-word family that includes only three words, *waif, chafe,* and *unsafe.*

Other words like *bulb, film,* and *tablet* stand alone, since they have no rhyming mates. Can you think of more words to add the "Singles Club"?

Singles Club

bulb	sixth
donkey	tablet
druggist	wasp
exit	Wednesday
film	zebra
hundred	
infant	
month	
noisy	
nothing	
orange	

Write It Right (Spelling)

My Own Spelling Demons

Are there some words that you find difficult to spell? Chances are your words and any misspellings you use are in the list that begins on page 171. If not, add them to the list.

One Sound, Many Spellings

Most of us are not bad spellers. We just have problems when a sound can be spelled more than one way. The *ik* sound, for example, is spelled *ick* in words such as *pick* and *sick*. But the *ik* sound is spelled *ic* in words such as *picnic* and *plastic*. Look at the many spellings of the *oos* sound:

oose as in *goose*	*The goose is loose!*
uce as in *spruce*	*We planted a spruce tree.*
uice as in *juice*	*I had apple juice for lunch.*
eus as in *Zeus*	*Zeus was the father of Apollo.*
use as in *use*	*All of the computers are in use now.*

Using the rhyming-word lists beginning on page 97, can you find two or more other ways to spell each of these sounds?

ar as in *fair*	*urt* as in *dirt*
o as in *sew*	*ep* as in *keep*
e as in *fee*	*i* as in *cry*
ol as in *hole*	*an* as in *cane*

Spell-Well

Using the word list beginning on page 171, copy a correct or misspelled word onto each of several note cards. Try for an equal number of correctly spelled words and misspelled words. Place all the cards in a deep bucket or box. Take turns with a friend to draw a card from the "well" and tell whether the word is spelled "well" or incorrectly. Can you correct the misspelled words?

Spell-Around WHOOPS!

Invite friends or family members to play. The first player names any word's first letter. The next player thinks of any word that begins with that letter and adds the second letter, while being careful not to complete a two-letter word. Proper names and abbreviations cannot be used. Spell-Around WHOOPS continues until an actual word is spelled. The first time a player's letter completes a word, the player receives a *W*. The second time, the player receives an *H,* and so on. Play continues until any player accumulates *WHOOPS* and is out of the game. A dictionary may be used during play, but a player who incorrectly challenges a word is "rewarded" with a *WHOOPS* letter.

Down, Up, and Across

Write a word vertically down the left side of a sheet of paper. Write the same word in reverse up the right side of the paper. Then write a related word on each line such that the word begins with the letter on the left and ends with the letter on the right.

S	softballs	**S**
P	point	**T**
O	oar	**R**
R	rodeo	**O**
T	trap	**P**
S	skis	**S**

Mountain Climbing

Think of a category, such as *music.* Write the word to form the first step of an upward climb. Using words that relate to the category, form the first riser with a word, such as *cello,* that begins with the last letter in *music.* Continue to see how high you can "climb."

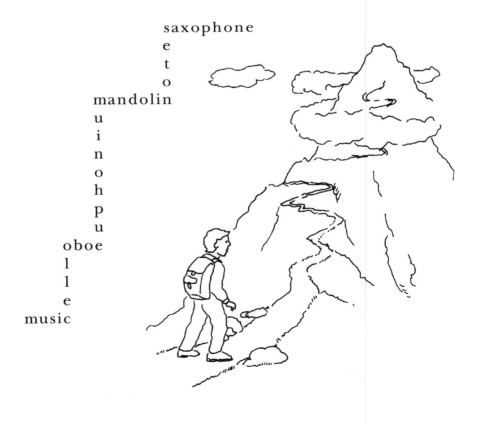

```
                    saxophone
                    e
                    t
                    o
          mandolin
          u
          i
          n
          o
          h
          p
          u
     oboe
     l
     l
     e
  music
```

Another Way to Say It (Synonyms, Metaphors, Similes)

Is It All the Same?

Using figurative language and synonyms, how many ways can you say the same thing? Let's see—

I figured I'd get in trouble for doing it.
My guess was I'd get sent to my room.
I reckoned I'd be in for it.
I knew I was skating on thin ice.
Chances were I'd end up in the doghouse.
I hardly expected to be rewarded for what I'd done.

And you can add to the list! Challenge a friend or family member to help you list other ways to express each of these ideas:

- You lose a favorite pair of jeans.
- Your favorite TV show is about to begin.
- You have to explain why you don't have your homework.
- You think no one agrees with you.

Going "Word Shopping"

Invite a friend or family member to go "word shopping" with you. Look for metaphors and similes on store signs and on product packages. If an outing is not possible, "shop" at home or "shop" the advertisements in magazines and newspapers.

This Way or That?

In his poem "Fog," Carl Sandburg used a *metaphor* to compare the fog to a cat—"The fog comes on little cat feet." If the poet had used a simile with *like* or *as*, he might have described the fog like this: "The fog moves as stealthily as a cat." or "The fog sneaks into the harbor like a cat."

How might you change these similes to metaphors and metaphors to similes?

- Julianna ran the bases *like a bolt of lightning.*
- My friend's room is *a sports Hall of Fame.*
- That guy is *an accident waiting to happen.*

A Picture Is Worth a Thousand Words

Figures of speech, metaphors, and similes "paint pictures" as they present images in our minds. Draw or paint the pictures you see when you think of these ideas:

couch potato
something crossed my mind
raining cats and dogs
walking on air
combing the newspaper
pulling someone's leg

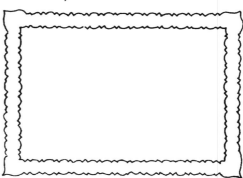

That's Just Like . . .

Analogies help us create similes and metaphors. When we think about the *analogy* "grapes are to vines as oranges are to trees," we think about how grapes grow on vines while oranges grow on trees. Can you complete the following analogies? Then write some analogies of your own.

People are to **houses** as **birds** are to _____.

Ten years are to **decade** as **one hundred years** are to _____.

Girl is to **sister** as _____ is to **brother**.

Curtains are to **windows** as _____ are to **beds**.

_____ are to **gymnasium** as **students** are to **classroom**.

Getting Specific

Some words are more specific than others. Suppose you were going to draw a picture to illustrate the sentence, "Sam went to the front of the line." The word *went* is a general word that doesn't tell you much about why the line was formed, nor how Sam was feeling as he took his place in that line. But how might you illustrate that sentence if Sam **glided, sauntered, meandered, sneaked, advanced, trekked, strode, ambled, trudged,** or **slinked** to the front of the line?

See if you can substitute synonyms that are more specific for each of the boldfaced general words in these sentences:

That's a **nice** shirt.
I'm having a **bad** day.
This school is **big**.
I **ran** when I heard the noise.

Sharing Your Words

(Publishing Markets for Young Writers)

Some writers write only for themselves. Other writers want to share their words and ideas with others. One way to share your writing with others is to have it published in a magazine or your local newspaper.

The names and addresses of newspapers in your area can be found in the Yellow Pages® of your phone book. The list on the next page gives the names and addresses of some magazines that welcome young writers' manuscripts. You will find issues of some of the magazines in your school or public library or in a bookstore near you.

Before you submit your writing to the editor of a magazine or newspaper, you will want to send a short letter to ask for the publisher's guidelines for writers. Guidelines tell writers how to submit a manuscript and the kinds of manuscripts a publisher would like to receive. Writer's guidelines are free.

When requesting writer's guidelines, be sure to include a SASE (self-addressed stamped envelope). Attach one first-class stamp onto your SASE, fold the envelope if necessary, and include it with your letter. If you do not send a SASE with your request, you will probably receive no response.

If a magazine is not available in a library or bookstore in your community, ask in your letter to the publisher how you can obtain a sample copy. There is often a fee for a sample copy. Before sending any money, it is wise to send for and then study the writer's guidelines. This way you will have a better idea whether the magazine is right for your manuscript.

Some of the magazines listed are published outside of the United States. As with any mail you send out, you will use a U.S. stamp on your envelope to request information from a publisher in another country. But a publisher in another country cannot use a U.S. stamp to send a response to you. So you must enclose International Reply Coupons (IRCs) with your SAE (self-addressed envelope). An employee at your local post office will help you decide how many IRCs you need to include with your letter and SAE.

Editors like to know something about a young writer who wants to submit a manuscript. When you write for information, you may want to tell the editor your age or grade in school. Here is a sample of how your letter might look:

> (your street address)
> (your city, state, zip)
> (today's date)
>
> Editor
> (name of magazine)
> (publisher's street address)
> (publisher's city, state, zip)
>
> Dear Editor:
>
> I would like to submit my writing to your magazine. I am (your age) years old. Please send me your writer's guidelines. I would also like information about how to receive a sample copy of your magazine. Thank you.
>
> Sincerely,
>
> (your name)

List of Magazines

The Acorn, 1530 7th St., Rock Island, IL 61201

American Girl Magazine, 8400 Fairway Place, Middleton, WI 53562

Attention Please!, RR 1, Box 1913, Lopez Island, WA 98261

Boodle: By Kids, For Kids, P.O. Box 1049, Portland, IN 47371

Boys' Life Magazine, 1325 W. Walnut Hill Lane, P.O. Box 152350, Irving, TX 75015-2350

Calliope: World History for Young People, 7 School St., Peterborough, NH 03458

Chalk Talk, 1550 Mills Rd. RR2, Sidney, British Columbia V8L 3S1, Canada

Chickadee Magazine, 25 Boxwood Lane, Buffalo, NY 14227

Child Life, 1100 Waterway Blvd., P.O. Box 567, Indianapolis, IN 46202

Children's Digest, 1100 Waterway Blvd., P.O. Box 567, Indianapolis, IN 46202

Children's Playmate, 1100 Waterway Blvd., P.O. Box 567, Indianapolis, IN 46202

Counselor, P.O. Box 632, Glen Ellyn, IL 60138

Creative Kids, GCT Inc., P.O. Box 6448, Mobile, AL 36660

Creative with Words, P.O. Box 223226, Carmel, CA 93922

Flying Pencil Press, P.O. Box 7667, Elgin, IL 60121

The Goldfinch: Iowa History for Young People, State Historical Society of Iowa, 402 Iowa Ave., Iowa City, IA 52240

Hawaii Funday, 3138 Waialae Ave., Honolulu, HI 96816

High Adventure, 1445 Boonville Ave., Springfield, MO 65802-1894

Highlights for Children, 803 Church St., Honesdale, PA 18431

Hopscotch: The Magazine for Young Girls, P.O. Box 164, Bluffton, OH 45817

Humpty Dumpty's Magazine, 1100 Waterway Blvd., P.O. Box 567, Indianapolis, IN 46202

Ink Blot, 7200 Burmeister, Saginaw, MI 48609

Jack and Jill, 1100 Waterway Blvd., P.O. Box 567, Indianapolis, IN 46202

Kid City, Children's Television Workshop, One Lincoln Plaza, New York, NY 10023

Kids and Computers, 200 Oakview Rd., High Point, NC 27265

Kid's Korner Newsletter, P.O. Box 413, Joaquin, TX 75954

Kids N' Sibs, 191 Whittier Rd., Rochester, NY 14624

Kidsart, P.O. Box 274, Mt. Shasta, CA 96067

The McGuffey Writer, 5128 Westgate Dr., Oxford, OH 45056

National Geographic World, 1145 17th and M St. NW, Washington, DC 20036-4688

Our Literate Legacy, Bonding Times, P.O. Box 736, Dept. MG, Lake Hamilton, FL 33851

Pikestaff Forum, P.O. Box 127, Normal, IL 61761

Savannah Parent, 31 W. Congress St., Suite 203, Savannah, GA 31401

Skipping Stones, P.O. Box 3939, Eugene, OR 97403

Skylark, 2200 169th St., Hammond, IN 46323

Spark!, 1507 Dana Ave., Cincinnati, OH 45207

Spring Tides, Savannah Country Day Lower School, 824 Stillwood Dr., Savannah, GA 31419

Stone Soup, The Magazine by Children, Children's Art Foundation, P.O. Box 83, Santa Cruz, CA 95063

Teen Power, P.O. Box 632, Glen Ellyn, IL 60138

Thumbprints, 928 Gibbs, Caro, MI 48723

Turtle Magazine, 1100 Waterway Blvd., P.O. Box 567, Indianapolis, IN 46202

U*S* Kids, 1100 Waterway Blvd., P.O. Box 567, Indianapolis, IN 46202

The Writers' Slate, P.O. Box 734, Garden City, KS 67846

Young Authors Magazine, P.O. Box 81847, Lincoln, NE 68501-1847

Young Voices, P.O. Box 2321, Olympia, WA 98507

More Reference Tools

Downing, David. *303 Dumb Spelling Mis*s *takes . . . and What You Can Do About Them.* Lincolnwood, IL: National Textbook Company, 1992.

This author makes spelling fun by presenting playful ways to look at words that are often misspelled. Fun illustrations encourage spellers to remember a word's spelling by concentrating on a troublesome letter, associating a picture with part of a word, or focusing on a little word within a larger word.

Elster, Charles Harrington. *There Is No Zoo in Zoology and Other Beastly Mispronunciations.* New York: Macmillan, 1988.

The author gives the correct (and the incorrect) pronunciations for four-hundred words that are often mispronounced. Examples are *zoology,* where *zoo* is pronounced so that it rhymes with *go,* and *envelope,* where *en* is pronounced so that it rhymes with *then.*

Henderson, Kathy. *Market Guide for Young Writers: Where and How to Sell What You Write,* 4th ed. Cincinnati, OH: Writer's Digest Books, 1993.

This book lists the names and addresses of magazines that welcome stories, poems, articles, jokes, riddles, and plays written by young writers. Also included are tips on how to prepare and submit a manuscript, sample cover letters to include with manuscripts, how-to's of submitting a manuscript online, and writing contests open to young writers. The book includes stories by several young writers, including persons who later became well-known authors.

Hendrickson, Robert. *Encyclopedia of Word and Phrase Origins*. New York: Henry Holt and Company, 1987.

The author presents a fun-to-read history of the origins or possible origins of more than seven thousand words and phrases in the English language. Some of the words and phrases included in this book are no longer in use.

Lees, Gene. *The Modern Rhyming Dictionary: How to Write Lyrics*. Port Chester, New York: Cherry Lane Books, 1981.

The author and songwriter presents hundreds of rhyming-word families that are especially useful to songwriters. The book includes a list of more than three hundred words that have no rhyming mates.

Lent, Penny. *Young Writer's Contest Manual*. Puyallup, WA: Kaleidoscope Press, 1993.

This booklet includes addresses and entry requirements for more than forty-eight contests open to young writers.

____. *Young Writer's Manuscript Manual: A Guide on How to Send Writing for Publication*. Puyallup, WA: Kaleidoscope Press, 1994.

This booklet includes explanations of terms used by writers and publishers, samples of various kinds of writing, sample query and cover letters, and many tips for revising and improving a manuscript.

Lerner, Sid, and Gary S. Belkin. *Trash Cash, Fizzbos, and Flatliners: A Dictionary of Today's Words*. New York: Houghton Mifflin, 1993.

This book gives the meanings of hundreds of words you may never find in any dictionary. Many of the words have been coined or invented for use in modern-day science and technology. "Street talk" and "faddish" words, words that are in use now but may not be used in the near future, are included.

Lyman, Darryl. *Dictionary of Animal Words and Phrases*. Middle Village, NY: Jonathan David Publishers, 1994.

This dictionary gives the origins of more than three hundred animal names and animal-related words, such as *tail* or *zoo*. The book includes the origins of phrases and expressions related to the animal world and words for animal homes and habits. An index makes it easy to find any entry word.

Rosenthal, Peggy, and George Dardess. *Every Cliché in the Book*. NY: William Morrow and Company, Inc., 1987.

The authors present hundreds of clichés in a fun way. Clichés are grouped by ideas or subjects, and many of the expressions are accompanied by illustrations.

Silverman, Jay, Elaine Hughes, and Diana Roberts Wienbroer. *Rules of Thumb: A Guide for Writers*. New York: McGraw Hill, 1990.

This book provides writers with easy-to-use basic information about the use of grammar and punctuation. Other information includes tips on editing and proofreading, note-taking, test-taking, and essay writing. A topic index makes the book a useful tool for writers.

Tuleja, Tad. *Marvelous Monikers: The People Behind More than 400 Words and Expressions*. New York: Harmony Books, 1990.

This book tells the story behind eponyms, names that have been borrowed to name other things. The book includes words and expressions such as "Lazy Susan," "Charley Horse," and "Goody Two Shoes."

Why Do We Say It? The Stories Behind the Words, Expressions and Cliches We Use. Secaucus, NJ: Castle, 1985.

The author tells a short story about the origins of more than six hundred words and expressions. A reader can review the information by taking the ten quizzes whose answers are in the back of the book.

Writer's Thesaurus. Glenview, IL: Scott, Foresman and Company, 1994.

This reference book presents hundreds of basic words, each word's part of speech, and several synonyms for each word. Figures of speech, information about a word's origin, and tips for using a word are included for many words. Colorful illustrations add interest, and an index provides a quick reference for locating a word or its synonym.

Young, Sue. *The New Comprehensive American Rhyming Dictionary*. New York: William Morrow and Company, Inc., 1991.

This book contains thousands of rhyming words and phrases, including numerous slang expressions. Words that are pronounced differently in different parts of the country are found under all possible pronunciations.

Glossary

Acronym

A word formed from the first letters or parts of a series of words.

Antonym

A word that means the opposite of another word.

Cliché

An overused figure of speech.

Collective noun

A noun that includes a group of members acting as one.

Compound word

A word made up of two or more smaller words.

Contraction

A shortened form of two words where an apostrophe is used in place of a missing letter or letters.

Dewey Decimal System

A system that classifies library books into ten main categories.

Ellipsis

Three periods indicating that one or more words have been omitted.

Figurative language

Picturesque expressions whose meanings are other than their literal or actual meanings.

Figure of speech

An expression that has a meaning other than its literal or actual meaning.

Formal writing

Writing, such as a business letter or manuscript, that is intended to be read by people other than oneself or friends.

Hink-pink

A one-syllable rhyme that is often humorous.

Hinkety-pinkety

A three-syllable rhyme that is often humorous.

Hinky-pinky

A two-syllable rhyme that is often humorous.

Homograph

A word that is spelled like another word but has a different meaning and is sometimes pronounced differently.

Homophone

A word that sounds like another word but has a different spelling and different meaning.

Idiom

An expression that has a meaning other than its literal or actual meaning.

Imperfect rhyme

Rhyming words that have the same consonant before their rhyming sound.

Informal writing

Writing, such as a note or friendly letter, that is intended to be read by oneself or friends.

Irregular verb

A verb whose past and past participle forms do not follow any rule.

Library of Congress System

A system that classifies library books into main categories noted by a letter of the alphabet.

Metaphor

A figure of speech that compares two ideas.

One-syllable rhyme

One-syllable word endings that sound alike.

Onomatopoeia

A word, such as *woof*, whose pronunciation imitates an actual sound.

Palindrome

A word, phrase, sentence, or number that reads the same way backward or forward.

Parts of speech

Eight ways a word may be used in a sentence: noun, pronoun, adjective, verb, adverb, preposition, conjunction, interjection.

Perfect rhyme

Rhyming words that have different consonants before their rhyming sound.

Plural

A word that refers to a set having more than one item.

Prefix

A letter or letters that when attached to the beginning of a word or root word, changes the word's meaning.

Proofreader

A person who corrects a piece of writing.

Publishing market

Publishers who may want to publish a person's writing.

Regular verb

A verb whose past and past participle forms are made by adding *d* or *ed* to the present tense form.

Rhyming sounds

Word endings that sound alike.

Rhyming word family

A group of words whose endings sound alike.

Simile

A figure of speech that uses the word *like* or *as* to compare two ideas.

Slant rhyme

Words such as *ready* and *Betty* that are pronounced as rhyming words, though the spellings suggest no rhyme.

Subject-verb agreement

The requirement that both the subject of a sentence and the verb must be singular or both must be plural.

Suffix

A letter or letters, that when attached to the end of a word or root word, changes the word's meaning.

Synonym

    A word whose meaning is the same or nearly the same as that of another word.

Three-syllable rhyme

    Three-syllable word endings that sound alike.

Two-syllable rhyme

    Two-syllable word endings that sound alike.

Verb tense

    The form of a verb that tells whether an action takes place in present, past, or future time.

Word origin

    The history of how a word and its meaning came to be used.

Index of Rhyming Sounds

One-Syllable Rhymes

a as in *play*
a as in *spa*
ab as in *crab*
ach as in *notch*
ach as in *catch*
ad as in *grade*
ad as in *dad*
ad as in *broad*
af as in *safe*
af as in *calf*
aft as in *raft*
ag as in *snag*
aj as in *page*
ak as in *make*
ak as in *pack*
aks as in *tax*
akt as in *fact*
al as in *sale*
al as in *pal*
al as in *fall*
am as in *game*
am as in *jam*
amp as in *stamp*
an as in *cane*
an as in *can*
anch as in *ranch*
and as in *grand*
ang as in *rang*
anj as in *range*

ank as in *thank*
ans as in *dance*
ant as in *paint*
ant as in *chant*
ap as in *shape*
ap as in *map*
aps as in *perhaps*
ar as in *fair*
ar as in *bar*
arch as in *march*
ard as in *hard*
arj as in *large*
ark as in *park*
arm as in *farm*
arn as in *yarn*
arp as in *sharp*
art as in *smart*
arv as in *starve*
as as in *chase*
as as in *gas*
ash as in *crash*
ask as in *mask*
asp as in *grasp*
ast as in *paste*
ast as in *last*
at as in *plate*
at as in *fat*
at as in *what*
ath as in *path*
av as in *gave*
aw as in *straw*
awd as in *sawed*
az as in *glaze*
az as in *jazz*

e as in *fee*
ech as in *beach*
ech as in *fetch*
echd as in *stretched*
ed as in *bead*
ed as in *head*
ef as in *beef*
ef as in *deaf*
eft as in *left*
eg as in *league*
eg as in *leg*
ej as in *ledge*
ek as in *creek*
ek as in *deck*
ekt as in *collect*
el as in *heal*
el as in *fell*
eld as in *field*
eld as in *weld*
elf as in *self*
elm as in *realm*
elp as in *yelp*
elt as in *melt*
elth as in *wealth*
elv as in *twelve*
em as in *seam*
em as in *hem*
en as in *clean*
en as in *pen*

e

ench as in *trench*
end as in *friend*
ength as in *strength*
ens as in *fence*
enst as in *sensed*
ent as in *sent*
ep as in *keep*
ep as in *step*
ept as in *kept*
er as in *dear*
erd as in *weird*
es as in *geese*
es as in *guess*
esh as in *fresh*
esk as in *desk*
est as in *feast*
est as in *test*
et as in *feet*
et as in *jet*
eth as in *teeth*
eth as in *death*
ev as in *sleeve*
ex as in *flex*
ext as in *text*
ez as in *these*

i as in *cry*
ib as in *tribe*
ib as in *rib*
ich as in *rich*
id as in *ride*
id as in *did*
if as in *life*
if as in *sniff*
ift as in *sift*
ig as in *fig*
ik as in *like*
ik as in *lick*
iks as in *fix*
ikt as in *strict*
il as in *mile*

il as in *spill*
ild as in *wild*
ild as in *build*
ilk as in *silk*
ilt as in *quilt*
im as in *dime*
im as in *swim*
imp as in *shrimp*
in as in *line*
in as in *skin*
inch as in *pinch*
ind as in *kind*
ind as in *pinned*
ing as in *sing*
inj as in *fringe*
ink as in *sink*
inks as in *lynx*
inkt as in *winked*
ins as in *since*
int as in *print*
ip as in *ripe*
ip as in *drip*
ipt as in *script*
ir as in *hire*
is as in *rice*
is as in *miss*
ish as in *wish*
isk as in *risk*
isp as in *wisp*
ist as in *list*
it as in *kite*
it as in *sit*
ith as in *with*
iv as in *drive*
iv as in *give*
iz as in *prize*
iz as in *quiz*

o as in *sew*
ob as in *robe*
ob as in *job*
och as in *coach*
och as in *watch*
od as in *road*
od as in *broad*
od as in *sod*
of as in *off*
oft as in *soft*
og as in *fog*
oi as in *toy*
oid as in *void*
oil as in *soil*
oin as in *join*
oint as in *point*
ois as in *voice*
oist as in *moist*
oiz as in *noise*
oj as in *lodge*
ok as in *joke*
ok as in *knock*
oks as in *hoax*
oks as in *fox*
ol as in *hole*
ol as in *fall*
old as in *bald*
old as in *fold*
olk as in *walk*
olt as in *colt*
olt as in *malt*
oltz as in *waltz*
olv as in *solve*
om as in *home*
om as in *mom*
omp as in *romp*
ompt as in *romped*
on as in *phone*
on as in *gone*
on as in *lawn*
ond as in *bond*
ong as in *long*

ont as in *won't*
ont as in *want*
onz as in *bronze*
ood as in *good*
ood as in *mood*
oof as in *proof*
ook as in *cook*
ook as in *spook*
ool as in *cool*
oom as in *room*
oon as in *moon*
oop as in *soup*
oos as in *juice*
oost as in *roost*
oot as in *suit*
ooth as in *tooth*
oov as in *move*
ooz as in *choose*
op as in *soap*
op as in *shop*
or as in *pour*
orch as in *torch*
ord as in *lord*
orf as in *wharf*
ork as in *fork*
orm as in *storm*
orn as in *corn*
ors as in *horse*
ort as in *fort*
orth as in *fourth*
os as in *gross*
os as in *loss*
osh as in *wash*
ost as in *most*
ost as in *cost*
ot as in *goat*
ot as in *hot*
ot as in *taught*
oth as in *growth*
oth as in *moth*
ov as in *drove*
ow as in *cow*
owch as in *pouch*
owd as in *loud*
owl as in *growl*
own as in *down*

ownd as in *found*
owns as in *pounce*
ownt as in *mount*
owr as in *sour*
ows as in *house*
owt as in *pout*
owth as in *south*
oz as in *nose*
oz as in *cause*

u as in *chew*
u as in *few*
ub as in *rub*
uch as in *such*
ud as in *mood*
ud as in *good*
ud as in *flood*
udj as in *fudge*
uf as in *proof*
uf as in *gruff*
ug as in *rug*
uk as in *spook*
uk as in *duck*
ukt as in *duct*
ul as in *cool*
ul as in *fuel*
ul as in *skull*
ul as in *full*
ulch as in *mulch*
ulk as in *sulk*
ulp as in *pulp*
ult as in *result*
um as in *room*
um as in *sum*
ump as in *jump*
un as in *moon*
un as in *fun*
unch as in *lunch*
ung as in *young*
unj as in *sponge*
unk as in *skunk*

unts as in *hunts*
up as in *soup*
up as in *pup*
ur as in *her*
ur as in *tour*
urb as in *verb*
urch as in *search*
urd as in *third*
urf as in *surf*
urj as in *urge*
urk as in *work*
url as in *girl*
urld as in *world*
urm as in *germ*
urn as in *learn*
urs as in *verse*
urst as in *first*
urt as in *dirt*
urth as in *earth*
urv as in *serve*
us as in *juice*
us as in *bus*
ush as in *push*
ush as in *crush*
usk as in *tusk*
ust as in *roost*
ust as in *must*
ut as in *suit*
ut as in *cut*
ut as in *put*
uth as in *soothe*
uth as in *tooth*
uv as in *move*
uv as in *love*
uz as in *amuse*
uz as in *choose*
uz as in *fuzz*

a

Two-Syllable Rhymes

a-bul as in *cable*
a-bur as in *labor*
a-chur as in *scratcher*
a-de as in *daddy*
a-ded as in *shaded*
a-dik as in *attic*
a-ding as in *grading*
ad-le as in *sadly*
a-dud as in *shaded*
a-dul as in *saddle*
a-dur as in *grader*
a-dur as in *chatter*
af-ter as in *laughter*
a-juz as in *pages*
ak-tiv as in *active*
ak-tur as in *factor*
a-kur as in *baker*
a-kur as in *stacker*
a-le as in *daily*
al-le as in *tally*
a-lur as in *sailor*
al-us as in *palace*
am-bul as in *scramble*
am-les as in *nameless*
am-pur as in *hamper*
a-mur as in *hammer*
an-de as in *candy*
an-ded as in *landed*
an-dul as in *handle*
an-e as in *nanny*
ang-kur as in *tanker*
ang-ul as in *tangle*
a-nik as in *panic*
an-jur as in *ranger*
an-se as in *fancy*
an-sez as in *dances*
an-ted as in *planted*
a-nur as in *manner*

a-pur as in *shaper*
a-pur as in *rapper*
ar-e as in *fairy*
ar-o as in *narrow*
ar-ut as in *carrot*
a-sez as in *bases*
a-sez as in *glasses*
ash-ez as in *crashes*
a-shun as in *nation*
a-ted as in *dated*
a-tul as in *rattle*
a-vur as in *saver*
a-zez as in *gazes*
a-zur as in *blazer*

e-chez as in *peaches*
e-chur as in *teacher*
e-de as in *greedy*
e-de as in *ready*
e-ded as in *needed*
e-ded as in *headed*
e-ding as in *feeding*
e-ding as in *getting*
e-dul as in *pedal*
e-dur as in *reader*
e-dur as in *spreader*
e-ing as in *seeing*
e-jez as in *pledges*
e-king as in *leaking*
e-king as in *pecking*
ek-shun as in *section*
e-kur as in *weaker*
e-kur as in *wrecker*
e-ling as in *feeling*
el-ling as in *selling*
el-lo as in *hello*
el-lur as in *speller*
em-bur as in *member*

e-mur as in *screamer*
en-ded as in *blended*
en-ding as in *sending*
en-dur as in *fender*
e-ne as in *genie*
e-ning as in *meaning*
en-shun as in *tension*
en-tal as in *rental*
en-ted as in *rented*
e-pe as in *sleepy*
er-e as in *cheery*
e-shun as in *session*
e-sing as in *guessing*
e-sted as in *tested*
e-ted as in *sweated*
e-thing as in *teething*
e-ting as in *meeting*
e-tul as in *petal*
e-tur as in *meter*
e-vur as in *never*
e-zhur as in *pleasure*
e-zing as in *teasing*
e-zur as in *freezer*

i-bul as in *nibble*
i-chez as in *riches*
i-ded as in *guided*
i-dul as in *bridal*
i-dul as in *middle*
i-dur as in *spider*
if-te as in *thrifty*
if-tur as in *sifter*
i-ful as in *rifle*
i-gul as in *jiggle*
i-ing as in *drying*
i-jit as in *midget*
i-ke as in *sticky*
i-ket as in *ticket*

i-king as in *striking*
ik-li as in *sickly*
ik-shun as in *fiction*
i-kur as in *quicker*
il-e as in *chili*
il-nes as in *stillness*
il-yun as in *million*
im-bul as in *symbol*
i-ming as in *rhyming*
i-ming as in *swimming*
im-ping as in *limping*
im-pul as in *pimple*
in-ding as in *finding*
in-e as in *skinny*
ing-ing as in *singing*
ing-ke as in *slinky*
ing-kul as in *twinkle*
i-nur as in *winner*
i-pe as in *drippy*
i-pur as in *wiper*
i-pur as in *shipper*
ir-ing as in *wiring*
i-shun as in *mission*
i-sing as in *pricing*
is-tic as in *artistic*
is-tur as in *sister*
i-sul as in *missile*
it-le as in *nightly*
i-tur as in *sitter*
i-vur as in *shiver*
i-ze as in *dizzy*
i-zul as in *sizzle*

O

o-be as in *hobby*
o-bing as in *sobbing*
o-bul as in *gobble*
o-ching as in *coaching*
o-de as in *spotty*
o-ding as in *prodding*
o-dul as in *waddle*
o-dur as in *totter*

o-ing as in *rowing*
o-ken as in *spoken*
o-ket as in *pocket*
o-kur as in *soccer*
ol-dur as in *colder*
ol-le as in *jolly*
o-ne as in *pony*
o-nik as in *tonic*
o-pur as in *shopper*
o-pe as in *poppy*
or-dur as in *porter*
or-e as in *story*
or-mur as in *warmer*
or-ul as in *floral*
o-se as in *glossy*
o-shun as in *motion*
o-shus as in *ferocious*
o-tur as in *totter*
ow-dur as in *louder*

U

u-be as in *hubby*
u-bul as in *trouble*
u-de as in *study*
u-dul as in *puddle*
u-dur as in *tutor*
u-dur as in *shutter*
u-fing as in *puffing*
ug-lur as in *struggler*
u-ke as in *lucky*
uk-tiv as in *destructive*
u-kul as in *chuckle*
u-le as in *truly*
u-lur as in *ruler*
um-bul as in *stumble*
u-me as in *tummy*
um-pe as in *lumpy*
u-mur as in *rumor*
u-mur as in *summer*
un-dur as in *wonder*
u-ne as in *money*
ung-ur as in *younger*

un-ke as in *monkey*
u-nur as in *tuner*
u-pur as in *super*
ur-dul as in *turtle*
ur-e as in *worry*
ur-le as in *surely*
u-shun as in *solution*
u-siv as in *exclusive*
u-ste as in *dusty*
u-sul as in *muscle*
u-thur as in *mother*
u-zez as in *chooses*
u-zul as in *nuzzle*
u-zur as in *loser*

Three-Syllable Rhymes

a-be-est as in *crabbiest*
a-bur-ing as in *neighboring*
ach-u-bul as in *patchable*
a-de-um as in *stadium*
al-i-te as in *legality*
al-ur-e as in *salary*
a-ze-nes as in *laziness*

o-bur-e as in *snobbery*
o-ji-kul as in *logical*
o-me-tur as in *thermometer*
or-i-te as in *majority*
o-si-te as in *curiosity*
o-tur-e as in *pottery*
o-ze-est as in *nosiest*

e-di-kat as in *medicate*
e-di-tor as in *editor*
e-de-ur as in *speedier*
ek-tiv-le as in *objectively*
e-pi-le as in *sleepily*

un-dur-ing as in *wondering*
ur-e-us as in *furious*
ur-i-te as in *maturity*
ur-u-bul as in *durable*
u-ste-est as in *dustiest*
uth-ful-nes as in *youthfulness*
u-tur-ing as in *muttering*

i-e-ting as in *quieting*
il-i-te as in *mobility*
i-se-ning as in *glistening*
i-si-kul as in *icicle*
is-tur-e as in *mystery*

Index of Synonyms

abandon (see *stop*)
abandoned (see *empty, went*)
abashed (see *ashamed*)
abhor (see *hate*)
able, 16
able-bodied (see *able*)
ably (see *well*)
abnormally (see *very*)
abode (see *home*)
abominate (see *hate*)
about (see *almost*)
aboveboard (see *right*)
abruptly (see *suddenly*)
absconded (see *went*)
absolutely (see *very*)
absorbed (see *busy*)
absorbing (see *interesting*)
absurd (see *crazy*)
abused (see *hurt*)
accelerate (see *hurry*)
accelerated (see *fast*)
accept (see *take*)
acceptable (see *good*)
accident-prone (see *awkward*)
accomplished (see *won*)
accomplishment (see *act*)
accurate (see *careful, good, right, true*)
accuse (see *blame*)
achieve (see *take*)
achieved (see *won*)
achievement (see *act*)

aching (see *painful*)
acknowledge (see *answer, believe*)
acme (see *top*)
acquaintance (see *friend*)
acquire (see *buy, have, take*)
acres (see *lots*)
act, 16
action (see *act*)
active (see *busy*)
actual (see *true*)
added (see *said*)
address (see *home, talk*)
adequately (see *well*)
admire (see *love*)
admit (see *let*)
admitted (see *said*)
admonished (see *said*)
adopt (see *choose*)
adore (see *love*)
advance (see *walk*)
advanced (see *went*)
adventure (see *story*)
advisor (see *teacher*)
aerial (see *tall*)
affluent (see *rich*)
afraid (see *scared*)
aged (see *old*)
agitated (see *excited*)
agreeable (see *nice, ready*)
aid (see *help*)
ailing (see *ill*)
airy (see *cold, light*)
alarmed (see *scared*)
alarming (see *dangerous*)
alert (see *careful, smart*)
alike, 16

alive (see *excited*)
alley (see *street*)
allied (see *alike*)
allow (see *let*)
all right (see *good, safe*)
ally (see *friend*)
almost, 16
alone (see *lonely*)
alter (see *change*)
altogether (see *very*)
amble (see *walk*)
ambled (see *went*)
ambush (see *catch*)
amiable (see *nice*)
ample (see *fat, full, wide*)
amplify (see *grow*)
amputate (see *cut*)
amusement (see *fun*)
amusing (see *enjoyable, funny, interesting*)
ancestors (see *family*)
ancestry (see *family*)
anchor (see *stay*)
ancient (see *old*)
anecdote (see *story*)
angelic (see *good*)
angry, 16
animated (see *excited*)
announced (see *said*)
annoy (see *bother*)
annoying (see *painful*)
answer, 16
answered (see *said*)
ant-sized (see *little*)
antique (see *old*)
anxious (see *worried*)
apartment (see *home*)

boulevard (see *street*)

bounce (see *jump*)

bound (see *jump*)

boundless (see *wide*)

brag, 19

bragged (see *said*)

brainy (see *smart*)

brave, 19

bread (see *money*)

break, 19

breathed (see *said*)

breezy (see *cold*)

bridge (see *join*)

brief (see *little*)

bright (see also *shiny, smart*), **19**

brilliant (see *bright, smart*)

brimming (see *full*)

bring (see *carry*)

brisk (see *fast*)

broad (see *fat, wide*)

broke (see *poor*)

broken (see *hurt*)

broken-hearted (see *sad*)

bruised (see *hurt*)

brush (see *rub*)

brutal (see *cruel*)

bucks (see *money*)

buddy (see *friend*)

budged (see *went*)

buffaloed (see *confused*)

bug (see *bother*)

build, 19

bulge (see *grow*)

bulky (see *fat*)

bumbling (see *awkward*)

bumpy (see *rough*)

bungalow (see *home*)

buoyant (see *light*)

burn, 19

burning (see *hot, painful*)

bushed (see *tired*)

business (see *work*)

bustle (see *hurry*)

bustling (see *busy, excited*)

busy, 19

butcher (see *kill*)

buy, 20

cabin (see *home*)

caboose (see *car*)

cackle (see *laugh*)

called (see *said*)

calm (see also *quiet*), **20**

camouflage (see *hide*)

canny (see *careful*)

canter (see *run*)

capable (see *able, smart*)

capacious (see *wide*)

capture (see *catch*)

car, 20

career (see *work*)

careful, 20

careless, 20

caress (see *touch*)

carry, 20

cart (see *carry*)

carve (see *cut*)

cascade (see *fall*)

castle (see *home*)

catch, 21

catnap (see *sleep*)

cautioned (see *said*)

cautious (see *careful*)

cavernous (see *deep*)

cease (see *stop*)

ceiling (see *top*)

celebrate, 21

celebrated (see *famous*)

censor (see *blame*)

center (see *middle*)

century (see *time*)

certain (see *clear*)

chagrined (see *ashamed*)

chair (see *seat*)

challenged (see *said*)

chancy (see *dangerous*)

change (see also *money*), **21**

char (see *burn*)

charge (see *blame, cost*)

charming (see *interesting*)

chase, 21

chatter (see *talk*)

cheap, 21

cheat, 21

cheer (see *shout*)

cheerful (see *happy*)

cheerless (see *sad*)

cherish (see *love*)

chic (see *pretty*)

chief (see *first*)

chiefly (see *especially*)

childlike (see *young*)

children (see *family*)

chilly (see *cold*)

chip (see *part*)

choice (see *best*)

choose, 22

chore (see *work*)

chortle (see *laugh*)

chosen (see *best*)

chubby (see *fat*)

chuckle (see *laugh*)

chum (see *friend*)

chunk (see *part*)

circumvent (see *avoid*)

claimed (see *said*)

clamor (see *noise*)

clamorous (see *loud*)

classmate (see *friend*)

clatter (see *noise*)

clean (see also *shiny*), **22**

clear, 22

clever (see *smart*)

closing (see *last*)

cloudburst (see *storm*)

clouded (see *dull*)

cloudless (see *clear*)

clumsy (see *awkward*)

clutch (see *catch*)

coach (see *car, teacher*)

coarse (see *rough*)

cobble (see *fix*)

c

damaged (see *hurt*)

damp (see *wet*)

dangerous, 24

daring (see *brave*)

dark (see also *night*), **24**

darkness (see *night*)

dart (see *run*)

dash (see *run*)

dashing (see *brave*)

dawdling (see *slow*)

day (see *time*)

dazzling (see *bright*)

dead, 24

deafening (see *loud*)

debate (see *argue*)

deceased (see *dead*)

deceive (see *cheat*)

decidedly (see *very*)

declare (see *talk*)

declared (see *said*)

decree (see *rule*)

dedicate (see *begin, celebrate*)

deduce (see *understand*)

deed (see *act*)

deep, 24

deepen (see *grow*)

deeply (see *very*)

defected (see *went*)

defective (see *bad*)

deficient (see *few*)

definite (see *clear*)

defraud (see *cheat*)

dehydrated (see *dry*)

dejected (see *disappointed, sad*)

delayed (see *late*)

deliberate (see *careful, slow*)

delicate (see *light, pretty, weak*)

delicious (see *good*)

delighted (see *happy*)

delightful (see *enjoyable, nice, pretty*)

deliver (see *carry*)

demand (see *ask*)

demanded (see *said*)

demanding (see *hard*)

demented (see *crazy*)

demolish (see *break*)

demure (see *shy*)

denounce (see *blame*)

dense (see *dull*)

depart (see *run*)

departed (see *dead, went*)

dependable (see *true*)

deposit (see *money*)

depressed (see *sad*)

depressing (see *cold*)

descend (see *fall*)

descended (see *went*)

described (see *said*)

deserted (see *empty, went*)

desire (see *want*)

desirous (see *jealous*)

desolate (see *lonely*)

despise (see *hate*)

despondent (see *sad*)

destitute (see *poor*)

destroy (see *break*)

detailed (see *careful*)

detect (see *find*)

detest (see *hate*)

develop (see *build, grow*)

developed (see *full*)

devise (see *build*)

devour (see *eat*)

differ (see *argue*)

different, 24

difficult (see also *painful, rough*), **24**

dilapidated (see *old*)

diluted (see *weak*)

dim (see *dark*)

din (see *noise*)

dine (see *eat*)

diner (see *car*)

dinky (see *little*)

dippy (see *crazy*)

dirty, 25

disagree (see *argue*)

disagreeable (see *ugly*)

disappeared (see *went*)

disappointed, 25

disapprove (see *blame*)

discern (see *find, understand*)

discerned (see *saw*)

discombobulated (see *confused*)

disconcerted (see *confused*)

discontinue (see *stop*)

discounted (see *cheap*)

discouraged (see *disappointed, sad*)

discover (see *catch, find*)

discreet (see *careful*)

discuss (see *argue*)

diseased (see *ill*)

disenchanted (see *disappointed*)

disfigured (see *ugly*)

disguise (see *hide*)

disheartened (see *sad*)

dishonest (see *bad*)

disillusioned (see *disappointed*)

disinteresting (see *dull*)

dislike (see *hate*)

dismal (see *dark, dull, sad*)

dispatch (see *carry*)

displeasing (see *ugly*)

dispute (see *argue*)

dissect (see *cut*)

dissimilar (see *different*)

distant (see *cold*)

distinct (see *clear*)

distinctive (see *different*)

distinguished (see *famous*)

distressed (see *worried*)

district (see *country*)

disturb (see *bother*)

disturbed (see *confused, worried*)

diversify (see *change*)

divide (see *cut*)

divine (see *pretty*)

division (see *part*)

dodge (see *avoid*)

dog (see *chase*)

dog-tired (see *tired*)

dollar (see *money*)

expense (see *cost*)
experienced (see *able*)
explain (see *answer, argue*)
explained (see *said*)
exposed (see *clear*)
express (see *fast, talk*)
exquisite (see *pretty*)
extensive (see *wide*)
extinct (see *dead, old*)
extra (see *lots*)
extraordinarily (see *very*)
extraordinary (see *different, new*)
extravagantly (see *very*)
extremely (see *very*)
exultant (see *happy*)
eye-catching (see *pretty*)
eyed (see *saw*)

fable (see *story*)
fabricate (see *build*)
factual (see *true*)
faint (see *dark, weak*)
fair (see *pretty, right*)
fall, 26
family (see also *people*), **26**
famished (see *hungry*)
famous (see also *big*), **26**
fancy (see *want*)
fantasy (see *story*)
fare (see *cost*)
far-flung (see *wide*)
fascinating (see *interesting*)
fashion (see *build*)
fast, 26
fastened (see *tight*)
fastidious (see *careful*)
fat, 27
fathom (see *understand*)
fathomless (see *deep*)
fatigued (see *tired*)

faultless (see *innocent*)
fearful (see *careful, scared, worried*)
fearless (see *brave*)
feast (see *eat*)
feat (see *act*)
feathery (see *light*)
feeble (see *weak*)
feel (see *touch*)
fellow (see *teacher*)
ferry (see *carry*)
fetch (see *carry*)
fetching (see *pretty*)
feverish (see *hot*)
few, 27
fiery (see *hot*)
filled (see *full*)
film (see *picture*)
filthy (see *dirty*)
final (see *last*)
find, 27
fine (see *best, good, pretty*)
finger (see *touch*)
finicky (see *careful*)
finish (see *stop*)
first, 27
fitting (see *good, nice*)
fix, 27
fixed (see *tight*)
flaming (see *hot*)
flat (see *smooth*)
flaunt (see *brag*)
flawed (see *wrong*)
flawless (see *good, right, true*)
fled (see *went*)
flee (see *run*)
flew (see *went*)
flexible (see *soft*)
flimsy (see *weak*)
flock (see *crowd*)
flourish (see *grow*)
flush (see *smooth*)
flustered (see *confused*)
focus (see *middle*)
foggy (see *confused*)
folks (see *family*)

folktale (see *story*)
follow (see *chase*)
foolish (see *crazy*)
foremost (see *first*)
forgetful (see *careless*)
forlorn (see *lonely, sad*)
fortissimo (see *loud*)
foul (see *bad, dirty*)
found (see *build*)
fracas (see *noise*)
fraction (see *part*)
fracture (see *break*)
fragile (see *weak*)
fragment (see *part*)
frail (see *weak*)
freeway (see *street*)
freezing (see *cold*)
frequently (see *often*)
fresh (see *clean, new, young*)
fretful (see *worried*)
friend, 27
friendless (see *lonely*)
friendly (see *nice, warm*)
frightened (see *scared*)
frigid (see *cold*)
frisky (see *playful*)
frolicsome (see *playful*)
frosted (see *cold*)
frosty (see *cold*)
full, 27 (see also *wide*)
full-grown (see *tall*)
fume (see *complain*)
fun (see also *enjoyable*), **27**
funny, 28
furious (see *angry*)
fussy (see *careful*)

gaiety (see *fun*)
gain (see *come, take*)
gale (see *storm*)
gallant (see *brave*)

gallivanted (see *went*)

gallop (see *run*)

game, 28

gamesome (see *playful*)

gargantuan (see *big*)

gash (see *cut*)

gasped (see *said*)

gather (see *take*)

gaunt (see *thin*)

gawky (see *awkward*)

genial (see *nice*)

genuine (see *good, true*)

germinate (see *grow*)

gigantic (see *big*)

giggle (see *laugh*)

glad (see *happy*)

glamorous (see *pretty*)

glaring (see *bright*)

gleaming (see *bright, shiny*)

gleeful (see *happy*)

glimpsed (see *saw*)

glistening (see *shiny*)

gloat (see *brag*)

gloomy (see *dark, sad*)

glorious (see *big*)

glossy (see *shiny, smooth*)

glowing (see *bright, shiny*)

go (see *walk*)

gobs (see *lots*)

godly (see *good*)

gone (see *dead*)

good (see also *nice*), **28**

good-looking (see *pretty*)

good-natured (see *nice*)

goofy (see *crazy*)

gorge (see *eat*)

gorgeous (see *pretty*)

grab (see *catch*)

graceless (see *awkward*)

gracious (see *nice*)

grand (see *big*)

grasp (see *catch, take, understand*)

great (see *big, famous, good*)

grill (see *ask*)

grim (see *hard*)

grimy (see *dirty*)

grip (see *catch, take*)

gripe (see *complain*)

gripping (see *interesting*)

groom (see *rub*)

grouch (see *complain*)

groundless (see *wrong*)

grow, 28

growl (see *complain*)

grumble (see *complain*)

guarded (see *careful, safe*)

guffaw (see *laugh*)

guide (see *teacher*)

guideline (see *rule*)

guiltless (see *innocent*)

guilty (see *ashamed*)

gung-ho (see *excited*)

gutsy (see *brave*)

habitually (see *often*)

haggle (see *argue*)

hair-raising (see *scared*)

half-baked (see *poor*)

halt (see *stay, stop*)

hammer (see *hit*)

handle (see *touch, use*)

handsome (see *pretty*)

happy, 29

harass (see *bother*)

hard (see also *difficult*), **29**

hardy (see *strong*)

harmed (see *hurt*)

harmful (see *bad*)

harmless (see *safe*)

harsh (see *cruel, loud*)

harvested (see *won*)

hassle (see *bother*)

hasten (see *hurry*)

hastily (see *suddenly*)

hate, 29

haul (see *carry*)

have, 29

hazardous (see *dangerous*)

hazy (see *confused*)

healthful (see *good*)

healthy (see *clean*)

heaps (see *lots*)

heart (see *middle*)

heartbroken (see *sad*)

heartless (see *cruel*)

hearty (see *warm*)

heated (see *hot, warm*)

heavenly (see *high*)

heavy (see *big, fat*)

heckle (see *bother*)

heedful (see *careful*)

heedless (see *careless*)

hefty (see *big*)

heighten (see *grow*)

help, 29

helper (see *friend*)

helpful (see *good*)

Herculean (see *strong*)

heritage (see *family*)

heroic (see *brave*)

hesitant (see *careful, shy, slow*)

hide, 29

hideous (see *ugly*)

high (see also *tall*), **29**

highchair (see *seat*)

highest (see *best*)

highly (see *very*)

highway (see *street*)

hilarious (see *funny*)

hindmost (see *last*)

hint (see *whisper*)

hinted (see *said*)

hire, 29

history (see *dead*)

hit, 30

hit-or-miss (see *careless*)

hobby (see *fun*)

hold (see *catch, have, take*)

holler (see *shout*)

hollow (see *empty*)

home, 30

homely (see *ugly*)

mad (see *angry, crazy*)
magnificent (see *good, pretty*)
magnify (see *grow*)
main (see *first*)
mainly (see *especially*)
majestic (see *big*)
major (see *first*)
make (see *build*)
malnourished (see *hungry*)
manipulate (see *touch*)
mannerly (see *good*)
manufacture (see *build*)
many (see *lots*)
marry (see *join*)
massacre (see *kill*)
massage (see *rub*)
masses (see *crowd, lots, people*)
massive (see *big, fat, wide*)
master (see *teacher*)
match (see *game*)
matchless (see *best*)
mature (see *grow*)
meager (see *few*)
mean (see *bad, cruel, middle*)
meander (see *walk*)
measly (see *few, little*)
median (see *middle*)
meditate (see *think*)
meet (see *game, join*)
melancholy (see *sad*)
memorialize (see *celebrate*)
memory (see *story*)
mend (see *fix*)
mentioned (see *said*)
merge (see *join*)
merry (see *happy*)
messy (see *careless, dirty, ugly*)
meticulous (see *careful*)
middle, 33
midpoint (see *middle*)
midsection (see *middle*)
mighty (see *strong, very*)

migrated (see *went*)
mindful (see *careful*)
mini (see *little*)
miniature (see *little*)
miniscule (see *little*)
minor (see *little, young*)
minute (see *time*)
mirthful (see *happy*)
miserable (see *sad*)
mislead (see *cheat*)
mistaken (see *wrong*)
mistreated (see *hurt*)
mixed-up (see *wrong*)
moan (see *cry*)
mob (see *crowd*)
mock (see *bother*)
model (see *teacher*)
modern (see *new*)
modest (see *shy*)
modify (see *change*)
moist (see *wet*)
mold (see *build*)
moment (see *time*)
money, 33
moneyed (see *rich*)
monsoon (see *storm*)
monstrous (see *big*)
month (see *time*)
monumental (see *big*)
moral (see *good, right*)
morsel (see *part*)
mortals (see *people*)
mortified (see *ashamed*)
mostly (see *especially*)
motionless (see *calm*)
motorcar (see *car*)
mouthed (see *said*)
move (see *carry*)
movie (see *picture*)
much (see *lots*)
muddy (see *dirty*)
multiply (see *grow*)
multitude (see *crowd*)
multitudinous (see *lots*)
mumble (see *whisper*)
murder (see *kill*)

murky (see *dark*)
murmur (see *whisper*)
murmured (see *said*)
mutate (see *change*)
mutilate (see *break*)
mutter (see *whisper*)
mystified (see *confused*)
myth (see *story*)

nag (see *complain*)
naive (see *young*)
nap (see *sleep*)
narrative (see *story*)
narrow (see *thin*)
nasty (see *bad, ugly*)
nation (see *country, people*)
natural (see *easy, true*)
nearly (see *almost*)
neat (see *pretty*)
need (see *want*)
needle (see *bother*)
needy (see *poor*)
neglectful (see *careless*)
negligent (see *careless*)
neighborly (see *nice*)
nervous (see *worried*)
nervy (see *brave*)
net (see *catch*)
netted (see *won*)
never, 33
new (see also *young*), **33**
nice (see also *pretty*), **33**
night, 34
nighttime (see *night*)
nimble (see *light*)
noise, 34
noisy (see *loud*)
nominal (see *few*)
nonfictional (see *true*)
nonchalant (see *careless*)
nonsensical (see *crazy*)

nosy (see *curious*)
notably (see *especially, very*)
note (see *find, write*)
noted (see *saw*)
notice (see *find*)
noticed (see *saw*)
notorious (see *bad*)
novel (see *story*)
nucleus (see *middle*)
numb (see *dead*)
nurse (see *help*)

obedient (see *good*)
obese (see *fat*)
objectionable (see *ugly*)
observant (see *careful*)
observe (see *celebrate*)
observed (see *saw*)
obsolete (see *old*)
obtain (see *buy, have, take*)
obvious (see *clear, easy*)
occupied (see *busy*)
occupy (see *use*)
odd (see *different*)
offered (see *said*)
official (see *true*)
offspring (see *family*)
oft (see *often*)
often, 34
okay (see *good, safe*)
old, 34
ominous (see *dangerous*)
once (see *time*)
oodles (see *lots*)
opaque (see *dark*)
open (see *begin*)
opening (see *first*)
opera (see *story*)
operate (see *use*)
optimistic (see *happy, hopeful*)
opulent (see *rich*)

order (see *rule*)
ordered (see *said*)
origin (see *family*)
original (see *first*)
originate (see *begin, build*)
outdated (see *old*)
outlined (see *said*)
outrageously (see *very*)
outstanding (see *best, big*)
outwit (see *cheat*)
overdue (see *late*)
overflowing (see *full*)
overjoyed (see *happy*)
overweight (see *fat*)
own (see *have*)

pace (see *walk*)
paced (see *went*)
pack (see *carry*)
packed (see *full*)
pad (see *home, walk*)
pained (see *hurt*)
painful, 34
painstaking (see *careful*)
painting (see *picture*)
pal (see *friend*)
paltry (see *few*)
pandemonium (see *noise*)
panted (see *said*)
parallel (see *alike*)
paralyzed (see *scared*)
parched (see *dry*)
part, 34
particle (see *part*)
particular (see *careful*)
particularly (see *especially*)
party (see *celebrate*)
passé (see *old*)
passed (see *went*)
passive (see *quiet*)
pastime (see *fun*)

pat (see *rub*)
patch (see *fix*)
pausing (see *slow*)
pavement (see *street*)
pay (see *money, buy*)
payment (see *cost*)
peaceful (see *quiet*)
peak (see *top*)
pedagogue (see *teacher*)
pedigree (see *family*)
peer (see *friend*)
peeved (see *angry*)
peewee (see *little*)
pen (see *write*)
penniless (see *poor*)
people (see also *country, family*), **35**
perceived (see *saw*)
perfect (see *best, right, true*)
performance (see *act*)
perilous (see *dangerous*)
period (see *time*)
periodically (see *often*)
perished (see *dead*)
permissible (see *good*)
permit (see *let*)
perplexed (see *confused*)
perplexing (see *difficult*)
persons (see *people*)
perturb (see *bother*)
perturbed (see *worried*)
pester (see *bother*)
pet (see *rub, touch*)
petition (see *invite*)
petrified (see *scared*)
pew (see *seat*)
photograph (see *picture*)
pick (see *choose, take*)
picky (see *careful*)
picture, 35
pictured (see *saw*)
piddling (see *little*)
piece (see *part*)
pigment (see *color*)
pilfer (see *steal*)
pinnacle (see *top*)

pinpoint (see *find*)
pitiable (see *sad*)
place (see *find*)
placid (see *calm*)
plagiarize (see *cheat*)
plain (see *clear, easy, ugly*)
play (see *fun, story*)
playful (see also *enjoyable*), **35**
playmate (see *friend*)
plead (see *ask, invite*)
pleaded (see *said*)
pleasant (see *nice*)
pleased (see *happy*)
pleasing (see *nice, pretty*)
pleasurable (see *enjoyable*)
pleasure (see *fun*)
pliable (see *soft*)
plod (see *walk*)
plodding (see *slow*)
pluck (see *catch*)
plummet (see *fall*)
plump (see *fat*)
plunder (see *steal*)
plush (see *soft*)
pointless (see *dull*)
polar (see *cold*)
polish (see *rub*)
polished (see *clean, shiny, smooth*)
polite (see *nice*)
ponder (see *think*)
ponderous (see *big*)
poor (see also *bad*), **35**
popular (see *famous*)
population (see *people*)
portion (see *part*)
portly (see *fat*)
portrait (see *picture*)
positive (see *happy*)
possess (see *have, take*)
posterior (see *last*)
posthaste (see *suddenly*)
postponed (see *late*)
pounce (see *jump*)
pound (see *hit*)
power (see *rule*)

powerful (see *strong*)
practice (see *use*)
praise (see *celebrate*)
praised (see *said*)
praiseworthy (see *good*)
prance (see *walk*)
prank (see *game*)
prayed (see *said*)
preached (see *said*)
precise (see *careful, right, true*)
prefer (see *choose, want*)
prehistoric (see *old*)
premiere (see *first*)
prepare (see *fix*)
prepared (see *ready*)
preposterous (see *crazy*)
preserve (see *save*)
press (see *touch*)
pretty, 35
prevent (see *help*)
price (see *cost*)
primarily (see *especially*)
primary (see *first*)
prime (see *best*)
primed (see *ready*)
principal (see *first*)
principle (see *rule*)
prize (see *love*)
probe (see *ask*)
probed (see *saw*)
proceeded (see *went*)
proclaim (see *talk*)
procure (see *buy, find, have, take*)
produce (see *build*)
professor (see *teacher*)
profoundly (see *very*)
project (see *act, work*)
prominent (see *big, clear, famous*)
promised (see *said*)
prompt (see *ready*)
promptly (see *suddenly*)
proper (see *nice, true*)
properly (see *well*)
proposed (see *said*)

prosper (see *grow*)
prosperous (see *rich*)
protect (see *save*)
protected (see *safe*)
province (see *country*)
prudent (see *careful*)
prune (see *cut*)
Pullman (see *car*)
pulverize (see *break*)
punctual (see *ready*)
puny (see *weak*)
purchase (see *buy*)
pure (see *clean, innocent, true*)
pursue (see *chase*)
puzzling (see *difficult*)

qualified (see *able*)
quarrel (see *argue*)
query (see *ask*)
question (see *ask*)
questioning (see *curious*)
quibble (see *argue*)
quick (see *fast*)
quickly (see *suddenly*)
quiet, 35
quipped (see *said*)
quit (see *stop*)
quite (see *very*)
quiz (see *ask*)
quizzical (see *curious*)
quoted (see *said*)

race (see *hurry, people, run*)
racket (see *noise*)
radiant (see *bright, shiny*)

r

radically (see *very*)
raging (see *angry*)
raise (see *build*)
ramble (see *walk*)
rambled (see *went*)
ranted (see *said*)
rap (see *talk*)
rapid (see *fast*)
rapidly (see *suddenly*)
rare (see *few*)
rarely (see *never*)
rash (see *careless*)
rational (see *right*)
rattletrap (see *car*)
ravage (see *eat*)
ravenous (see *hungry*)
raw (see *painful*)
reach (see *come*)
ready, 35
real (see *good, true*)
realize (see *understand*)
realized (see *saw, won*)
reaped (see *won*)
rear (see *build*)
rearmost (see *last*)
reason (see *think*)
reasonable (see *cheap, right*)
receive (see *catch, have, take*)
recent (see *new, young*)
recited (see *said*)
reckless (see *careless*)
reckon (see *understand*)
reclusive (see *shy*)
recognize (see *believe*)
record (see *write*)
recreation (see *fun, game*)
rectify (see *fix*)
recycle (see *save*)
red-faced (see *ashamed*)
refined (see *nice*)
reflect (see *think*)
refrain (see *avoid*)
refrigerated (see *cold*)
region (see *country*)
regularly (see *often*)
regulation (see *rule*)

relate (see *talk*)
relatives (see *family*)
relentless (see *hard*)
reliable (see *good, true*)
relish (see *love*)
reluctant (see *shy*)
remain (see *stay*)
remarkably (see *very*)
remarked (see *said*)
remedy (see *fix*)
remember (see *celebrate*)
reminded (see *said*)
remiss (see *careless*)
remorseful (see *ashamed*)
remote (see *cold*)
renowned (see *famous*)
reorganize (see *change*)
repair (see *fix*)
repeatedly (see *often*)
replace (see *change*)
replied (see *said*)
reply (see *answer*)
report (see *story*)
reported (see *said*)
reprimand (see *blame*)
repugnant (see *ugly*)
repulsive (see *ugly*)
request (see *ask, invite*)
require (see *ask*)
rescue (see *help, save*)
resembling (see *alike*)
reserve (see *save*)
reside (see *stay*)
residence (see *home*)
residents (see *people*)
respectable (see *good*)
respected (see *famous*)
respond (see *answer*)
responded (see *said*)
responsible (see *right*)
restful (see *calm*)
restless (see *tired*)
restore (see *fix*)
restricted (see *tight*)
retain (see *have, hire*)
retaliate (see *answer*)

reticent (see *shy*)
retire (see *sleep*)
retreat (see *avoid, run*)
retreated (see *went*)
rich, 36
riches (see *money*)
ridiculous (see *funny*)
right (see also *good, nice, well*), **36**
righteous (see *good, innocent*)
rightful (see *right*)
rigid (see *hard, tight*)
rigorous (see *difficult*)
riot (see *argue*)
riotous (see *funny*)
rip (see *cut*)
risky (see *dangerous*)
riveting (see *interesting*)
road (see *street*)
roam (see *walk*)
roar (see *laugh, shout*)
roared (see *said*)
roaring (see *loud*)
roasting (see *hot*)
rob (see *steal*)
rocker (see *seat*)
roof (see *top*)
roomy (see *wide*)
roots (see *family*)
rotten (see *bad*)
rough, 36
roughly (see *almost*)
route (see *street*)
roved (see *went*)
R.S.V.P. (see *answer*)
rub (see also *touch*), **36**
ruckus (see *noise*)
rude (see *bad*)
rugged (see *strong*)
ruin (see *break*)
ruined (see *hurt*)
rule, 36
run, 36
rush (see *hurry, run*)
ruthless (see *cruel*)

S

sacked (see *won*)
sad, 36
safe (see also *good*)**, 37**
safeguard (see *save*)
saga (see *story*)
said, 37
salary (see *money*)
salvage (see *save*)
same (see *alike*)
sample (see *try*)
sanction (see *let*)
sanded (see *smooth*)
sandstorm (see *storm*)
sassed (see *said*)
satiny (see *smooth*)
satisfactorily (see *well*)
satisfactory (see *good, nice*)
satisfied (see *happy*)
satisfy (see *answer*)
saturated (see *wet*)
saunter (see *walk*)
savage (see *cruel*)
save, 37
savings (see *money*)
savor (see *love*)
savvy (see *understand*)
saw (see also *cut*)**, 38**
say (see *talk*)
scads (see *lots*)
scamper (see *run*)
scanty (see *few, little*)
scared, 38
schizo (see *crazy*)
schoolmaster (see *teacher*)
schoolwork (see *work*)
scold (see *blame*)
scoot (see *run*)
scorch (see *burn*)
score (see *cut*)
scored (see *won*)
scour (see *rub*)
scoured (see *clean*)

scramble (see *run*)
scrammed (see *went*)
scrap (see *part*)
scrawny (see *thin*)
scream (see *shout*)
screamed (see *said*)
screwy (see *wrong*)
scribble (see *write*)
scribe (see *write*)
scrub (see *rub*)
scrubbed (see *clean*)
scrutinized (see *saw*)
scurry (see *hurry, run*)
seam (see *join*)
seamless (see *smooth*)
sear (see *burn*)
searching (see *curious*)
seat, 38
second (see *time*)
section (see *part*)
secure (see *buy, have, safe, save,*
    take, tight)
sedan (see *car*)
seek (see *chase, invite, try*)
seemly (see *pretty*)
seething (see *angry*)
segment (see *part*)
seize (see *catch*)
select (see *best, choose*)
send (see *carry*)
senile (see *old*)
sensible (see *smart*)
separate (see *lonely*)
serene (see *calm, quiet*)
serial (see *story*)
serve (see *help*)
settle (see *stay*)
sever (see *cut*)
severe (see *cruel*)
shabby (see *cheap*)
shade (see *color*)
shadow (see *chase*)
shadowy (see *dark*)
shaky (see *weak*)
shamefaced (see *ashamed*)
shape (see *build*)

share (see *part*)
sharp (see *smart*)
shatter (see *break*)
shave (see *cut*)
shear (see *cut*)
sheepish (see *ashamed*)
shelter (see *home*)
sheltered (see *safe*)
shift (see *time*)
shiftless (see *lazy*)
shining (see *bright*)
shiny (see also *bright, clean*)**, 38**
ship (see *carry*)
shirk (see *avoid*)
shivering (see *cold*)
shoplift (see *steal*)
short (see *little*)
short-change (see *cheat*)
shout, 38
shouted (see *said*)
shred (see *part*)
shrieked (see *said*)
shuffle (see *change, walk*)
shun (see *avoid*)
shy, 38
sick (see *ill*)
sickly (see *ill*)
sidekick (see *friend*)
side-splitting (see *funny*)
sigh (see *whisper*)
sighed (see *said*)
sighted (see *saw*)
sightly (see *pretty*)
silent (see *quiet*)
silly (see *crazy, funny*)
similar (see *alike*)
simple (see *easy*)
sincere (see *true, warm*)
singe (see *burn*)
sinister (see *wrong*)
sink (see *fall*)
sinless (see *innocent*)
skedaddle (see *hurry*)
skeletal (see *thin*)
skillfully (see *well*)
skimpy (see *few*)

studious (see *busy*)

stuffed (see *full*)

stumble (see *fall*)

stunning (see *pretty*)

stupid (see *crazy*)

sturdy (see *strong*)

stuttered (see *said*)

stylish (see *pretty*)

substitute (see *change*)

succeeded (see *won*)

successfully (see *well*)

suddenly, 40

sufficiently (see *well*)

suffocated (see *dead*)

suggested (see *said*)

suitable (see *good, nice*)

sultry (see *hot*)

summit (see *top*)

summon (see *ask, invite*)

sunny (see *bright, happy*)

sunset (see *night*)

super (see *best, good*)

superb (see *best, good*)

superhighway (see *street*)

superior (see *good*)

superlative (see *best*)

supplement (see *grow*)

support (see *help*)

supreme (see *best*)

supremely (see *very*)

surly (see *angry*)

surveyed (see *saw*)

swagger (see *walk*)

swallow (see *believe*)

swap (see *buy, change*)

swarm (see *crowd*)

sweating (see *hot*)

sweeping (see *wide*)

swell (see *grow*)

sweltering (see *hot*)

swept (see *clean, won*)

swift (see *fast*)

swiftly (see *suddenly*)

swindle (see *cheat, steal*)

switch (see *change*)

symmetrical (see *alike*)

synonymous (see *alike*)

tail (see *chase*)

take (see also *carry, catch*), **40**

tale (see *story*)

talk, 40

tall (see also *high*), **41**

tardy (see *late*)

tarnished (see *dull*)

task (see *act, work*)

taste (see *try*)

taunt (see *bother*)

taut (see *hard, tight*)

taxicab (see *car*)

taxing (see *difficult*)

teacher, 41

teammate (see *friend*)

tear (see *break, cut*)

tearful (see *sad*)

tease (see *bother*)

teasing (see *playful*)

tedious (see *difficult*)

tee-hee (see *laugh*)

teeny (see *little*)

tell (see *answer*)

tempt (see *invite*)

tempting (see *interesting*)

tense (see *hard*)

tent (see *home*)

tepid (see *warm*)

term (see *time*)

terminated (see *dead*)

terrible (see *bad*)

terribly (see *very*)

terrified (see *scared*)

territory (see *country*)

test (see *try*)

testified (see *said*)

Texas-sized (see *big*)

thick (see *wide*)

thicken (see *grow*)

thieve (see *steal*)

thin, 41

think, 41

thirsty (see *dry*)

thorough (see *careful, full*)

thoroughfare (see *street*)

thoroughly (see *very*)

thoughtful (see *careful, nice*)

thoughtless (see *careless*)

thought-provoking (see *interesting*)

threadlike (see *thin*)

thrilled (see *happy*)

thrive (see *grow*)

throbbing (see *painful*)

throne (see *seat*)

throng (see *crowd*)

thump (see *hit*)

thunderous (see *loud*)

tickled (see *happy*)

tidy (see *clean*)

tie (see *join*)

tight, 41

time, 41

time-honored (see *good*)

timid (see *shy*)

tinge (see *color*)

tint (see *color*)

tiny (see *light, little*)

tiptoe (see *walk*)

tired (see also *dead*), **41**

tiresome (see *dry*)

titanic (see *big*)

titter (see *laugh*)

toasty (see *warm*)

toil (see *work*)

told (see *said*)

toll (see *cost*)

tone (see *color*)

tons (see *lots*)

top, 41

topple (see *fall*)

tops (see *best*)

torment (see *bother*)

tormented (see *hurt, worried*)

utter (see *talk*)
uttered (see *said*)

vacant (see *empty*)
vacuumed (see *clean*)
valid (see *good, true*)
valuable (see *good*)
value (see *believe, cost*)
vamoosed (see *went*)
van (see *car*)
vary (see *change*)
varying (see *different*)
vast (see *big, wide*)
vastly (see *very*)
vault (see *jump*)
vehicle (see *car*)
veil (see *hide*)
vent (see *talk*)
verified (see *true*)
versed (see *able*)
very, 43
vicious (see *cruel*)
viewed (see *saw*)
virtuous (see *good, innocent*)
visualize (see *think*)
vivid (see *bright*)
vocation (see *work*)
vociferous (see *loud*)
void (see *empty*)
volumes (see *lots*)
volunteered (see *said*)
voracious (see *hungry*)

wacko (see *crazy*)
waddle (see *walk*)
wail (see *cry*)

wailed (see *said*)
walk, 43
wander (see *walk*)
wandered (see *went*)
want, 43
war (see *argue*)
warm, 43
warned (see *said*)
wary (see *careful*)
washed (see *clean*)
waste (see *kill*)
wasted (see *hurt*)
watched (see *saw*)
wax (see *grow*)
weak, 43
wealth (see *money*)
wealthy (see *rich*)
weary (see *tired*)
wee (see *little*)
week (see *time*)
weep (see *cry*)
weightless (see *light*)
welcome (see *nice*)
well, 44
well-behaved (see *good*)
well-known (see *famous*)
well-lit (see *bright*)
well-mannered (see *good*)
well-off (see *rich*)
went, 44
wept (see *said*)
wet, 44
whack (see *hit*)
wheels (see *car*)
whimper (see *cry*)
whine (see *cry*)
whisper, 44
whispered (see *said*)
wholesome (see *good*)
wicked (see *cruel, dark*)
wide (see also *fat*), **44**
wide-eyed (see *curious*)
widen (see *grow*)
willing (see *ready*)
willowy (see *thin*)
windy (see *cold*)

wintry (see *cold*)
wishful (see *hopeful*)
wispy (see *thin*)
witchy (see *cruel*)
withdrawn (see *lonely*)
withdrew (see *went*)
witnessed (see *saw*)
witty (see *funny*)
woebegone (see *sad*)
woeful (see *sad*)
won, 44
wondered (see *said*)
work (see also *act, help*), **45**
worked-up (see *excited*)
working (see *busy*)
worn (see *old*)
worried, 45
worship (see *love*)
worth (see *cost, money*)
worthless (see *cheap*)
wounded (see *hurt*)
wrangle (see *argue*)
wreck (see *break*)
wretched (see *sad*)
write, 45
wrong, 45

yammer (see *complain*)
yap (see *shout*)
yarn (see *story*)
year (see *time*)
yearn (see *want*)
yearning (see *jealous*)
yell (see *shout*)
yelled (see *said*)
yelling (see *noise*)
yelp (see *shout*)
yield (see *stop*)
yip (see *shout*)
young, 45
youthful (see *young*)

zap (see *kill*)
zoom (see *run*)

Index